DOOLITTLE RAID PILOT

This book is dedicated to **Eva Streeter**, who died young, leaving four children behind.

To **Laura Bolte**, who lost four children.

To **Marie Crouch**, who lost her husband.

And to **Donna Marie Smith**, who grew up with stories instead of memories.

Strong and courageous women, in times of uncertainty.

DOOLITTLE RAID PILOT

THE STORY OF CAPTAIN DONALD SMITH, SURVIVOR OF THE BOMBING OF TOKYO IN 1942

GEERT ROTTIERS

AIR WORLD

AIR WORLD

DOOLITTLE RAID PILOT

The Story of Captain Donald Smith, Survivor of the Bombing of Tokyo in 1942

First published in Great Britain in 2026 by
Air World
An imprint of
Pen & Sword Books Ltd
Yorkshire – Philadelphia

Print ISBN 978 1 03619 650 9
ePUB ISBN 978 1 03619 652 3
ePDF ISBN 978 1 03619 653 0

Typeset by SJmagic DESIGN SERVICES, India.
Printed and bound in the UK by CPI Group (UK) Ltd.

The Publisher's authorised representative in the EU for product safety is Authorised Rep Compliance Ltd., Ground Floor, 71 Lower Baggot Street,
Dublin D02 P593, Ireland.
www.arccompliance.com

For a complete list of Pen & Sword titles please contact:

PEN & SWORD BOOKS LTD
George House, Units 12 & 13, Beevor Street, Off Pontefract Road,
Barnsley, South Yorkshire, S71 1HN, England
E-mail: enquiries@pen-and-sword.co.uk
Website: www.pen-and-sword.co.uk

or

PEN AND SWORD BOOKS,
1950 Lawrence Road, Havertown, PA 19083, USA
E-mail: uspen-and-sword@casematepublishers.com
Website: www.penandswordbooks.com

FSC
www.fsc.org
MIX
Paper | Supporting responsible forestry
FSC® C013604

Contents

Prologue – More Than a Name on a List

In 2025, my book *The Tokyo Sixteen* was published – a tribute to the sixteen pilots who took part in the legendary Doolittle Raid on Japan in April 1942. Sixteen young men, each with their own background, character, dreams, and fate. Some were taken prisoner, a few never returned. But all dared the impossible, and in doing so, they made history.

While writing, I found myself deeply moved by the story of one of them: Capatain Donald Smith, pilot of Crew 15. At first, his name was merely one among sixteen – listed between Crew 1 (Doolittle) and Crew 16 (Farrow) in *The Tokyo Sixteen* – but his life story stood out. How could a boy from the heart of South Dakota, after a childhood marked by loss and hardship, rise to become a pilot on one of the most perilous missions of the war – only to lose his life on a second deployment a few months later. The question would not leave me.

I wanted to know who he truly was. Not just the pilot who bombed Kobe, Japan, but the son – the boy who lost his mother very young, was rejected by his father, placed in an orphanage, and grew up in silence and simplicity – yet became a man of resolve and duty.

What began as a chapter in *The Tokyo Sixteen* grew into a mission of its own. I contacted Donald's family in the United States, and they granted me their full cooperation to write a book about his life. The schools he attended, the church community of his parents, the orphanage that sheltered him, and the people who had known him – for whom Donald is still more than a name from the past – all contributed. So did veteran associations of the units he served in. For he was more than a soldier: a farmer's son, a modest young man raised on the South Dakota prairie in the spirit of the pioneers – where hardship, simplicity, and endurance were daily realities.

After the Doolittle Raid, Don was offered a safer post back in the United States – as an instructor, liaison officer, or in a propaganda role – but he firmly refused. Officially, the decision lay with army leadership, yet as a Doolittle Raider he possessed some leverage: his prestige and experience meant his wishes were taken seriously. At a time when the US Army Air Forces faced a severe shortage of experienced pilots, his request to return to combat duty was granted. Where others chose the safety of a training field, Don saw it as his duty to keep fighting. That choice took him to England, to the 319th Bomb Group (Medium) – a decision that would ultimately cost him his life.

Despite the many losses he endured at a young age – including the death of loved ones and estrangement from his father – Donald learned to survive in a world that offered him little comfort. Instead of breaking under those conditions, he became determined and resilient. He found strength in sports, where he could channel his energy, and in his studies, where he sought intellectual fulfilment. That same dedication and perseverance eventually brought him into the cockpit. He proved an exceptional pilot – admired by his comrades and respected by his instructors. His skill, discipline, and composure made him a natural leader – qualities that did not go unnoticed. It was no coincidence that he was chosen for the Doolittle Raid, one of the most daring operations of the Second World War. That mission marked the beginning of a military career that would forever secure his place in history.

Donald possessed a remarkable inner strength. Every time life pushed him down, he fought his way back. Adversity could strike him, but never defeat him. He refused to surrender to fate and always found the courage to go on – head held high, gaze steady.

Donald Smith was one of the many young men who gave their lives in the service of freedom. But he was also a unique individual. With this book, I want to ensure that he will not be forgotten.

On 12 November 1942, the B-26 Marauders of the 439th Squadron, 319th Bomb Group, to which Donald Smith belonged, prepared for the continuation of their ferry flight to North Africa. Ten aircraft were scheduled to depart from RAF Attlebridge in Norfolk, England, with RAF St Eval in Cornwall as an intermediate stop en route to the North African front. There, they would join operations supporting Operation Torch – the Allied landings in Algeria and Morocco that had begun just days earlier.

Although weather forecasts were unfavourable, the mission was given the go-ahead. At nearby RAF Horsham St Faith, the aircraft of the 437th and 438th Squadrons of the same Bomb Group were ordered to remain grounded. Only the 439th squadron took off. According to the 319th Bomb Group's official diary, theirs were the only USAAF planes in the air over the United Kingdom that day. Conditions were already poor at departure and were worsening rapidly.

Around two o'clock in the afternoon, Captain Donald Smith took off from RAF Attlebridge in his B-26 Marauder, serial number 41-17751, nicknamed 'SNAFU'. Nine other aircraft followed. Smith was no ordinary pilot in the unit – it was just seven months since his participation in the Doolittle Raid on Japan as pilot of Crew 15, a mission that had captured the world's attention.

What followed was catastrophic.

The weather over England deteriorated swiftly; thick cloud cover, gusting winds, freezing temperatures, rain, and dense fog. Navigation became nearly impossible. Radio contact was largely lost. The formation broke apart.

Five of the ten Marauders eventually returned to RAF Attlebridge. The other five were lost.

Two aircraft made emergency landings in England – at RAF Warmwell and RAF Graveley. Both were destroyed, but all crew members survived.

Two others drifted so far off course that they crossed the Channel into enemy territory. Both were intercepted by German fighters, shot down, and crashed southwest of Cherbourg, France. All crew members were killed, save one survivor.

The fifth lost aircraft was that of Captain Donald Smith. His B-26 Marauder ran into trouble over Cambridgeshire, apparently attempting an emergency landing at RAF Alconbury. Around three o'clock that afternoon, the plane crashed in a field south of the airfield, near Wild Goose Leys, Abbots Ripton, in Cambridgeshire. There were no survivors.

Donald Smith was 24 years old. His final mission ended not over Tokyo or North Africa, but over the English countryside – far from his birthplace in Whitewood Township, Kingsbury County, South Dakota, yet close to his enduring sense of duty.

The 319th Bomb Group (Medium) was the first USAAF unit to complete the transatlantic ferry flight to Britain largely on its own. Without the aid of ferry crews or transport commands, the pilots had to bring their B-26 Marauders across the North Atlantic – a route notorious for its treacherous weather, barren outposts, and razor-thin margin for error. In September and October 1942, they made that pioneering crossing, from the US mainland via Newfoundland, Greenland, and Iceland to Great Britain – traversing some of the most perilous airspace on earth.

Captain Smith, like his comrades of the 439th Squadron, had flown the northern route. At Bluie West One in Greenland he had to descend through the fjord and land under extreme conditions: icebergs in the water, minimal visibility, and a runway that allowed no mistakes. The landing demanded skill and composure – qualities Smith possessed in abundance as a former Doolittle Raider.

Who was this Donald Smith? What drove a humble farm boy to risk his life not once, but twice, in the fiercest moments of war? What shaped a quiet orphan into a pilot? And why has his name faded from the pages of history, when his deeds deserve remembrance?

This book seeks those answers – in the letters he wrote, in the records he left behind, and in the voices of those who knew him, served with him, or survived him. It is not just the story of a soldier, but of a man – one with dreams, doubts, humour, courage, and vulnerability.

The crash near RAF Alconbury ended his life. But with this book, I hope it will not end his memory.

Introduction

by Denise Mack – Great-Niece of Captain Donald G. Smith

Open the first chapter of this book, and you step onto the wind-swept prairies of South Dakota at the close of the nineteenth century. You meet George and Nancy Streeter, pioneers who left the familiar farmlands of Wisconsin for the promise – and the hardship – of the Dakota Territory. Their journey was long, their challenges many. They crossed rivers and mud roads in ox-drawn wagons, endured storms and isolation, and faced the endless horizon with faith as their only compass. Yet they persevered, building a life from nothing through hard work, self-reliance, and the quiet courage that comes from facing the unknown.

Those values did not fade with time. Passed from parent to child, they shaped not only a way of life but a way of thinking – one that prized endurance over ease, honesty over comfort, and duty over self. That inheritance, carried through decades of change, found its truest expression in the generations who grew up beneath the same vast Dakota sky.

Among them was Donald Gregory Smith, George and Nancy's grandson. Long before he wore a flight suit or sat in the cockpit of a B-25 Mitchell, Don carried the legacy of the prairie within him: determination in the face of risk, resilience in adversity, and loyalty to those beside him. These were not lessons taught in classrooms, but learned through seasons of scarcity, blizzards on the plains, and the steady rhythm of rural life – a rhythm that demanded persistence, humility, and faith in one's purpose.

This book tells the full story of Don – from his roots on the prairie to his final mission in 1942. It traces his journey through the formative years of the Great Depression, his studies at South Dakota State College, his decision to join the Army Air Corps, and his path to becoming one of the Doolittle Raiders – the airmen who carried America's first strike against Japan after Pearl Harbor. Their mission, launched from the deck of the USS *Hornet* in April 1942, remains one of the most daring operations of the Second World War. Yet behind every historic act lies an individual life, and behind every act of courage, a lifetime of quiet preparation.

Don's story is, at its heart, about more than war. It is a story about family, about duty, and about the unseen forces that shape a person long before they step into history's light. It is about a boy who grew up gazing at the open skies of South Dakota and came to meet those skies again – this time in the service of his country, halfway across the world.

To reconstruct that life in full required a return to its beginnings. This book draws upon a wide range of primary sources: church and baptismal records from Kingsbury and Butte Counties, South Dakota; archival documents from the orphanage where Donald spent part of his childhood; school registers, census lists, and military personnel files preserved in the National Archives. Just as vital are the family letters – many written in Don's own hand from the training fields of Texas, Georgia, and Washington – along with the oral histories and recollections passed down through generations, stories told around kitchen tables long after the war had ended.

Together, these sources form a mosaic – fragments of faith, hardship, and hope that reveal the full measure of a man shaped by both love and loss. Each letter, each record, and each family memory helps restore his voice to the world he left behind.

As you turn these pages, I hope you will see Donald Smith not only as a figure of history, but as the man his family remembers – shaped by the same wind that once swept the prairie, bound by love and duty, and carried, finally, into the uncertain sky with the courage of his forebears in his heart.

The Kingsbury Years (1918 – 1926)

Chapter 1

The Dream of the West

George M. Streeter was born in Crawford County, Pennsylvania, in 1853. When he was 6 years old, his father Norman, and stepmother Ellen, moved the family west to Wisconsin, settling near Fennimore in Grant County. There, George grew into a strong and capable young man. He and his brothers worked in the surrounding area, often in railroad and mining labour – trades that demanded endurance, discipline, and ingenuity.

It was in Fennimore that George met a local woman, Nancy Elizabeth Andrew. The two married on 31 August 1873, beginning a partnership that would endure hardship, distance, and change.

Ten years after their marriage, George and Nancy joined the flow of settlers heading westward to Dakota Territory. They carried with them not only their possessions but the resilient values of the Wisconsin frontier: work, modesty, and cooperation. The move would shape not only their own lives but the character of generations to follow.

At the end of the nineteenth century, thousands of American families left the relative security of the settled Midwest in search of a better life on the still-untamed plains of the Dakota Territory. They were drawn by the promise of the Homestead Act of 1862, which offered 160 acres of free land to anyone who would live on and cultivate it for five years. The frontier was shrinking but not yet gone, and for many, the chance to own land – real land, not rented acres – was worth every risk. Among those who set their hopes towards the horizon were George and Nancy Streeter and their three young children. They left behind a modest but established farm in Grant County, Wisconsin, to begin again as pioneers beneath an immense western sky.

The Streeter family's westward movement was not a sudden impulse but the continuation of a generational journey. It had begun decades earlier in the wooded hills of upstate New York, where Horace Hayman

Streeter and his wife Rebecca Cole raised their children near Sackets Harbor. After Horace's early death, his eldest son, Norman S. Streeter, carried the family's ambitions westward to Pennsylvania and later to Wisconsin. There, in Grant County, the Streeters became part of the wave of farmers who cleared oak groves and built small frame houses along the rolling ridges. In 1888, Norman extended the family's reach once more, filing a homestead claim in the Dakota Territory. Two years later, his son, George Milton Streeter, established his own adjoining claim, ensuring that the family name would take root on the prairie.

The territory that would later become Kingsbury County was formally ceded by the Yankton Sioux to the United States in 1858 and, prior to its opening for non-Native settlement, had formed part of an Indian reservation. Systematic surveying began in the early 1870s, and during the summer of 1873 the land was divided into townships measuring six by six miles. Survey maps recorded lakes, sloughs, Indian mounds, and other visible features of the landscape, establishing the framework for settlement and development. That same year, Kingsbury County was formally established and named after George Kingsbury, an early settler and legislator in Dakota Territory.

The Streeter homestead was located in Kingsbury County, South Dakota, approximately 22km (14 miles) southeast of the Ingalls homestead near De Smet, the former home of Laura Ingalls Wilder, author of the *Little House on the Prairie* series. While no direct connection existed between the two families, this geographical proximity places the Streeter farm within the same homesteading landscape that later came to symbolise the nineteenth-century pioneer experience in American historical memory.

The relative locations of the Ingalls homestead and the Streeter farm can be precisely identified using the Public Land Survey System. Charles Ingalls settled on the northeast quarter of Section 3, Township 110 North, Range 56 West, while the Streeter homestead was situated on the northwest quarter of Section 23 within the same township and range in Kingsbury County. Each township measured 6 by 6 miles and was divided into thirty-six 1-mile square sections. Both locations formed part of the same surveyed landscape, firmly situating the Streeter homestead within close geographical proximity to the Ingalls homestead.

George and Nancy's journey west covered nearly 960km. It took between eight and ten weeks under favourable weather, sometimes longer when rain turned the tracks into deep mud. They travelled in a covered wagon drawn by a pair of oxen, carrying everything they owned: bedding, clothing, tools, seed grain, and the simplest household furniture. Each morning began before sunrise. After the animals were fed and harnessed, the wagon creaked back onto the trail. By dusk they had covered perhaps 16 to 24km. A broken wheel, a lame animal, or a flooded creek could bring a day's progress to nothing.

They followed roughly the route that led from Dubuque, on the Mississippi River, towards the prairies of Minnesota and South Dakota. Major rivers such as the Mississippi, and further west the Missouri were natural obstacles for some wagon trains, their crossings made by ferry – slow, risky operations in high water. Nights were spent in makeshift camps, wagons drawn into circles for safety and companionship. The dangers were many: disease, exhaustion, and accident were constant companions, while wolves, coyotes, and the occasional wandering bear reminded them that the prairie still belonged to the wild.

Sometimes the road offered brief moments of wonder: fields of sunflowers stretching to the horizon, a sky so wide it seemed to bend with the earth. Yet there were darker memories too – a child feverish with dysentery, a sudden storm tearing at the canvas cover, the silence that followed when a family's wagon fell behind and was not seen again. Every kilometre demanded resilience.

They passed small settlements and military posts – Fort Ridgely, Sioux Falls, De Smet – where supplies could be replenished. De Smet, named after a Belgian missionary, showed the first fragile signs of community: a schoolhouse, a blacksmith, a few false-fronted stores. Still, beyond its edge stretched an ocean of grass where wind was the only sound. One night in Minnesota they were startled by the shrill howls of coyotes circling the camp; another afternoon, a black bear wandered close enough that George reached for his rifle, but let the creature amble away. Such encounters reminded every settler of how exposed they truly were.

At last they reached Kingsbury County, South Dakota. Here the prairie rolled gently towards the west, unbroken except for occasional sloughs and the shimmering surface of Lake Thompson. George chose a rise of ground in the north-central part of the township, between De Smet and Oldham, as the place to settle. When the wagon halted and the oxen were unyoked, the family knew the long journey had ended. Later they would travel to the land office in Watertown to make the claim official, but their decision was already fixed in the soil.

This migration was more than a change of residence; it marked a passage from dependence to freedom, from the known to the unknown. The values that sustained the Streeters – perseverance, self-reliance, and quiet fellowship – would echo through the generations. For Donald Smith, a descendant of this line, that inheritance was not abstract. His courage, like theirs, grew from the hard soil of the prairie rather than from the field of battle.

In the summer of 1883 the Streeters began the work of turning wilderness into home. Their first shelter was a sod house cut from the very earth they intended to cultivate. George's priority was water. With a hand auger, wooden bucket, and patience, he dug until a cold stream rose from below. The well was victory enough to begin. Next came a crude barn of cottonwood logs, then the breaking of the virgin sod with a borrowed plough. Over the years the holdings expanded: a granary, a livestock barn, two wells, and, finally, a clapboard house with an addition that caught the morning light.

For seven years the Streeters cultivated wheat, oats, flax, and rye. Their harvests sustained not only themselves but also contributed to the young farming community forming around Oldham, the nearest settlement. On 14 November 1890, after proving their claim through continuous residence and cultivation, George and Nancy received their official land patent – Homestead Certificate No. 6420 – signed by President Benjamin Harrison. It represented more than legal ownership; it embodied seven years of endurance and moral fortitude. Two neighbours, George Huttenhow and Herman Woestman, testified on their behalf, calling the Streeters 'model settlers'.

George's father, Norman S. Streeter, had been the first of the family to reach the Dakota plains, claiming land in Section 10 of Township 109 North, Range 55 West, in 1882. Two years later his son George settled nearby in Section 23, followed by George's brother Wayne in Section 15. Within a few years the three Streeters occupied adjoining quarter-sections – a small family enclave on the open prairie of Kingsbury County.

The exact location of the homestead of George and Nancy Streeter is preserved on the Map of Kingsbury County, South Dakota, compiled and published in 1898 by E. Frank Peterson of Mitchell. That hand-coloured lithograph, with its carefully inked township lines and property divisions, shows George M. Streeter's claim in Township 109 North, Range 55 West, Section 23 – one of the earliest established in what would become Whitewood Township. Surrounded by neighbouring claims belonging to Gust H. Hanson, Ingeborg M. Hartvedt, and Andrias J. Kringsrud, the Streeters formed part of a small but enduring farming cluster on the Dakota plains.

Seen through Peterson's map, the Streeter homestead becomes more than a patch of land; it stands as a symbol of the greater movement that carried American families westward in search of independence. Here, on 160 acres of wind-swept prairie, George and Nancy Streeter built a life of substance and integrity. From their labour grew not only a farm but a legacy – one that would reach far beyond the fences they raised and live on in the courage of those who followed.

The Streeter farm soon became an anchor in the region. Over time, other family members joined them on the prairie, and three generations came to live within sight of one another. The homestead offered more than food and shelter – it became a social centre.

George was remembered as a practical, resolute man who preferred quiet work to words. He guided his family calmly and with purpose. Nancy Elizabeth Andrew, born in 1856, was strong-willed yet patient, devoted to her children's welfare and quick to adapt to hardship. Together they embodied the pioneer spirit – not one of romantic adventure, but of endurance, improvisation, and faith in the future.

It was in Oldham that George's physical strength became local legend. The story was often told of the day when the Christensen Brothers offered a challenge at their store: anyone who could lift a 300lb barrel of salt onto his wagon could take it home. George, smiling quietly, walked over, lifted the barrel onto his shoulder, and carried it out without help – winning both the bet and the admiration of his neighbours. In later years, he served as a 'bouncer' at local dances and was known for his love of horse races, a touch of light-heartedness amid the rigours of prairie life.

Even before their title was granted, the Streeter family helped establish a nearby district school: Whitewood School No. 6. This humble one-room schoolhouse, built in the early 1880s, played a vital role in shaping the community. Heated by a coal stove, with no running water or electricity, it offered basic education to the children of surrounding homesteads.

Inside, the teacher had few materials. The ever-present *McGuffey Readers* and spelling books formed the core of language instruction, while *Ray's Arithmetic* introduced the principles of mathematics. Students wrote on slates, as paper was too precious for daily use. A large chalkboard dominated the front wall, and in one corner stood a worn globe and an old geography book – their window to the wider world. Bible passages and psalms were often read aloud, serving both literacy and moral instruction. The teacher supplemented lessons with simple nature studies drawn from the prairie itself. In this way, the sparse furnishings and limited resources reflected the settlers' determination to preserve education and community even in the harshest conditions.

The 1899 map of Kingsbury County shows how the Streeter family had become firmly rooted in Whitewood Township. George M. Streeter's original homestead occupied the northwest quarter of Section 23, while his eldest son, Clarence D. Streeter, established his own claim just to the north, in Section 14. On Clarence's land stood the small district school that served the children of nearby settlers – including his younger siblings and cousins. Though his name appears in parentheses on the map, suggesting a later transfer of ownership, Clarence's role in the community remained unmistakable. He maintained the schoolhouse, repaired its roof after storms, and sometimes organised evening lessons for adults – acts of quiet civic duty that reflected the Streeters' enduring spirit of service and education.

In the broader context of military history, the story of the Streeter family illustrates the kind of communities from which future American servicemen emerged. Families like the Streeters formed the social, cultural, and moral foundations of the nation. Their lives revolved around duty, perseverance, cooperation, and devotion – values that, decades later, would define the men and women who served in the First and Second World Wars.

The Streeter farm in Kingsbury County was no outpost of power, but a cradle of character. From such humble origins arose men and women who, when their time came, served the country they first came to know through the plough, the school desk, and the prairie storm.

Chapter 2

Pioneers – Roots of Duty and Character

George Milton Streeter and his wife, Nancy Andrew, belonged to a generation of Americans who not only built a physical existence on the untamed plains of South Dakota, but also laid a moral foundation on which later generations could build. As homesteaders in Whitewood Township, Kingsbury County, at the crossroads of nineteenth- and twentieth-century America, they embodied the core values of the young nation: work, family, faith, and perseverance.

Their family of six children grew into a close-knit unit. The eldest three – their sons Clarence Delbert (1875), Harry Norman (1878), and William Edward (1881) – were born in Wisconsin and Iowa before the move to the South Dakota prairie. Each developed into a distinct type: Clarence as a worker and leader, Harry as a problem-solver and thinker, and William as a thoughtful observer rooted in the land.

Clarence, the firstborn, took on responsibility at an early age. He worked the fields alongside his father and, while still young, began cultivating a plot of his own – proving not only his independence but also carrying forward the pioneering spirit that defined his parents. His work ethic and paternal bearing made him a pillar within the family and the wider community.

Harry became the farm's practical engineer. He devised more efficient methods of irrigation and mechanisation and later served as a mail carrier in Lake Preston, South Dakota – a role in which he enjoyed the community's daily trust. William chose a different path: as a brakeman with the Great Northern Railroad in Watertown, South Dakota, he left farm life and found his calling amid the rhythms between stations, balancing freedom of movement with responsibility.

In South Dakota the three daughters of George and Nancy were born: Flora Belle (1884), Jessie Mabel (1889), and Eva Emmeline

(1892). They played a central role in the household's social fabric. Flora became the linchpin of domestic life; Jessie, with imagination and diaries, captured prairie life; and Eva, the youngest, brought liveliness and curiosity – traits that would later shape her role in the church and social communities of Oldham.

Only a few days' journey south of the Streeter farm lay the valley of Wounded Knee Creek, where, on 29 December 1890, the 7th Cavalry surrounded a camp of Lakota Sioux. What began as a tense disarmament ended in a hellish volley of rifles and Hotchkiss guns. Hundreds of men, women, and children were left in the snow – dead in the last major clash of the Indian Wars. It was a wound in the land itself, a shadow that lingered for decades over the South Dakota prairies. For the generation of George and Nancy Streeter, settling as pioneers in those same years, Wounded Knee was no distant history but a tangible reality, retold in hushed stories by the fireside.

The family knew joyful moments, such as the arrival of foster child Rolla Harrison, who was briefly taken into the household. But there was tragedy as well; in September 1905, Laura Myrtle Faris, the newlywed wife of son Harry, died – likely of tuberculosis. She was only 21. Laura's death brought mortality harshly into a household that until then had been marked chiefly by building and progress.

Not long after the Streeter homestead had become firmly established, George's father, Norman S. Streeter, and Nancy's mother, Sarah Ditto, both spent periods of time living with the family in Whitewood Township. Their presence brought stability and continuity – a living link to the older pioneer generation that had first crossed from the wooded hills of Wisconsin to the open plains of Dakota.

In their later years, both left the farm to live closer to relatives. Sarah Ditto passed away in Lake Preston, South Dakota, on 8 May 1906, only a few kilometres from the Streeter homestead. Norman Streeter returned to Wisconsin in his final years and died in Rewey in 1912. Though they did not both end their days on the family farm, their influence lingered in the household – in its rhythm of work, faith, and cooperation. Their passing marked a quiet turning point: the close of the pioneer era and the rise of a new generation, their children, now citizens of a young and growing state.

At the dawn of the twentieth century, the sons left the parental homestead. Clarence remained closest, on his own plot across from the family farm, where he also supported the nearby Whitewood No. 6 school. Harry stayed active in Lake Preston and continued to advise and assist the family. William settled permanently in Watertown with the railroad, yet his letters and visits sustained ties to home.

With their sons gone, George and Nancy made a momentous decision: they retired to a farm parcel owned by son Harry – land that allowed them to grow old on familiar soil. The original Streeter farm was later transferred to daughter Eva and her husband Chas Gregory – a logical step in the continuation of the family story.

The farm remained more than an economic unit. It was a place of transmission: of experience, norms, stories, and belonging. Fireside tales – of settlers trapping bears, of harsh winters and abundant harvests – did not become mere folklore, but a moral memory. Every child and grandchild who stepped onto the yard was unconsciously shaped by the echo of those stories.

Clarence, Harry, and William carried their Streeter legacy into their respective lives – as farmer, mail carrier, and railroad man – all forms of service to land and community. Their children – the next generation – would grow up with the same sense of duty and perseverance, qualities that would later reappear in descendants, including Donald Smith.

While George and Nancy's sons left the homestead in the early twentieth century, the daily rhythm of prairie life continued. Cows had to be milked, fields cultivated, bread baked. In that same period, the youngest daughters – Flora, Jessie, and Eva – came of age amid farm work and school days in a small schoolhouse on land owned by their brother Clarence.

Between 1897 and 1899, the three girls attended Whitewood School No. 6 together – affectionately called 'the Streeter School'. This modest one-room wooden schoolhouse symbolised the hope, solidarity, and progress of a young community. Within its simple walls – warmed by a cast-iron stove and lit by sunlight pouring through tall windows – generations of children learned not only to read and write, but also to cooperate, dream, and persevere.

At the head of this class stood a dedicated teacher with quiet authority. Her lessons, lively and adapted to farm life, offered more than knowledge – they offered direction. Flora, the thoughtful eldest, often helped younger pupils. Jessie, sensitive and dreamy, kept diaries. Eva, curious and energetic, asked endless questions and brightened the room. Each of them grew within those walls not only as students but as people.

In their spare time, prairie children often turned to homemade games – simple in form but rich in imagination. A favourite pastime was corn-cob darts: a piece cut from a dried cob with a nail inserted, sometimes adorned with a chicken feather, so it resembled a primitive dart. They aimed at a wooden door or plank, testing skill and daring. It was a game that cost little but yielded great fun – and reflected the inventive character of farm life: where toys were scarce, you fashioned them from harvest remnants.

In winter, when farm work slowed, adult learners also came to the school for evening classes. Harry and William Streeter took their seats with roughened hands, determined to improve their skills. The teacher encouraged them, knowing that education could also open a window to a wider world for adults. During her years at the Streeter School, Eva began to blossom socially, becoming a warm and well-liked presence among her classmates and in the life of the community.

The school functioned as a miniature community. Plays, storytelling evenings, and communal meals formed a cultural fabric that offered warmth and cohesion against the prairie's raw wind. As the sisters outgrew Whitewood No.6, their education carried them beyond the district to a larger graded school in Oldham, located some 8km from the family farm. Attendance there required a weekly separation from home. During the school days the girls stayed with relatives near the town; at weekends they returned to the farm, where agricultural labour, shared meals, and family life resumed their familiar rhythm.

In Oldham, the sisters encountered a broader intellectual and social environment than the one-room school could provide. Flora developed a strong interest in literature, Jessie showed particular talent in drawing, and Eva gravitated toward geography and storytelling. The move to Oldham signified more than academic advancement. It marked a transition from the enclosed rhythms of prairie life to a world structured around graded instruction, specialised subjects, and wider horizons.

By the late 1890s, Oldham itself had emerged as a regional centre for public schooling. After an initial one-room schoolhouse opened in 1892–1893, a purpose-built two-storey public school was erected in 1898 on the town's designated school block, adjacent to City Park. Designed to accommodate multiple grades and teachers, the building reflected a growing commitment to structured, graded education that went beyond the limitations of rural district schools.

For families such as the Streeters, this educational opportunity lay beyond walking distance and depended on extended kinship networks. Census records list Eva Streeter, born in 1892, as a student in Oldham at the age of 12, indicating her attendance at the town's graded public school in the early years of the twentieth century. Like many prairie families, the Streeters relied on periods of residence away from the farm to sustain continued schooling. By 1910, Eva was living in the household of her older brother William Streeter, no longer recorded as a schoolchild but as a young woman contributing to the domestic economy — a natural progression from education into adulthood.

After their studies, Flora and Jessie set out on their own: Flora married and moved to Cedar Falls, South Dakota, and Jessie found love in Pierre, South Dakota. Eva remained on the farm – the beating heart of the household – and took care of her parents. Her continued presence gave the family continuity and deepened ties with the community.

For a military-historical work, the story of the Streeter School is more than a nostalgic portrait. It is a lens on the formation of character and citizenship. In classrooms like that of the Streeter School, future generations learned the values of discipline, service, cooperation, and resilience – values that would later prove essential for servicemen like Donald Smith, a son of Eva Streeter. His decision to serve in wartime was rooted not only in duty, but in a culture that began in prairie schoolrooms – among chalkboards, corn cobs, and fireside tales.

In the early years of the Streeter School, Lottie Rotluff and Nellie Dailey stood before the class as its first teachers. The first generation of pupils to attend the Streeter School in 1893 were the children of pioneers George and Nancy Streeter: Clarence, Harry, William, Florence, Eva, and Jessie. In the early twentieth century a second generation followed – the children of Clarence Streeter, whose farm lay beside the school. Clyde, Glen, Hazel, Mae, and Grace grew up with the same sparse yet meaningful education that had shaped their uncles and aunts. Thus the schoolhouse reflected not only the development of a community, but also the enduring family bonds that, from generation to generation, sustained education and shared life on the prairie.

After completing their teacher training, both Mae and Hazel Streeter returned to teach at the Streeter School – Whitewood No. 6 – the small one-room schoolhouse that had once been their own classroom. Their work there continued the family's long tradition of teaching on the prairie, a legacy that began with their grandfather George Streeter, who had helped establish the school in the 1880s.

In later years, Hazel – by then Hazel Streeter Hatch – remained among its teachers, while Mae also devoted her career to education. By the 1930s, former pupils remembered names such as Miss Starkey, Miss Maxam, and Miss Sneesby, who guided a new generation of children. The school's story reflects not only the dedication of its teachers, but also the Streeter family's enduring commitment to education and community life on the South Dakota prairie.

A symbolic turning point in the school's history came in September 1941; the *Oldham Register* reported that, for the first time since its founding in 1894, no child from the Streeter family was enrolled. Under Miss Sneesby, who then had seven pupils in her care, teaching continued – but the school had undeniably entered a new era. In the early 1950s the Streeter School closed its doors for good.

The Streeter School may be gone, but its legacy lived – and lives – on in the lives of those it formed, and in the deeds of those who emerged from that community to serve their country, wherever in the world they were called.

Chapter 3

A New Love on the Prairie

It was a crisp spring morning in 1912 when Eva Streeter first met Charles Levi Gregory – or Chas, as he introduced himself. She was 20, the youngest of six children, and although she had always been the little sister, she was slowly beginning to make her own way. Her brothers and sisters were scattered across South Dakota. At home on the farm it was Eva – the only one of the six – who still lived with her parents. Her sisters, Flora and Jessie, lived farther away.

The days were long but full; work in the fields, household chores, and above all her service to the Methodist Church, which still held services in Oldham's modest Baptist chapel. There Eva found not only faith but belonging. She helped with collections, visited families in need, and felt useful – though she likely wondered at times whether another life might also be meant for her, a life like the ones her brothers and sisters had built: with a family, a home.

That morning she had hitched up the wagon early; Daisy – her trusty mare – was already waiting. The drive to Oldham was calm, birds chattering in the ditches, the spring air bright and light. At the chapel she began loading baskets and parcels for a poor family on the edge of Whitewood Township. As she wrestled with a heavy basket, a stranger stepped in to help. His clear blue eyes, weathered skin, and steady bearing made an immediate impression. He introduced himself as Chas Gregory, a handyman from Bryant who was temporarily working with his cousin in Lake Preston.

What began as a chance encounter grew into a familiarity that surprised Eva. Charles started appearing more often. He helped with church collections, brought surplus from his cousin's harvest, and sometimes lingered a little longer. Their conversations turned to farm life, the seasons, family, community – and slowly something took root between them, gentle yet solid at once. They felt at home with each other, a feeling that didn't need to be named.

Summer brought colour and warmth across the prairie, and in Eva's heart grew a feeling she hardly dared to name. Chas was not a farmer, not a man of the land like her brothers and father, but he worked hard, listened sincerely, and showed a kind of respect that moved her. She understood that love does not always follow what seems logical. Sometimes it simply appears.

When Eva discovered she was pregnant, she told her mother. The response was one of emotion, a blessing. The news set the family in motion: brothers and sisters offering cautious congratulations, parents slowly opening themselves to what lay ahead.

Chas understood he had to choose: for Eva, for their child, and for a future that would not come by itself. One summer evening out in the field he asked her to marry him. His hands were rough, his voice hesitant, but his heart was open. Eva said yes.

On 7 October 1913, in the parental home on the Streeter land, surrounded by brothers, sisters, neighbours, and Reverend Wilson, Eva and Chas were married. No grand church, no ceremonial display – but a house full of people who cared for them. Her dress was simple, hand-sewn by her mother; Chas's suit was borrowed from his cousin and a bit too loose. But their looks, their smiles – those fit perfectly.

After the ceremony came a simple yet warm celebration. Long tables in the autumn sun, wildflowers picked by her sisters, stews and apple pie, cider and music. Even Clarence and William, who had harboured doubts about Chas, raised a toast. Nancy spoke words of a mother's blessing; George watched in silence, his heart full.

Later that evening, Eva and Chas stood by the fence, the stars above them, the land before them. They said little. Their silences were filled with promise. They knew life would test them, that days of doubt and hardship would come. But in that moment they were simply two young people, united in hope.

Eva and Chas began something as old as it was new: a life together. Not without struggle, but with the conviction that love could be built – like a house, a field, a future.

The roots of both the Streeters and the Gregorys lay in England. Their ancestors crossed the Atlantic in the seventeenth century and settled in the colonies of New England. The Streeters found their calling in the land; they were farmers, accustomed to the rhythm of the seasons and the hard work of the fields. For generations they raised crops and livestock, including in Wisconsin, where they were part of close-knit farming communities.

The Gregorys followed a different path. They were craftsmen and labourers – men who made their living working metal and wood, repairing tools, and taking on all manner of practical jobs. Chas Gregory followed that track, trained as a handyman, like his father before him, who worked as a blacksmith.

In the 1880s, George and Nancy Streeter went west as pioneers to the Dakota Territory, drawn by the promise of fertile land under the Homestead Act. The Gregorys came later but also found their place there. In time the families met on the South Dakota prairies, where Eva Streeter – a farmer's daughter – married Chas Gregory, a blacksmith's son. Two worlds came together: one rooted in agriculture, the other in craft.

It is not for me, as the author, to pass judgment on later events during and beyond their marriage. What is certain is that tensions grew over the years, ultimately leading to their son Donald and youngest daughter Grace spending a period of time in an orphanage. The reasons remain disputed to this day; within the father's family there is the conviction that there was no other choice at the time, while within the mother's family the prevailing feeling is that it should never have happened. I confine myself to the facts, allowing the reader to see how the circumstances and backgrounds of both families helped shape the course of this story.

Chapter 4

A Place for the Young Family

In the autumn of 1913, shortly after their marriage, Eva Streeter and Chas Gregory were given the opportunity to build a new life on Eva's parents' farm in Whitewood Township, Kingsbury County, South Dakota. With their first child on the way, George and Nancy Streeter – both elderly and aware of the physical limits of farm life – decided to retire to a smaller property that had once belonged to their son Harry. The family farm, with its fertile fields, spacious barn, and sturdy farmhouse, was entrusted to the next generation. For Eva and Chas, this meant more than a practical arrangement: it was a symbolic passing on of responsibility, heritage, and hope for the future.

In the first years after moving in, Eva and Chas threw themselves into the work. Chas, not born to the prairie, had embraced farming with conviction. His efforts were intense, driven by love for his wife and the promise of a growing family. Quietly, he sometimes struggled with doubt – was this truly his calling? – but he kept such thoughts to himself. Eva, who had grown up among the fields, recognised his effort and valued it all the more.

On 14 January 1914, their first child was born: George Edward Gregory, named after Eva's father. Two years later, on 9 February 1916, their daughter Dorothy Mae Gregory came into the world. In these early years a close, hardworking household took shape. George grew up with a sense of responsibility beyond his age, and Dorothy brought light and laughter to the home. Chas found joy in fatherhood and worked tirelessly to secure the family's future.

When the United States entered the war in Europe on 6 April 1917, even men whose lives were rooted in the soil of the prairie were drawn into the machinery of national mobilisation. On 5 June 1917, Chas reported to De Smet to register with the Selective Service System, as required by law. As the father of two young children and an established farmer, he qualified for deferment. Yet the act of registration itself marked a decisive moment: for the first time, the distant conflict in Europe pressed directly upon daily life on the prairie.

That same awareness soon reached the kitchen table of George and Nancy Streeter's farm. Under the provisions of the Selective Service Act, all men between the ages of 21 and 45 were required to register for the draft, regardless of profession, family obligations, or geographic isolation. The war made no distinction between city and countryside.

For Clarence, Harry, and William Streeter, the official notice did not imply immediate induction, but it nevertheless carried a sobering weight. The letter was brief, formal, and impersonal, yet its meaning extended far beyond the paper on which it was written. It confirmed that even the remote prairies of South Dakota were no longer beyond the reach of a global conflict.

George Streeter watched his sons in silence. All three fell within the mandated age range, though at its upper limits. Clarence was 43, Harry 39, and William 36 – men with established livelihoods, land to maintain, and responsibilities that extended well beyond themselves. Their lives were firmly anchored in agriculture, a sector increasingly recognised by federal authorities as strategically indispensable.

The question, therefore, was not whether they would register – that was compulsory – but what role they would ultimately be called upon to play. The American war effort demanded far more than soldiers alone. It required food, transport, maintenance, and industrial output on an unprecedented scale. Farmers, in particular, formed the backbone of this logistical system.

In September 1917, the three brothers travelled together to De Smet, the administrative centre of Kingsbury County, to complete their registration. The draft office was crowded with men of widely varying ages and backgrounds. Young adults at the threshold of their lives stood beside fathers of large families, craftsmen, railroad workers, and agricultural labourers. The process was efficient and unceremonious. Names, dates of birth, and occupations were recorded; physical descriptions carefully noted.

When their occupation was entered – *farmer* – its significance was unmistakable. No assurances were given, but the implication was clear. As many in rural communities already suspected, deferment was likely.

Food production had been officially designated as essential to the success of the American Expeditionary Forces overseas.

That assessment proved correct. In the months that followed, official correspondence confirmed that none of the three brothers would be called to active service. Clarence continued to manage his own land, Harry applied his mechanical skills to improving agricultural equipment, and William worked closely with his father on the family farm. Their contribution to the war effort was indirect, but no less vital.

While thousands of younger men departed for training camps and, eventually, for the battlefields of France, the Streeter brothers remained at work. Their duty was not carried out in trenches or under fire, but in the fields of South Dakota – where grain, livestock, and sustenance were produced to support a war fought an ocean away.

In quiet perseverance, they served the same cause: far from the front lines, yet firmly embedded in the national war effort.

Chapter 5

Signs of Change

It did not change in a single day. There was no storm, no upheaval, no loud signal. The prairie remained what it was, and yet it was felt: something had shifted. Gently, almost imperceptibly, but irreversibly.

Where time had once been measured in seasons, harvests, and Sundays, another rhythm began to assert itself. Faster. Tighter. Directed from elsewhere. Change did not arrive on horseback, but with steam, electricity, and steel. At first as a rumour, distant and vague. Then closer, tangible, at once promise and threat.

By the middle of the second decade of the twentieth century – when Europe was already at war, but America still stood on the sidelines – the outlines of a new age were becoming visible even on the prairie.

Farmers who had broken the land by hand watched as their sons dreamed of electricity instead of inheritance, of machines instead of ploughs. Women leafed through mail-order catalogues filled with objects no one had ever needed – until they existed. And in the mailbox appeared letters from cities no one had ever visited, yet which everyone began to long for.

These were not shocks that made the earth tremble. They were details. An automobile on a dirt road. A telephone wire stretching across a cornfield. A jingle drifting from a radio. A new railroad line drawn onto maps. They were signs of change. And those who listened closely could hear them coming, long before the train actually ran.

One of the most visible signs of change on the prairie was the arrival of the railroad. De Smet, the county seat of Kingsbury County, had been connected to the outside world since 1880 through the Chicago & North Western Railway. But in the years that followed – especially between 1905 and 1917 – plans emerged to extend additional lines toward smaller farming communities such as Bryant and Willow Lake.

In some places, wooden ties were already stacked along the fields. Elsewhere, surveyors stood in the shimmering heat with measuring rods and taut lines. The prairie was measured, divided, opened up.

The railroad brought not only goods and people, but also ideas, commerce, and speed. For farmers it meant new possibilities: grain, corn, and livestock could be shipped farther than ever before – to Minneapolis, Sioux City, or even Chicago. The landscape did not grow larger, but distances suddenly seemed shorter.

On a sweltering morning, neighbour Harold Evans rode his horse into George Streeter's yard. His face was red from the heat, his shirt soaked with sweat, but his words carried news.

'They're extending the line to Willow Lake,' he said as he dismounted and removed his hat. 'I heard it in Bryant, at the grain elevator. Next season we might be able to ship our harvest to the city by rail.'

George said nothing. He looked eastward, where the land rose gently toward the shimmering horizon. The prospect was tempting: no more days-long journeys by horse and wagon, no wasted time, no spoiled loads. But the thought did not come alone.

If the rails came, they would not come for him alone.

Farmers from Nebraska, Kansas, or even Illinois would ship their grain to the same markets via that very line. Larger operations, better machinery, lower costs. Prices would fall. The old certainties – that you knew your neighbours, that labour and return were in balance – began to fade.

The prairie, once slow and familiar, suddenly felt open and vulnerable.

Signs of progress appeared everywhere. In Oldham he had recently seen an automobile pass by, a gleaming Ford that raised less dust than a horse and yet moved faster. In Lake Preston, a cousin said the church now had electric light. In De Smet, telephone poles had recently gone up along the main street, linked by thin black wires that carried voices from place to place. And in the mailbox lay a thick Montgomery Ward catalogue, filled with appliances, fabrics – even radios.

George thought of his barn, whose roof had leaked for years. Of his workhorses, slowly losing their strength. Of his son Clarence, who preferred reading about electricity and coils of wire to seed calendars and ploughing depths. And of his youngest daughter, Eva, who on Sundays sat at the neighbours' house around a strange wooden box, listening to crackling static and fragments of distant voices – as if the world were larger than wheat fields and silence.

The train brought progress, but also unrest.

The sound of metal on rails was still far away, yet in George's mind it already rang.

Chapter 6

As the Family Continues to Grow

On 15 January 1918, the third child of Eva and Chas was born: Donald Owen Gregory. Conditions were modest, the winter severe, but the household radiated resilience. Donald grew into a quiet, observant boy with an unusual fascination for everything that moved through the air. Airplanes and birds soaring high above the prairie caught his attention more than life on the ground. From early on, he seemed different – thoughtful, focused, as if destined for something not yet revealed.

He must have been a sturdy baby; in an old photograph he lies beside his cousin Ruth Streeter in a wooden crib, eyes wide open, body solid and heavy. According to family recollections, Eva remarked at his birth that 'his name would one day be heard across the fields and high into the clouds'. A few months later, a local newspaper even mentioned him as a crowd favourite at a Red Cross fundraising fair – the 'big, heavy baby' who drew curious townsfolk to the square of Lake Preston, South Dakota.

In August 1918, unexpected news reached the Gregory family: Lawrence Gregory, Chas's 23-year-old brother, had been killed in an explosion in Willow Lake, South Dakota. The tragedy left a deep mark. The funeral, held in Bryant, brought the family together in grief. Lawrence's death reminded them that loss did not always come from distant wars – it could strike just as cruelly at home.

In September 1918, the US government expanded the draft. Eva's brothers – Clarence, Harry, and William – all registered. Each ultimately received deferment based on their work in agriculture or transportation, sectors vital to the nation's wartime supply. The family remained spared from military service. In November, the war ended. For the Streeters and Gregorys, it did not mean the return of soldiers, but rather the quiet confirmation that their contribution on home soil had been of national importance.

On 29 January 1920, Grace Lola Gregory was born. Eva and Chas now had four children. Life on the farm settled into a steady rhythm. Eva cared for the household, raised the children, and kept the family together, while Chas worked the land – despite his recurring uncertainty about whether farming was truly his path. Yet the growth of the family gave him deep fulfilment. The children, each with distinct personalities, made the hard life bearable.

At the end of their lives, George and Nancy Streeter looked out across the fields they had once broken themselves. The house was quieter now, the rooms emptier, but their work endured – in every furrow of soil, in every timber of the little schoolhouse, in the letters of their sons, the prayers of their daughter, and the love of their grandchildren. The farm had not become a relic, but a living monument to labour, resilience, and family devotion.

In the autumn of 1920, the family lost its patriarch: George Streeter died on 23 September of a heart attack. His death marked the end of an era. George was more than a farmer; he was a pioneer, a father, and a pillar of stability for his children and grandchildren. His passing was felt as a collective loss – by Eva, her brothers and sisters, and most of all by his widow, Nancy, who had shared his life's long journey, from the gruelling ox-wagon trek to the building of the family homestead.

Eva and Chas carried on, now aware that they were the bearers of the family's story.

In the early 1920s, the Gregory farm was a place of work, simplicity, connection, and remembrance. Eva kept the family together; her mother, Nancy, helped where she could, and the children found their place within this carefully built life. Donald, still young but already with his head in the clouds, brought a new dimension to the family – a promise of something different, something greater. His fascination with the sky grew quietly, nourished by stories and by the dreams of his mother, Eva, who had once wished to see the world.

Life on the prairie demanded sacrifice but offered purpose in return. Following in the footsteps of their forebears, Eva and Chas built a future – rooted in tradition yet open to the possibilities still to come.

Chapter 7

The Spanish Flu

As the children grew, the world around them began to change in subtle yet unsettling ways. News of war and illness reached even the prairie, carried by newspapers, letters, and rumours from nearby towns like Oldham. What had first seemed a distant threat slowly began to cast its shadow over the rhythms of farm life.

Eva noticed it in her neighbours' behaviour, in the hush that settled over the fields, in the way people began to avoid one another. The Spanish Flu, which since 1918 had claimed millions of lives around the world, suddenly appeared closer to home. Even South Dakota was not spared. In Oldham, church pews grew emptier, the baker closed his doors, and wagons carrying the sick moved quietly through the villages.

Chas and Eva took precautions. The children stayed on the farm, hands were washed more often, and visitors were turned away. But against an unseen enemy there was no perfect defence. In the spring of 1921, as the snow slowly withdrew from the prairie, the first symptoms appeared in Eva – coughing, fatigue, shortness of breath. Then fever – heavy and unrelenting.

The illness swept through the household. Eva became gravely ill. Chas kept vigil at her bedside while Nancy cared for the children. Dorothy and Grace showed mild symptoms. Only Donald remained oddly unaffected, though he understood the seriousness from the looks on the faces of his father and grandmother.

The doctor confirmed what they feared: Eva had contracted the Spanish Flu. There was little to be done beyond rest, cool compresses, and prayerful waiting. For days her condition rose and fell. Her body fought on while the family maintained a hushed routine around her. Donald and his siblings lingered near the bedroom door, searching for reassurance.

Gradually Eva began to recover. The fever broke; her breathing steadied. But recovery was slow and left its mark. She was weakened, thin, her strength never fully returning. Something within her had been broken – not a visible wound, but a deep exhaustion that clung to her. Chas saw it, though he said nothing. Nancy, too, kept her observations to herself.

Life resumed its course. That spring, the doors of the Streeter School opened once more. But nothing felt the same. Some children were missing – taken by illness or moved away – and their absence weighed heavily on those who remained.

Clarence, Eva's brother, continued to maintain the building as he always had, but the little schoolhouse now felt like a relic of another time. The Spanish Flu might not have destroyed the community, but it had marked it deeply. The shadow of the pandemic lingered over the prairie, even as the skies cleared and children returned to their lessons.

By the spring of 1923, life on the Gregory farm began to steady once again. Yet the effects of the influenza were still fresh in memory. Eva, though convalescent, struggled to regain her former strength. She went about her chores with discipline, but her energy was limited. The doctor had warned her that the illness had left permanent damage to her lungs.

On the first morning George and Dorothy were allowed to return to school, Eva insisted on walking them herself. She saw it as a personal victory. The walk to the schoolhouse, hand in hand with her children, marked a symbolic moment of recovery. But along the way she felt a sudden dizziness. At the schoolhouse door, her vision went briefly dark – a sign of how fragile her health remained.

Soon afterward, her condition worsened again. What began as fatigue and mild chest pain developed into persistent fever and shortness of breath. The doctor confirmed that Eva was suffering from severe pneumonia, a complication of her earlier influenza.

In the days that followed, Eva lay bedridden, her condition declining steadily. Family gathered at the farm. Her mother Nancy kept vigil by her side; her brothers Clarence, Harry, and William, and her sisters Flora and Jessie came to help. The children moved quietly through the house, sensing the gravity of the moment.

On Friday, 13 April 1923, Eva Emmeline Gregory, née Streeter, passed away at the age of 30. Her death was sudden but not unforeseen. Influenza and its complications had finally overcome her weakened body. The loss struck the family deeply. Chas lost his wife, the children their mother, and Nancy her beloved daughter.

Three days later the funeral was held. The casket stood in the farmhouse parlour, surrounded by wildflowers and simple wreaths. Reverend Richard Linstrom led a modest service at the Methodist Church of Oldham. Eva was then laid to rest in the Oldham cemetery, among generations of settlers from Whitewood Township.

Eva's death broke the rhythm of family life. Chas was left with four young children. George soon took on a protective role within the household. Dorothy helped with chores and cared for little Grace. Donald, still small, often withdrew into silence, seeking his mother's presence in memory and routine. From contemporary newspaper accounts it is clear that Eva was a very social person, surrounded by a wide circle of friends and neighbours, whose sympathy and presence at her passing spoke volumes about the place she held within her community.

Life on the farm continued – carried by duty and remembrance. Eva's legacy endured in the family's habits, in the care they gave one another, and in the quiet strength they spoke of without words. Spring came again, and the fields were sown once more. Yet on the prairie of Whitewood Township, Kingsbury County, an empty space remained – silent, but lasting.

Chapter 8

The Aftermath

After Eva's burial in Oldham, the mourners returned to the farm – a home that would now have to go on without her voice or presence. Family from the region stayed for several days to help fill the first hollow silence. Clarence, Harry, and William worked the fields beside Chas, while Flora and Jessie tended to the household. Nancy, Eva's mother, was there every day. She cared for the children and comforted Chas without words. Her presence gave the family a fragile sense of steadiness.

When the relatives departed, the silence deepened. The house, once alive with Eva's warmth, now echoed with absence. Chas returned to his work but struggled with exhaustion and grief. Donald, only 5, bore the loss in bewildered silence. Dorothy tried to impose order, while Nancy's daily visits became the family's anchor.

In the weeks that followed, the impact of Eva's death proved not only emotional but practical. She had managed the household finances. When Chas spread the bills and ledgers across the kitchen table, discouragement set in. The farm was under strain.

He turned to Clarence, Eva's eldest brother. Together with William, Harry, Flora, Jessie, and their mother Nancy, the Streeters convened to support the Gregory family. Clarence took over part of the fieldwork. William arranged for schoolbooks. Harry's wife provided weekly meals. Flora and Jessie contributed money. Nancy assumed care of little Grace.

The Streeter family became a collective safety net, joined by the Oldham community. Neighbours helped with food, clothing, and small financial gifts. The Methodist Church organised support gatherings and kept the family in prayer. In the midst of sorrow, Chas felt hope for the first time in months.

In September 1923, the new school year began. George, Dorothy, and Donald attended Whitewood No. 6, the one-room schoolhouse on

Clarence's property. Grace, still too young, stayed with her grandmother. George, now 9, was solemn and responsible. Dorothy, 7, watched over Donald and guided him through his first school day with gentle determination.

That morning, Chas waved them off. The simplicity of their departure – Donald with his homemade satchel and slate board – was likely seared into his memory. He must have thought of Eva, of all she had been to their children, and felt the weight of single fatherhood. But he also knew he was not alone.

With the Streeters' support, the solidarity of the community, and his own perseverance, Chas Gregory entered a new chapter of fatherhood. The household slowly adjusted to its loss, and the farm found a fragile rhythm once more. The future remained uncertain, yet the enduring bonds of kinship and care gave them strength.

Across the fields of Kingsbury County, the sounds of life and growth began, tentatively, to return.

Chapter 9

A Hard Choice

The summer of 1923 brought not only the lingering weight of grief but also a devastating drought that swept across much of the United States, including South Dakota. Week after week, the sky remained empty. Without rain, the fields withered, the soil cracked open, and the lifeblood of the prairie seemed to evaporate. Crops failed, livestock weakened, and families who had endured war and loss now faced a new and merciless adversary: nature itself.

In Kingsbury County, the drought struck with particular cruelty. The once-green stretches of wheat and corn turned to dust and straw. The small rivers and ponds that had sustained livestock for generations shrank into muddy hollows. Winds swept across the flatlands, lifting dry earth into the air until even the horizon blurred. People spoke in low voices about the weather, about prices falling and debts rising, about neighbours packing up their wagons and leaving for towns farther east.

For Chas Gregory, widower and father of four young children, the drought became a trial that tested him to his limits. Already worn by the loss of Eva, he now faced the unthinkable: the possible collapse of the life they had built together. Without a harvest, there would be no income. Without income, there would be no way to keep the farm running. The animals had to be fed, tools repaired, taxes paid – all while grief still clung to the walls of the house.

By midsummer, Chas began to realise that survival alone might no longer be possible. He spent long evenings sitting on the porch, watching the sun set through a haze of dust, thinking about what he might have to do. Would he have to give up the land? Would he need to send his children away – to relatives, or even to institutions – just to ensure they were fed? The thought was unbearable. Yet he could not ignore the arithmetic of hunger.

The Streeter family, steadfast as ever, refused to let that happen. In a family council held at Clarence's farm, they gathered – Clarence, Harry, William, Flora, Jessie, and their mother Nancy. They decided together that Chas would not face this fight alone. Each would contribute what they could. Clarence took over the ploughing and field repairs. Harry arranged to transport feed and supplies from neighbouring farms that had fared slightly better. William, still working with the railroads, used his connections to help move grain at reduced cost. Flora and Jessie handled the paperwork and letters, negotiating credit and keeping track of expenses. And Nancy – steady, unyielding Nancy – stayed on at the Gregory farm, running the household and caring for the children as though she were holding the fabric of their lives together by sheer will.

Their cooperation brought a fragile order back to the farm. With his brothers-in-law tending to the heavier work, Chas focused on the livestock, whose care demanded less labour but offered something steady in return – milk, eggs, and a little food for the table. The animals, unlike the parched fields, still responded to effort and patience. That daily routine gave him a purpose when everything else seemed to crumble.

Despite the hardship, one principle remained sacred among the Streeters: the children's education. Even in the face of hunger and loss, the family insisted that George, Dorothy, and Donald continue attending the Whitewood No. 6 School. Education, they believed, was more than a privilege – it was a moral duty, an investment in dignity and future. Clarence repaired the school roof himself that autumn, refusing payment, and Flora supplied notebooks and pencils bought in town. In their small acts, the family turned despair into resolve.

As autumn approached, a faint sense of rhythm returned to the farm. There was no abundance, but there was stability. The barns were patched, the animals healthy enough to last the winter, and the fields – though barren – were ready for next season's planting. Chas worked quietly, his grief no longer sharp but ever-present, softened into a dull ache that accompanied every sunrise. The children grew – George taller and more serious, Dorothy thoughtful and helpful, Donald quiet and observant, Grace cheerful under her grandmother's watchful eye.

At times, Chas caught glimpses of Eva in them. In George's careful attention to chores. In Dorothy's habit of humming as she worked. In Donald's long silences, as if he were thinking about things beyond his years. Her absence remained a void, but her presence – her example, her gentleness – seemed to echo through all of them.

That autumn, when the first frost came and the fields turned pale under the morning sun, Chas stood outside the barn and felt, for the first time in months, a quiet sense of peace. The land had not yielded much, but it had not been lost. The family, held together by loyalty and faith, had endured.

The drought would ease the following year, though hardship would not vanish entirely. Yet in surviving this season, Chas and his children had proven something essential – that love, once rooted deeply, could withstand even the cruellest weather. And in each of the children, in ways both visible and hidden, a part of Eva's strength endured – the steadfast courage of a woman whose care continued to shape them long after her voice had fallen silent.

Chapter 10

The Break

In the months following Eva Gregory's death, life on the farm in Whitewood Township began to unravel. Without her as the steady heart of the household, Charles 'Chas' Gregory struggled more and more to keep up with the daily demands of running the place. Crops were harvested late or not at all. The cattle sometimes went without fresh water. The barns grew dirty, the fences unrepaired. What had once been a thriving homestead now bore the marks of fatigue and neglect.

Family members noticed the decline. Nancy Streeter, Eva's mother, came often to visit and saw the signs first-hand – the thinning cows, the smell of damp straw, the exhaustion in Chas's eyes. In October 1924, worried that things had gone too far, she asked her son Clarence to contact Arthur Smith, the local veterinarian. His inspection confirmed what everyone feared: the livestock was underfed, and the overall condition of the farm was deteriorating.

The situation forced the Streeter family to confront a painful reality. Eva's brothers – Clarence, Harry, and William – met to discuss what could be done. It was clear that Chas could no longer manage the farm and care for the children at the same time. After long and difficult conversations, a temporary plan was reached.

Dorothy, 8 years old, would move in with her uncle William Streeter and his wife, who lived near Watertown, where she could attend school and help around the house. George, 10, was placed with close family friends, Peter and Carrie Drilling, who had a farm nearby and could provide stability and schooling. For Donald and Grace, still very young, the hope was that they might remain with their father – provided he received extra help from relatives and neighbours.

The teacher of the Whitewood School had already expressed concern. She had written to the family earlier that summer, noting that the Gregory children often appeared tired and unkempt, sometimes missing classes for days at a time. Her words added urgency to the family's decision.

After a joint meeting that included Chas, it was agreed that he and the two youngest children, Donald (6½) and Grace (4½), would stay with his mother, Edna Gregory, in Bryant, South Dakota. The rest of the Streeter family would oversee the care of George and Dorothy and make sure the farm's property and debts were managed as best as possible.

Even with everyone's goodwill, however, the arrangement soon proved too fragile. The Gregory farm could not sustain itself, and Chas's mental and physical state worsened. The loss of his wife, the burden of debt, and the strain of separation from his older children weighed heavily on him.

Not all the details of this period can be reconstructed with certainty – memories differ among family descendants, and some accounts have faded into fragments of recollection. But the official records tell part of the story with quiet precision. On 2 September 1924, Charles L. Gregory brought his two youngest children, Donald and Grace, to the Children's Home Society in Sioux Falls, South Dakota. The admission register lists Edna Gregory – their grandmother – as temporary guardian and caretaker, the one who had been watching over them since Eva's death.

It was a heartbreaking decision, made not out of neglect but desperation. The Children's Home promised safety, schooling, and food – things the struggling farm could no longer guarantee. For Chas, leaving them there must have felt like both an act of love and a surrender.

In later years, those who knew the family would speak of that day in hushed tones. The journey to Sioux Falls marked the end of the Gregory family's time together under one roof. From that moment on, Donald's childhood changed forever – shaped not by the rhythms of the prairie, but by the corridors of an orphanage, where memory and longing became his quiet companions.

Chapter 11

The Road to the Orphanage

In July 1924, Charles Gregory loaded the last sacks and crates onto the wagon. The morning was cool and clear, the kind of prairie dawn that carried both promise and sorrow. Before him lay the long road to Bryant, Hamlin County, where his ageing parents still lived. Behind him stood the weathered house in Whitewood Township, the home he had shared with Eva – now marked by peeling paint, sagging fences, and the decay of absence.

He paused for a moment before climbing aboard, taking one last look at the house. The silence around it felt heavier than ever. Donald and Grace, the two youngest of his children, waited patiently, unaware of the finality of the moment. Charles had made the decision to bring them to his mother while he searched for work. It was not a choice born of will, but of necessity.

The children climbed onto the wagon. Donald, 6 years old, sat close to his father, while little Grace held a worn doll in her lap. As the horses started forward, the wheels rattled over the dry earth. The day stretched endlessly before them, a journey measured not only in miles but in resignation.

Along the road, Donald asked the question that Charles had dreaded: 'Why aren't George and Dorothy coming with us?'

Charles hesitated before answering. 'They're staying with family,' he said quietly. 'So they can go to school and have a place to grow.'

It was true – Dorothy had gone to live with Eva's brother William and his wife, while George was staying with Peter and Carrie Drilling, trusted friends of Eva's family. The children were scattered now, like seeds blown by a hard wind, each placed where there was still a chance to survive.

For the rest of the journey, the road offered only silence – broken by the clatter of wagon wheels and the steady rhythm of the horses' hooves. Charles kept his eyes fixed on the road, though his thoughts spiralled inward. He worried about his mother, Edna Gregory, whose health had begun to fail. Could she truly manage two small children? He had written to her, explaining his situation, but no reply had come.

That evening, they stopped at a small farm. A kind woman took pity on them and offered a night's rest – straw bedding in the barn, a jug of milk, and a loaf of bread. The children slept soundly; Charles did not.

The next day, they resumed their journey. By early evening, the wagon rolled into Bryant, South Dakota, bathed in the soft amber light of the setting sun. The old Gregory homestead stood quiet, its porch shaded by a wind-twisted tree. When they arrived, Donald and Grace ran ahead, calling out. Edna appeared in the doorway, frail but smiling, and opened her arms. She gathered them in as if to shelter them from everything the world had taken.

That night, after the children were asleep, Charles and his mother talked long into the dark. He told her of his plans to find work in Flandreau, South Dakota, his fears for the children, and his inability to provide for them properly. Edna listened, her lined face calm but weary. She promised to care for Donald and Grace as best she could, though she confessed her strength was waning. Charles nodded in silence, knowing she was telling the truth. He had run out of choices.

The next morning, he rose before dawn, packed his few belongings, and went into town. For $1.30, he bought a train ticket to Flandreau, with a transfer in Watertown. He found work first at a bakery, hauling flour sacks and stoking ovens. The job was hard and the pay meagre – four dollars a week for a rented room above a general store. He found a slightly better job at a grain mill, but even that left him with barely enough to live on. Each payday, he sent a small envelope of cash back to Bryant.

A month later, he returned home. His mother's health had worsened. Her hands trembled when she poured tea; her breath came short after the simplest task. The children clung to her skirts, happy but thin. Charles saw the strain in her eyes and knew he could not leave them there much longer.

That evening, around the kitchen table, they discussed what neither wanted to say aloud. Edna admitted she could no longer manage. Charles's father reminded him of their own financial struggles. There was one remaining option – the Children's Home Society in Sioux Falls.

Charles recoiled at the thought. He knew what people said about such places – the cold dormitories, the rigid rules. He imagined Eva's reaction and felt shame rise in his chest. But he also saw no alternative. His mother's health, his empty pockets, the harshness of prairie life – they all pressed him towards the same conclusion.

On the intake form from the Children's Home, written in precise handwriting, the facts appear stark and unfeeling:

> Gregory, Donald Owen – born 15 January, 1918
> Gregory, Grace Lola – born 29 February, 1920
> Guardian: Mrs. Edna Gregory (grandmother)
> Father, Charles L. Gregoy, employed, temporary placement requested.

Orphanage records further document the situation: Grace is listed under dossier number 2734, and Donald under dossier number 2744.

The matron at the orphanage assured him the children would receive food, schooling, and care. The paperwork was clinical, but Charles's hand shook as he signed his name. He wrote his signature slowly, the way a man does when each letter carries the weight of a promise he might never keep. He told himself it was temporary, that he would find steady work, save enough, and bring them home.

That night, back at his parents' table, he sat beneath the flickering light of an oil lamp. The farmhouse was silent except for the ticking of a clock. Before him lay the admission forms, the ink still damp. This was the hardest decision of his life.

Outside, the wind moved softly through the prairie grass. Inside, Charles bowed his head over the papers and whispered a quiet vow – that no matter how long it took, he would come back for Donald and Grace.

Chapter 12

A Decision in Silence

The admission papers made it official: Chas could no longer care for his children. Yet, in his mind, this was not the end of fatherhood. He believed, or perhaps needed to believe, that this was only a pause – a temporary arrangement until he could find work and rebuild his life. The form itself reflected that fragile hope: the notation beside the entry read 'temporary stay'.

Still, the decision carried the weight of defeat. He chose not to inform the Streeter family, fearing their judgment or pity. To them, it might appear as abandonment; to him, it was the only way to keep the children safe.

On Tuesday, 2 September 1924, Edna Gregory, acting as guardian for her son Charles, brought Donald and Grace Gregory to the Children's Home Society in Sioux Falls, South Dakota, for what the paperwork described as 'temporary care'. The morning of their departure was cold and still, the kind of morning when even the birds seemed hesitant to sing. Donald and Grace stood beside their father on the platform, clutching small bundles of clothes. They likely didn't understand the true nature of the journey. Donald, at 6½, may have sensed the gravity of the day; Grace, 4 years old, still saw it as an adventure. The train to Sioux Falls arrived in silence, steam hissing, iron wheels grinding against the rails. On the journey, Grace held tightly to Donald's arm, as if he were the last familiar piece of a vanishing world. Donald, solemn beyond his years, promised silently that he would take care of her – though he had no idea how.

The Children's Home Society, founded in 1893, was a place for children whose families could no longer care for them – whether through death, poverty, or circumstance. Its mission was rooted in compassion, but its methods were shaped by discipline and necessity. The intake ledger recorded Edna Gregory as the accompanying adult – 'Mrs. Gregory,

Dexter Hall, All Saints School' – and listed 'Chas L. Gregory, Flandreau, S.D.' as the father.

For the institution, these were routine details. For Donald and Grace they marked the beginning of a new existence – a childhood lived within walls not their own. Their arrival marked the second great rupture in their short lives. The first had been the loss of their mother, whose warmth had anchored their world. Now came the second: separation from their father and grandparents, and the realisation that the life they had known was gone.

Inside the orphanage, life followed a rigid rhythm. The staff provided food, lessons, and medical care, but affection was rationed, like everything else. The halls were clean, the rules clear, the punishments swift.

Donald learned quickly how to keep quiet, how to follow instructions, how to make himself small. Grace adapted more slowly, frightened at night, whispering his name across the dormitory until she fell asleep.

The wounds of separation were invisible but deep. In a time when families across the Midwest were torn apart by illness, drought, and hardship, their story was not unique – yet to them, it felt like the end of childhood itself.

Chapter 13

Inside the Children's Home

Four months later, on 3 January 1925, the entry in the register of the Children's Home changed. What had been temporary became permanent. Their father signed a formal transfer of guardianship, surrendering his parental rights to the Children's Home Society. From that moment, the staff no longer required his consent for future placement or adoption decisions.

The register makes no mention of a final visit – no record of Charles seeing his children again. Legally, it was a routine act; emotionally, it was an erasure. Donald and Grace, too young to understand the meaning of the paperwork, were never told. Their 'temporary stay' had become a permanent separation. The heavy wooden door of the orphanage had closed behind them that September morning, sealing one life away and opening another.

Inside, the air smelled faintly of soap and varnish. The building was solid – tall ceilings, long corridors, polished floors that echoed with footsteps. The staff guided them through a brief intake process: names, ages, health check, a bath, clean clothes. They were assigned to separate dormitories – boys on one side, girls on the other – each filled with neat rows of iron beds, thin mattresses, grey wool blankets, and a single nightstand.

The next morning began before dawn. A bell clanged, followed by prayer and a plain breakfast of porridge and milk. Duties were assigned: Grace helped in the dining hall, Donald worked in the garden. Then came school lessons – arithmetic, spelling, Bible study – taught in strict silence.

During breaks, the siblings sought each other out in the courtyard, sharing whispered memories of home: the fields at Whitewood, the sound of their mother's voice, their father's promise that this was not forever. These moments became their refuge.

In time, they began to adjust. The orphanage provided stability, if not comfort. There were routines, clean clothes, predictable meals. But there was little warmth. The children learned to survive within structure, to replace love with obedience.

And yet, both held on to hope – that someone, someday, would come for them.

Meanwhile, far away in Whitewood Township, the prairie lay buried under snow. In the kitchen of the old Streeter farmhouse, Nancy Streeter and her children gathered around the table in concern. They had not heard from Chas in months, nor did they know what had become of Donald and Grace.

Clarence, Flora, and Harry were present; William was expected later that day. Jessie had written from afar, urging that something be done. Letters to Chas went unanswered. The family decided that if no word arrived before the year's end, they would contact Edna Gregory directly, or travel to Bryant to uncover the children's whereabouts themselves.

Nancy, her voice trembling but firm, insisted that the children must know they were not forgotten. The family agreed – they would find a way to reach them.

Then, in early December 1924, a letter arrived at the Children's Home. It bore a simple envelope, no return address except 'Bryant, S.D.' Inside were two short notes – one from their father, the other from their grandmother Edna.

> My dear Donald and Grace,
>
> I think of you every day. I am working hard and doing my best to make things right. Be brave, and help each other. We will be together again one day.
>
> Your loving father,
> Chas.

> My sweet grandchildren,
>
> I keep you in my prayers each night. Remember, you are loved and not forgotten.
>
> Grandmother.

The matron handed the letters to Donald and Grace in a quiet corner of the common room. They read them together – Grace tracing the words with her finger, Donald reading aloud in a steady voice. When he finished, Grace wiped her eyes and smiled faintly.

For the first time in months, the children felt something more than routine. The words from home were simple, but in that sterile place, they carried the weight of a promise – that somewhere beyond those walls, love still waited for them.

Chapter 14

A Miracle in the Early New Year of 1925

The first days of January 1925 brought back the familiar routine at the orphanage. For Donald and Grace Gregory, the holidays had been difficult. They missed the smell of freshly baked bread, the warmth of the woodstove, and the familiar voices of their aunts and uncles.

Although the Children's Home offered order, safety, and care, it could not fill the emptiness left by the loss of their mother and the separation from their home. Still, Donald and Grace remained hopeful. The letters they had received from their father and grandmother gave them something to hold onto in uncertain times. They believed that their family still thought of them and that their father was working towards a future where they might be together again – at least, that was their hope.

After spending the Christmas holidays with their parents in Oldham, Hazel Streeter returned to Madison on Monday, 5 January, to register for the new term at the Eastern State Normal School. The following morning, her sister Mae arrived on the early train from Oldham to join her.

The sisters met at the Madison depot just as dawn broke over the frosted platforms. The next train – bound for Sioux Falls – stood ready, its cars shrouded in clouds of steam. Together, they boarded, joining a group of teachers and student educators on a field visit to the Children's Home Society orphanage. For Hazel, it was part of her training; for Mae, already teaching, it was an opportunity to observe new methods and reconnect with her sister before returning to her own classroom.

The train carried them across the frozen plains of South Dakota. When they arrived in Sioux Falls, a bitter wind drove the group towards the large brick building at the edge of town. Inside, the air smelled faintly of soap and varnish. The visitors were led through the classrooms, dormitories, and common rooms by one of the staff.

In a classroom of mixed ages, Mae suddenly stopped. Her eyes had caught a name scrawled in chalk on the edge of a desk: 'Donald G.' A few desks away, she noticed another: 'Grace G.'

When the group reached the teacher's desk, Mae's gaze fell upon the class register lying open. In neat handwriting she read: 'Gregory, Donald' and 'Gregory, Grace', along with their ages and birthplaces. The combination of surname, age, and place of origin left no doubt – these were the children of her late aunt, Eva Streeter Gregory.

Mae quietly called her sister over and pointed to the names. Together they confirmed their suspicion by discreetly asking the staff member accompanying the tour. The answer came without hesitation: Donald and Grace had been admitted several months earlier, from a small rural community.

For the two sisters, the discovery was shocking and deeply emotional. Without anyone in the family knowing, their young cousins were living in this very institution.

Mae and Hazel were granted permission to meet Donald and Grace. They found Donald sitting at a table, focused on a chess game with another boy. His posture was calm and disciplined, but when he noticed the two young women watching him, something in his expression changed. He rose quietly, approached them, and greeted them with a mixture of relief and shy joy. In their brief conversation, he made it clear that he knew who they were – family – and that he had missed them. When asked why he was there, he answered simply, 'Father brought us here. He said it would be better for us.'

Grace was found among a group of children playing in another room. She was cheerful and engaged, her laughter bright and unrestrained. When she spotted Mae and Hazel, she ran straight to them and threw her arms around their waists. Her joy was spontaneous and pure, yet beneath it Mae and Hazel sensed something fragile – a child's effort to stay strong in a world she did not yet understand.

The sisters asked the director of the Children's Home Society if they might take their cousins home. The answer was firm: that was not possible. Donald and Grace were no longer classified as temporary residents but as permanent wards of the institution. Only through a formal adoption procedure could they ever leave.

When the visit ended, Mae and Hazel stepped back out into the cold air with heavy hearts. The children were clearly being cared for, but it was equally clear that their stay would not be short.

What had begun as a simple academic visit had turned into a deeply personal encounter – a discovery that would ripple through their entire family. The train ride back to Madison that evening passed in silence. Both sisters understood that what they had stumbled upon by chance might change everything for Donald and Grace.

Upon returning home to Whitewood, Mae and Hazel brought the news to their parents, Clarence and Esther Streeter. The first reactions were a mix of shock and relief – shock at the circumstances that had led the children to the orphanage, and relief that they were alive, healthy, and together.

A family meeting was quickly convened. Around the table sat the immediate relatives, listening in silence as Mae and Hazel recounted what they had seen. Clarence Streeter made his decision before the evening was over: he would begin the adoption process himself. The plan was for Donald and Grace to come live with him and his wife, to grow up again within a stable, loving household.

Telegram messages were sent to other family members – Jessie, William, and others – to inform them and to ask for their support. The family agreed that each would contribute in whatever way possible to bring the children home.

A few days later, Clarence travelled to Sioux Falls. His arrival at the orphanage marked the turning point. When he left with Donald and Grace, it was as though a missing part of the family had been restored.

Their return to the farm in Whitewood became a moment of shared celebration. Grandmother Nancy was waiting at the door, joined by uncles, aunts, and cousins. To the children's astonishment, George and Dorothy – their older brother and sister – were there as well. The reunion was warm and emotional. For the first time since Eva's death, something like wholeness returned to the family.

Although the official adoption was not completed until 26 February 1925, from that January day onward, everyone considered Donald and Grace once more a true part of the Streeter family.

Yet the time spent in the orphanage had left its mark. The months of separation, the discipline, and the quiet nights in a strange bed had deepened their sense of loss and created a distance that would take years to heal.

Home brought comfort, but also change. Donald felt the difference most keenly. Though the farm, the fields, and the faces were familiar, he himself was not the same boy who had left. That realisation would stay with him, growing over the years into a powerful inner drive – a determination to prove himself, to rise above hardship, and to endure whatever life demanded of him.

It was a strength born of early struggle – one that would later define him in the cockpit, in combat, and in the long shadow of history.

Chapter 15

The Meeting with Arthur and Laura

Arthur Wendell Smith was a man of quiet dignity, known throughout Kingsbury County for his professionalism and compassion. A certified veterinarian and graduate of the Chicago Veterinary College, he was registered in South Dakota under licence number 348. His expertise lay in diagnosing and preventing tuberculosis in cattle, a disease that threatened not only livestock but the health of entire communities. With his mobile practice – a sturdy wagon car equipped with medical instruments, bottles of tuberculin, and hand-written ledgers – he travelled from farm to farm across the prairie, offering both care and counsel to farmers who relied on their animals for survival.

Arthur was well respected by the agricultural community, particularly around Oldham, where he and his wife Laura Bolte Smith had settled shortly after their marriage. Their small home stood on the northern edge of town, surrounded by lilac bushes and a white-painted fence that Arthur maintained himself when he wasn't tending to animals. The Smiths were active members of the Methodist church, where Arthur served as treasurer and Laura played the organ on Sunday mornings. Their reputation for kindness and reliability made them beloved in the community.

Among the many families who placed their trust in Arthur was the Streeter family. He had known them for years – first George and Nancy, and later their children, including Clarence Streeter, who had become both a client and a friend. Arthur often stopped by their farm to test the herd for tuberculosis or to tend to injured horses. Over time, these visits had grown into long conversations over coffee at the kitchen table, where weather, crops, and family matters were discussed with the easy familiarity of old friends.

Through Clarence, Arthur also came to know Eva Streeter Gregory and her husband Charles (Chas) Gregory, who managed the family's adjoining property in Whitewood Township. Arthur had visited their farm several times, examining livestock and sharing meals with the family. He remembered little Donald, a bright-eyed boy who followed him around the barn, asking questions about animals and treatments, and Grace, a shy little girl who peeked at him from behind her mother's apron.

When news reached Arthur that Eva had passed away and that her children had been placed in an orphanage, it weighed heavily on him. The Gregorys were not strangers – they were part of the same web of families that formed the lifeblood of the prairie.

In the spring of 1925, Arthur drove his car to the farm of Clarence and Esther Streeter to treat a horse that had injured its leg in a plough accident. The prairie was just beginning to thaw, and a pale green shimmer had returned to the fields. As Arthur examined the wound and wrapped the animal's leg with steady hands, he noticed that Clarence seemed distracted – weary, perhaps, in a way that went beyond the usual fatigue of farmwork.

After the task was done, Arthur suggested they rest a moment on the porch. The friendship between the two men was old enough to allow for honesty. Over mugs of coffee, Clarence spoke quietly about his worries. Though he and Esther had taken Donald and Grace into their home after rescuing them from the orphanage, the household had become crowded. Their own children filled every room, and the added mouths to feed strained both their finances and their patience.

Arthur listened without interruption. He knew the Streeters well enough to recognise that this was not complaint but confession – the honest words of a man who wanted to do right but was reaching his limits.

He thought back to the little boy he had once met – curious, observant, and already set apart by something in his eyes. When he looked up from his cup, he saw that very boy walking across the yard. Donald greeted him politely, then paused halfway to the barn, his gaze lifting towards the sky. A flock of geese was passing overhead, and for a moment the boy stood perfectly still, following their formation as if he could understand their language. That image would stay with Arthur for years: the orphaned child looking skyward, drawn instinctively towards something larger than himself.

Arthur and Laura Smith understood the ache of loss all too well. Their own lives had been marked by heartbreak two years earlier.

In the summer of 1923, Laura had given birth to twin daughters, whom they named Betty and Beatrice. The pregnancy had been difficult, and the twins arrived far too early. Despite the desperate efforts of the local doctor and the prayers of their friends, both babies died within hours of their birth.

The grief was overwhelming. The house that had been prepared with such care – the tiny cradle by the window, the folded quilts, the little white dresses Laura had sewn – fell silent. The sound of the wind across the prairie seemed sharper in those days, the evenings longer. For Laura, the quiet was unbearable.

A short notice appeared in the *Oldham Chronicle*, and a modest funeral was held. Reverend Disrud, the town's Methodist minister, led the brief service beneath the cottonwoods by the cemetery gate. There were no elaborate flowers, no music – only a handful of neighbours standing with bowed heads as the two small coffins were lowered into the earth.

Arthur, usually a man of few words, was transformed by the loss. He buried himself in his work, travelling farther, taking on more cases, avoiding the empty rooms at home. Laura, whose health had been fragile during the pregnancy, grew weaker under the weight of sorrow. The doctor who had cared for her gently advised that she should not attempt another pregnancy; the risk to her life would be too great. With that, the couple faced a painful truth: they would never have children of their own.

Arthur commissioned a simple gravestone from a local mason. It bore the names of their daughters, *Betty and Beatrice Smith*, followed by their own – *Arthur and Laura*. Above the names, he requested the carving of a lamb, an old Christian symbol of innocence and eternal peace. Beneath it, he had engraved the words:

'Safe in the Shepherd's arms.'

It became a place of quiet pilgrimage for Laura. On early mornings, when the town still slept and mist clung to the fields, she would walk to the cemetery carrying fresh flowers. There she would sit beside the little stone, her hand resting on its cool surface, whispering the names of her daughters as if the act alone could bridge the distance between the living and the dead.

Neighbours sometimes saw her from afar, a small, still figure among the gravestones, and turned away in silence. Everyone in Oldham knew that grief had taken up residence in the Smith home, and yet, within that grief, there remained tenderness – a compassion that deepened rather than hardened them.

It was in that space – between loss and duty – that Arthur and Laura Smith's path crossed once more with the Gregory children. Clarence's confession lingered with Arthur after that spring visit. As he drove home, the sky turning gold over the prairie, he found himself thinking of Donald and Grace, of Laura's empty arms, and of the lamb carved in stone.

In the weeks that followed, that thought would return again and again, taking shape not as pity but as possibility – the faint but growing idea that perhaps, through these children, something broken in both families might yet be made whole.

Chapter 16

The Conversation with Laura

That evening, as twilight settled over Spring Lake, Arthur Smith found his wife sitting by the parlour window, mending an old quilt. The rhythm of her needle through fabric was the only sound in the room – soft, steady, almost meditative. Arthur removed his hat, took a seat across from her, and began to tell her about his day – about his visit to Clarence and Esther Streeter, and the conversation that had taken place after he had tended to their injured horse.

He explained that Clarence and Esther had taken in Donald and Grace Gregory, the orphaned children of Clarence's late niece, Eva, but that the household was under growing strain. They had done all they could, yet their own family was large and money was tight. Clarence had confided that though the children were safe, he worried about how long he could manage.

Arthur paused, then spoke of the boy – Donald. He described him as self-contained and observant, with a calm dignity unusual for his age and a fierce protectiveness towards his younger sister. As Arthur spoke, Laura laid her sewing aside and looked up. Her eyes, still carrying the deep sadness of the children she had lost two years before, remained fixed on her husband's face.

He told her he had seen something in the boy – a quiet resilience, a kind of steadiness that reminded him of what they had both once hoped to nurture in their own children. 'Clarence doesn't say it,' Arthur said softly, 'but he needs help. And that boy – he needs a home.'

Laura did not answer at once. She folded the half-mended quilt on her lap and let her thoughts settle. What Arthur was proposing wasn't impulsive; it was a reflection of something that had been stirring in both of them for months – the instinct to give their love and care to someone who needed it most.

When she finally spoke, her voice was calm but resolute. 'If we can offer him a home,' she said, 'then we should.'

It was not a decision made out of a desire to replace what they had lost – nothing could bring back Betty and Beatrice, their twin daughters buried in the Oldham cemetery – but rather an act of renewal. The silence that had haunted their home could now find purpose again.

Arthur nodded. He suggested that they first spend more time with Donald, to be sure that he would feel at ease with them before any promises were made. Laura agreed. The decision was shared quietly between them – no dramatic words, just understanding. They both knew that their past sorrows had prepared them to give this boy something steadfast and enduring.

That night, a different kind of stillness filled the Smith home – not the silence of grief, but the gentle hush of hope.

By May 1925, spring activity had returned to Oldham. For several days, a small travelling fair operated near the main street, drawing families from the surrounding countryside. Temporary amusements and stalls brought a brief concentration of visitors and activity to the town centre. Donald walked between Arthur and Laura, visibly relaxed in their company. From time to time, he reached for Arthur's hand, a small gesture of trust amid the noise and colour of the fair. The outing had been arranged by Clarence and Esther Streeter, who believed it might help Donald spend time with the Smiths in a natural, easy setting before any formal steps were taken.

At the carousel, Arthur lifted the boy onto the largest painted horse and stood beside him as the machine began to turn. Donald said little, but he listened intently as Arthur spoke – casually at first, about farmwork and animals, and then, almost in passing, about flying. He told him that sometimes a person's dreams, no matter how impossible they seemed, could one day take wing. Donald looked at him, thoughtful, and for the first time responded in kind – not with questions, but with quiet understanding.

When dusk came and the lights of the fair faded behind them, Donald climbed into Clarence's wagon and looked back once. To others, it might have seemed an ordinary evening. But for those present, it marked a turning point – the beginning of a bond that would endure far beyond the dusty streets of Oldham.

After that day, Donald began joining Arthur on his veterinary rounds. For the boy, it was an entirely new experience – long drives across open country, visits to farms and stables, the company of animals, and the steady patience of Arthur's work. He observed closely, asked sharp, practical questions, and listened with quiet focus to every explanation. When possible, Arthur let him assist – holding a halter, preparing bandages, learning how to read an animal's posture.

At home, Laura gently wove him into the household routine. Donald helped set the table, fetched water from the pump, and learned to care for the garden. A small room at the back of the house was given to him. Gradually, it filled with his few belongings – a book or two, a wooden toy horse, a drawing pinned to the wall – until it no longer looked like a guest room but like a boy's own space.

By early May, Arthur and Laura spoke with Clarence and Esther again. They expressed their wish to raise Donald as their own son. Clarence, though solemn, agreed. He was convinced that Arthur and Laura could give Donald the structure and stability that he and Esther struggled to provide. The decision was made with mutual respect and a shared understanding of what was best for the boy.

In the *Oldham Register* of 12 March 1925, the adoption of Donald Gregory was reported explicitly. The article stated that Dr and Mrs A.W. Smith had 'legally adopted little Donald Gregory', who had for some time been living in the household of Clarence Streeter. The notice emphasised the pride of the adoptive parents and their intention to provide the child with devoted care and attention – language characteristic of the moral and social tone of the interwar period. Concluding with the words 'Congratulations all around', the brief announcement confirms that the adoption was public, formal, and socially acknowledged.

On 30 June, 1925, the adoption became official. From that day forward, his full legal name was Donald Gregory Smith – *Gregory* as a link to his origins, *Smith* as the family name of his new home. It was not a birth in the literal sense, but it marked the beginning of a clearly defined new chapter in his life. Interestingly, in the South Dakota State Census of 1925, Donald appears in the household of Arthur and Laura under the name Donald Owen Smith – a likely clerical variation, yet a small reminder of the complex path that led him from one identity to another.

The loss of both parents had left deep marks. Donald rarely spoke of it, yet in quiet moments the memories still showed in his expression – sharp, undiminished by time. The steady structure of Arthur and Laura Smith's household offered him a sense of stability. Arthur took him along on visits to local farms, teaching him the practical rhythms of work and responsibility; Laura included him in household routines, letting him share in the daily order of their lives. Those simple, predictable patterns gave him rhythm, discipline, and the comfort of belonging.

Maintaining contact with his siblings – Grace, Dorothy, and George – remained a priority. The Smiths and Streeters worked together to arrange visits, ensuring that Donald's connection to his original family was never severed. That continuity became an anchor – a reassurance that love could exist in more than one home.

Gradually, Donald began to open up. His questions grew more confident, his posture more relaxed; outings with Arthur and Laura brought genuine moments of ease. There were still days of silence, times when the absence of his mother, Eva, seemed to weigh heavily upon him. Yet beneath that silence, something stronger was taking root – a growing will to move forward, to live in a way that honoured both his past and his new beginning.

Chapter 17

The Background of Arthur and Laura

Arthur Smith was born on 20 November 1880, in Port Huron, Michigan. From an early age he showed a deep interest in agriculture and animal health – an inclination that led him to pursue a career in veterinary medicine, a vital profession in the rural Midwest. After graduating from the Chicago Veterinary College, he became a licenced veterinarian in South Dakota under registration number 348.

Arthur's work brought him into daily contact with farmers across the region. His practice required not only medical skill but also reliability, quick judgment, and a calm temperament – qualities that earned him both respect and trust. To most who knew him, he was simply 'Doc Smith', a title of affection that reflected not just his profession but his authority and kindness.

Laura Bolte, born 28 November 1886, in Denver, Colorado, came from a more urban background. Yet she adapted easily to the rhythms of rural life after her marriage to Arthur. Practical, warm, and community-minded, Laura became a stabilising force in both their home and the broader Oldham community.

The couple married in 1919 in Winona, Florence County, South Carolina, before settling in Spring Lake near Oldham, Kingsbury County, South Dakota where they rented a modest house on Smith Street. There, Arthur quickly established himself as the region's most dependable veterinarian, known for his long days on the road, travelling farm to farm with his medical kit and a Ford automobile packed with supplies.

When Donald came to live with Arthur and Laura in June 1925, he entered a household marked by structure, steadiness, and affection. Life with the Smiths was predictable in the best sense of the word. Arthur involved him actively in his work – Donald accompanied him on veterinary rounds, handling tools, observing procedures, and performing small, supervised tasks. Laura introduced him to the routines of domestic life: helping with meals, collecting eggs, chopping wood, and completing household chores.

These simple, repetitive activities became the foundation for something larger – an education in discipline, persistence, and cooperation. Donald adapted quickly to the rhythm of farm life and, for the first time since his mother's death, found comfort in order and predictability.

Around 1925, Oldham was a lively prairie town where farming, trade, and community life came together along its dusty main street. Solid brick buildings with wooden façades lined both sides of the road, housing shops, a bank, and various local businesses. The A.L. Hanson Hardware Store, filled with farm implements, stoves, and gleaming tools, stood as one of the town's main gathering places. Farmers arrived daily – some still with teams of horses, others now driving the first motor trucks – to purchase supplies, exchange news, or simply visit. The scent of oil, leather, and freshly milled grain drifted through the air, mingled with the clatter of wagon and car wheels and the hum of conversation. At the edge of town ran the rail line to Madison, where the train passed each day bringing mail, travellers, and goods that connected Oldham to the broader world of South Dakota. Board sidewalks, lampposts, and the neat fronts of the grocers, druggists, and clothing stores gave the main street a modest but orderly charm. In the late afternoon sun, the glass windows shimmered while neighbours paused to talk and children played nearby. Though small, Oldham in the mid-1920s was a thriving, self-reliant community – a true reflection of prairie life at the dawn of modern America.

It was in this setting that Arthur and his young stepson, Donald, went to the City Barber Shop, a small storefront operated by George W. Wareham, who had been cutting hair in town for nearly a decade. The shop had two chairs, both gleaming beneath the front window, where Arthur and Donald sat side by side while Mr. Wareham's scissors clicked in steady rhythm. The faint scent of bay rum and pipe tobacco hung in the air, mixing with the sunlight and quiet murmur of the barber's conversation. On the counter stood polished jars of tonic and a neat display of cigars and tobaccos from the Barnett Company, lending the place a grown-up dignity that fascinated the boy. When their hair was trimmed and brushed clean, they stepped back out into the brightness of Main Street – the hum of cars and wagons and voices rising around them – two figures bound by family, habit, and the small routines that defined life in Oldham.

Donald continued his elementary education in Lake Spring at the local one-room district school characteristic of rural Kingsbury County. Throughout this period, Arthur and Laura maintained strong family cohesion, arranging regular visits and gatherings that kept Donald closely connected to his siblings – Grace, Dorothy, and George. The result was a robust foundation – a blend of affection, structure, and continuity that nurtured in him qualities that would later define his military career: self-reliance, a strong sense of duty, endurance, and adaptability.

From 1924 onward, advertisements regularly appeared in the *Oldham Register* announcing that Arthur Smith, veterinarian, could be reached through the Loesch Bros' store. Residents who required his services left messages at the town's pharmacy, which doubled as Oldham's communication hub. A note or a telephone call to number 16-2 was enough to reach 'Doc' Smith, who checked the messages frequently, responding to routine visits and emergencies alike.

Arthur and Donald often stopped by the local store together to collect new calls. From there, they set out across the prairie in Arthur's Ford, travelling to farms throughout Oldham, Lake Spring, and Lake Preston, as well as neighbouring communities. For the townspeople, this system was second nature – the pharmacy served as a clearinghouse not only for medical needs but for veterinary emergencies as well.

By May 1925, everyday life in Oldham had settled into a familiar rhythm. The business street was active with residents and farmers from the surrounding countryside, drawn into town for supplies, news, and conversation. Donald accompanied Arthur on several of these visits, walking beside him past the grocery stores, hardware shops, and the small businesses that lined the street. Inside, men lingered longer than strictly necessary – discussing crops, prices, and recent events – while children waited quietly nearby. For Donald, these trips offered more than errands; they were lessons in responsibility, observation, and belonging, absorbed in the ordinary movements of a working prairie town.

Before Arthur's transfer in late 1926, Oldham's Loesch brothers – John and William – transformed their store from a simple pharmacy into the social and technological centre of the community. Together with local mechanic Alfred Nelson, described by residents as 'the best repairman Oldham ever had,' they built a small radio station with the call letters KDGY in the back room of the store.

The new radio studio, like the message board for 'Doc' Smith, became a gathering point for the town. The broadcasts offered local news, music, and even live sports commentary by Lou Loesch, later remembered as one of the state's earliest sportscasters. At the same time, the station promoted the sale of Majestic radios, which brought the voices of distant cities into Oldham's farmhouses for the first time.

The work of a rural veterinarian was demanding and unpredictable. Arthur cared for both livestock and household animals, often travelling long distances over unpaved roads. His duties included diagnosing and treating disease, advising farmers on preventive care, and monitoring herd health.

Beyond medical treatment, Arthur also served as a consultant on nutrition, breeding, and hygiene, translating veterinary journals and bulletins into practical advice farmers could use. The results were tangible: healthier herds, improved milk and meat production, and, ultimately, greater economic stability for the region's farmers.

Donald's exposure to this life was formative. His daily responsibilities at home – feeding animals, collecting eggs, helping with repairs – gave him a sense of purpose. On non-school days, he rode with Arthur, learning to observe closely, to ask precise questions, and to value careful craftsmanship. Arthur's habit of repairing and modifying his own tools introduced Donald to the practical side of mechanical problem-solving, planting the early seeds of the technical curiosity that would one day draw him to aviation.

Meanwhile, Laura provided emotional steadiness and gentle guidance. Her consistency turned the Smith household into a sanctuary – a place where routine and affection coexisted. Donald's later letters, written during his studies in Brookings, South Dakota, and later during his pilot training, referred to them affectionately as 'Papa' and 'Mama'. That simple choice of words reflected his complete sense of belonging.

Thanks to Arthur's respected work as a veterinarian, Arthur, Laura, and Donald soon found themselves at the centre of community life in Oldham. They were far from strangers – everyone in town knew 'Doc' Smith and his family. Through his daily rounds and late-night farm calls,

Arthur had earned a reputation for skill and reliability, and that trust naturally extended to Laura and Donald.

Articles appeared in the *Oldham Register* announcing that Arthur and Laura Smith had adopted a son. The brief notices reflected the town's close-knit character – they mentioned the family's decision with warmth and goodwill, and the community collectively wished them happiness and success.

For many in Oldham, the news felt personal. Arthur and Laura were already respected and well-liked, and their adoption of Donald was seen as an act of generosity – a gesture that fit perfectly with the character of the couple everyone knew simply as 'Doc and Mrs Smith.'

Donald, often seen accompanying his adoptive father, was warmly regarded by neighbours and farmers alike. People appreciated his dedication – the way he fetched tools, steadied frightened animals, and listened intently as Arthur worked.

In a small prairie town where everyone depended on one another, the Smith family stood for kindness, competence, and constancy. Their presence was not only respected but genuinely valued – a symbol of stability in a community built on hard work and shared care.

As the years passed, the lessons Donald absorbed in Oldham and later Belle Fourche – discipline, steadiness, and resolve – became part of his character. Under Arthur's guidance he learned precision and responsibility; from Laura he inherited patience and compassion. Together they shaped in him the habits of a man who would one day carry far greater duties.

When he later left the prairie for study and training, the foundations laid in that modest household endured. The same calm perseverance that had steadied frightened animals in Arthur's care would soon steady aircraft in flight – the quiet confidence of a boy from Oldham who had learned early how to stand his ground.

His cousin Ruth Streeter, in a 2007 radio interview, summarised it best: 'Arthur and Laura gave him all the love in the world. Their adoption of Donald was the best thing that could have happened after the loss of his mother.'

The *Oldham Register* of 30 December 1926 notes that Dr A.W. Smith and his family were preparing to leave Oldham for Belle Fourche, following Smith's appointment as Deputy State Veterinarian. This item appears to mark another important turning point in Don's early life. Once again, his surroundings changed, but this time under clearly positive circumstances, connected to professional advancement, stability, and opportunity:

> Dr A. W. Smith and family expect to leave Friday for their new home at Belle Fourche where the doctor now has his headquarters as Deputy State Veterinarian. While the many friends of the family deeply regret to see them leave Oldham, all good wishes go with them for happiness and prosperity.

The move to Belle Fourche on 31 December 1926, marked a turning point for Donald – a break from Oldham and the small town where he had spent his first stable years. His initial reluctance soon gave way to the understanding that change was inevitable, and that adaptability could be a strength rather than a burden.

What remained was the foundation laid in Oldham: strong family bonds, a growing technical curiosity, steady discipline, and an emerging sense of confidence. These traits, forged in the rhythms of prairie life, would follow him into every stage that lay ahead.

The Belle Fourche Years
(1927 – 1940)

Chapter 18

Belle Fourche

Belle Fourche lay on the northern edge of the Black Hills, linked by rail to the great livestock markets of the Midwest. Founded by Seth Bullock and Sol Star as a regional trading centre, it was by 1927 a compact but industrious town. The stockyards drew ranchers from three states, while the railway station served as a vital junction between herds from Montana and Wyoming and the meat markets of the East.

Arthur and Laura left Oldham for a home at 823 Day Street in Belle Fourche – a sturdy house with enough room for themselves, Donald, and a boarder named Margaret Moore, who worked in a local store. Laura soon found employment as a secretary with Eastern Clay Products in Colony, Wyoming, just across the state line. Her efficiency, warmth, and reliability quickly earned her the respect of her employers. The steady income provided the family with financial breathing room and confirmed Laura's growing independence within the household.

Arthur continued his veterinary work without a fixed clinic, operating instead from a car stocked with instruments and medicines. His clients were the ranchers of Butte County and beyond, and his reputation for competence and honesty grew steadily. Donald often accompanied him on his rounds, learning the fundamentals of animal care, the handling of tools, and the improvisation required to solve problems in the field. These experiences nurtured his technical curiosity and confidence – traits that would later define him in far more demanding circumstances.

In 1927 Donald resumed his schooling in one of the small one-room rural schools of Butte County. The wooden schoolhouse reminded him of the Streeter School in Whitewood Township. His classmates were children of ranchers, shopkeepers, and railroad workers – a new mix that stimulated him. At home, Arthur reinforced discipline and a sense of responsibility, while Laura encouraged curiosity and kindness. School became a springboard rather than a burden; Donald not only adapted but began to excel, driven by a developing interest in mechanics and a quiet determination to succeed.

Although Arthur's appointment as Deputy State Veterinarian of South Dakota had been confirmed in late 1926 – prompting the family's move west – the practical arrangements of relocation stretched well into the following year. In the summer of 1927, Arthur and his son briefly returned to Oldham to settle remaining matters. The *Oldham Register* of 21 July 1927, recorded: 'Dr A.W. Smith and son Donald arrived Thursday by Ford from Belle Fourche, and on Monday loaded their household goods for shipment to Bellefourche.'

The following Monday, 25 July, the last crates were taken to the depot for transport – the final, tangible act of departure. For Donald, then 9 years old, helping to lift boxes and mark their contents was both a task and a ritual: one more goodbye to familiar neighbours, streets, and faces.

For the community, the brief notice confirmed what many had known but hesitated to accept – that 'Doc' Smith had officially moved his headquarters to Belle Fourche. The tone in Oldham remained bittersweet: regret over losing a trusted veterinarian, mixed with heartfelt wishes from countless farm families for prosperity in the west.

The family's new life in Belle Fourche was steady, though not untouched by sorrow. On 14 October 1928, a daughter, Mae Jean Smith, was born but died the same day – the third child Arthur and Laura lost after the deaths of their twin daughters, Beatrice and Betty, in 1923.

Donald, now 10, felt the loss deeply. His response was quiet but profound: he became more helpful at home, more attentive to both Arthur and Laura. The tragedy drew the small family closer together and deepened Donald's empathy and sense of duty.

Belle Fourche offered stability, but also lessons in resilience. In a town sustained by hard work and mutual support, Donald grew up surrounded by examples of perseverance. From Arthur he learned diligence and precision; from Laura, gentleness and composure. Together they shaped a boy who understood, even at a young age, that endurance and responsibility were the foundations of strength.

Donald's interest in self-reliance and mechanics found a clear direction when a Boy Scout troop was established in Belle Fourche. It was a relatively new phenomenon for the town, intended to teach boys practical skills, discipline, and a spirit of service. Meetings were held in simple community halls or out in the open, where, under the guidance of experienced leaders, the boys practised map reading, tent building, safe tool handling, and teamwork.

From the beginning, Donald distinguished himself – not through loud confidence or bravado, but through the quiet certainty with which he completed every task. He worked methodically, followed instructions carefully, and showed a natural ability to find solutions when plans went astray. His uniform gradually filled with merit badges, each earned through demonstrated skill and persistence:

- Camping: spending a night alone in the open with minimal gear, building a fire, shelter, and securing food.
- Hiking: completing a 20 mile trek through hilly terrain using navigation and orientation techniques.
- Astronomy: identifying constellations and celestial bodies with a borrowed telescope, keeping detailed notes in a logbook.
- Agriculture: earning the troop's highest distinction for his sound knowledge of livestock and poultry, learned from working on local farms.
- Bird Observation: recording local species and tracking seasonal migration patterns.
- Carpentry: constructing a sturdy birdhouse that stood for years on the troop's grounds.

Within the group, Donald quickly became a model for younger scouts. He took responsibility during joint exercises, helped others earn their own badges, and served informally as a mentor. His approach was always practical – analyse the problem, assign the tasks, complete the work efficiently.

The habits and attitudes he developed through scouting – discipline, perseverance, cooperation, and the ability to act effectively under varying conditions – would later prove directly applicable to his military life.

Outside of scouting, Donald carried his own responsibilities. Every morning before sunrise, he delivered newspapers in Belle Fourche. The early hours, the steady rhythm of work, and the independence it demanded gave him a sense of self-worth and duty.

In his free time, he sought movement and camaraderie – American football with neighbourhood friends, long days roaming the fields, and swimming in the nearby river.

Many days he spent beside Arthur, travelling dusty prairie roads to remote ranches. He helped feed animals, clean barns, and hand over instruments during veterinary procedures. That shared work strengthened the bond between father and son and gave Donald a firm grounding in discipline, observation, and responsibility. It also taught him how to adapt to unpredictable situations.

Chapter 19

The Boy Who Watched Everything

From an early age, Donald developed a remarkable expertise in the care of poultry. While other boys his age spent their afternoons playing baseball or fishing in the river, he could often be found among the chicken coops and feeding troughs, watching the birds with a keen, almost scientific eye. He noticed small changes in behaviour that hinted at illness, and he seemed instinctively to know when something was wrong. His advice – always practical and occasionally innovative – went far beyond what anyone expected from a boy his age.

Before long, word spread through Belle Fourche and the surrounding farms; when the hens stopped laying, when chicks appeared weak, or when an unfamiliar illness swept through the flock, Donald Smith was the one to call. He asked precise questions, conducted careful inspections as if he were already a trained veterinarian, and offered recommendations that often produced quick results. His quiet confidence earned him a reputation that reached well beyond his neighbourhood.

Among friends and relatives, this reputation earned him a nickname – 'the chicken expert'. Years later, in the service, the label evolved into the teasing nickname 'chicken officer', a phrase immortalised by aviation journalist and cartoonist Dick Kirschbaum, who once sketched him under that title. Sergeant Dick Kirschbaum served with the US Army Air Forces Information Office and became known for his cartoons in Air Corps base newspapers; he portrayed Donald with characteristic humour as the 'chicken officer'. What began as a boyish curiosity had, in truth, revealed the traits that would later define him in uniform – a sharp eye for detail, methodical problem-solving, and calm efficiency under pressure. The humour carried affection rather than mockery, for the nickname captured something true about him: that early fascination with living systems, observation, and order.

In his final year at South Dakota State College in Brookings, Donald transformed his practical knowledge into leadership. He not only joined the Poultry Club but was elected its president, a natural progression for someone of his dedication and reputation. The position allowed him to develop organisational and leadership skills – planning meetings, overseeing competitions, and representing the club at regional events. In that role, the once self-taught 'chicken expert' grew into a capable coordinator, known for his reliability, discipline, and quiet ability to inspire others.

Chapter 20

The Black Hills Roundup

When the Black Hills Roundup was formally established in 1919, it reflected more than a celebration of ranching skill. Emerging in the immediate aftermath of the First World War, it grew out of earlier charity rodeos organised to raise funds for soldiers overseas and to support local communities affected by loss and return. What began as a modest, community-driven event soon took on broader significance, honouring local veterans while reaffirming the values of resilience and solidarity that had sustained the region through war and hardship.

By 1932, the Black Hills Roundup had become a well-established name in the Western tradition of the United States, drawing visitors from several states to Belle Fourche each summer. For the town, the Roundup was more than an annual spectacle: it had become a symbol of identity, unity, and pride. At a time when much of the nation was struggling through the Great Depression, the event offered a brief return to normalcy and hope – a reminder that endurance, community, and shared tradition still carried meaning on the prairie.

For Donald Smith, 14 years old that summer, the Roundup was the highlight of the year. After finishing his early morning paper route – while the streets were still quiet except for a few early visitors – he returned home, where Laura had carefully pressed his shirt and trousers. He dressed as if for an official ceremony, yet his eyes betrayed the eager anticipation of adventure.

The parade through the town centre was a carefully orchestrated celebration of colour and sound. Cowboys on horseback, their saddles richly decorated, rode past in measured rhythm. Their lassos hung loosely across their shoulders, while the horses beneath them snorted and pawed at the dry pavement. Marching bands provided a steady, rousing beat, the drums echoing in perfect cadence. From the crowd rose a mingled scent of dust, saddle oil, fresh bread, and cotton candy.

Donald stood at the edge of the procession, taking in every detail as if he wanted to store the entire scene in memory. What others saw as a simple community fair, he perceived as a series of distinct observations – the gleam of leather, the clink of stirrups, the exact moment a rider corrected his horse. The stories he had heard about freedom and the life of the frontier seemed tangible now, though tempered by the new awareness of someone standing on the threshold between childhood and youth.

That summer, however, he went beyond merely watching. Donald took part in one of the crowd-pleasing attractions: catching turkeys released into the arena. For a 14-year-old boy, it was a test of speed, agility, and nerve. He managed to seize one of the flustered birds, to the audience's delight. The moment brought him not only applause but a memory that would resurface years later during his pilot training.

In a letter dated 13 January 1941, written from Brooks Field near San Antonio, Don unexpectedly recalled the Black Hills Roundup. After a picnic at a 'dude ranch just outside of S.A.' – with 130lb of barbecue beef and horses to work up their appetites – someone produced a photograph from 1932. Don recognised himself and Arthur ('Dad') in the picture and spontaneously demonstrated a few rope tricks. The scene linked his flying days in Texas to his Belle Fourche past: the same blend of skill, showmanship, and tradition that had shaped him as a boy had travelled with him into adulthood.

For Donald, the Roundup was more than a local celebration. Without realising it, he had been practising alertness – reacting to unpredictable situations and performing under the gaze of an audience. It also strengthened his pride in belonging to a community that cherished the values of the West and its pioneering heritage.

The summer of 1932 marked a threshold between youth and maturity. Donald had finished grade school and stood at the beginning of a new chapter in his life. The loss of his mother and the estrangement from his father years earlier had left deep traces, but in the steady household of Arthur and Laura Smith he once again found the order and sense of belonging he had long been missing.

Chapter 21

Belle Fourche High School

In the fall of 1932, 14-year-old Donald Smith stood before the wide steps of Belle Fourche High School. The imposing grey-stone building, with its tall windows and heavy wooden doors, radiated a sense of solidity and ambition. Inside, the air was filled with the bustle of hundreds of students – the echo of voices down long corridors and the steady rhythm of footsteps across polished wooden floors.

Donald recognised a few faces from children he had met during trips with Arthur to nearby farms. A few nods and quick smiles gave him a first sense of belonging. His first class took place in a room overlooking the endless prairie. There he heard words that would stay with him: that school was not only about arithmetic, writing, and history, but also about discipline, responsibility, and the importance of community.

The transition from the small one-room schoolhouse to a large high school required adjustment. The structure was stricter, the pace faster, and the expectations higher. Yet within the first few weeks, Donald sensed that this was a place of opportunity – one that could broaden his world.

In the weeks that followed, Donald's interest in new subjects grew, especially in physics and mechanics. When assigned to build a lever system, he approached it methodically, with the patience and precision he had learned from working on farms. Where others were content with a simple model, he was already thinking about how it might lift heavier loads. The realisation that a small adjustment could produce a large effect sparked his curiosity further. At home, he searched through Arthur's books for topics on engineering and aviation. His curiosity went beyond the classroom – he wanted to know how things worked, and how they could be improved.

After school, Donald often assisted Arthur in his work as a veterinarian. Together they visited ranches across Butte County, tending to horses, cattle, and sheep, performing medical checks and treatments. Arthur gradually allowed him to take more initiative and emphasised the importance of precision – details made all the difference. Donald learned to handle animals confidently, responding quickly when situations demanded it.

At home, Laura created a warm and steady environment. She read the newspapers, listened to the radio with Donald, and nurtured his interest in new developments – especially in aviation. On days off, the family went on outings with Donald's cocker spaniel, Mugs. These moments of quiet companionship deepened his sense of belonging and gave him a firm foundation to fall back on.

That same school year, Donald's physical strength also became evident. During a friendly game of American football, he stood out for his power, speed, and instinct for the game. Soon after, he was invited to train with the Belle Fourche High School Broncs, the city's proud team.

In his first year, his role was limited to the bench, but he trained tirelessly. Over the following years, he became a regular player, taking the position of offensive guard. A minor injury restricted his play during his junior year, but in his final season he started every game. After the last home game in 1935, he received the coveted Varsity Letter of Belle Fourche High School – a visible symbol of years of dedication and effort.

Beyond sports, Donald was active in the student council and several school clubs. There he learned to collaborate, to take initiative, and to shoulder responsibility. By accepting tasks and completing them diligently, he earned a reputation as a hardworking and dependable team player.

By the time he graduated in 1936, Donald had developed skills that went far beyond academic learning – discipline, perseverance, the ability to make decisions under pressure, and an eye for detail. These qualities earned him respect in times of peace within his school and community – traits that, in years to come, would define him in far greater tests of endurance and courage.

Chapter 22

Early Independence

In the early 1930s, owning a car in and around Belle Fourche was far from common. On the dusty country roads, horses and wagons still dominated the traffic. Arthur Smith's car, a Ford, was a sturdy but simple vehicle – indispensable for his work as a veterinarian. It carried him quickly from ranch to ranch, often loaded with medical equipment, medicines, and instruments in the back.

One evening, after a long day on the road, Arthur climbed into the driver's seat, looked at his son, and said, 'It's time you learned to drive.' The 14-year-old Donald slid behind the large steering wheel, his feet searching for the pedals, while the dashboard confronted him with an array of unfamiliar dials and switches. With calm instructions, Arthur guided him along the quiet country roads, where only the hum of the engine and the crunch of gravel under the tyres broke the silence. The first few yards were hesitant, but with every turn and every shift of gear came growing confidence. In rural South Dakota during the 1930s, learning to drive at such a young age was not unusual, particularly in families where automobiles were an essential part of daily work and mobility. For Donald, it was more than a new skill – it was a tangible sign of his father's trust and a step towards adulthood.

Driving lessons also awakened a fascination with mechanics. Under Arthur's supervision, Donald learned to change oil, replace spark plugs, and perform minor repairs. He began to see how each part worked in concert to make the whole function, and he quickly understood that maintenance could mean the difference between reliable transport and being stranded on a lonely road.

Where he had first worked cautiously and uncertainly, a few months later he stood confidently with grease-stained hands, bent over an open hood in full concentration. His technical knowledge grew through experience and study; he read manuals, followed the advice of local mechanics, and took every opportunity to practice hands-on repair.

When the chance arose, he used his savings to buy a second-hand 1930 Ford Model A coupe with a rumble seat. It was a plain but rugged vehicle – without luxury but built to last – ideal as a learning project for an aspiring mechanic. Donald replaced worn parts, corrected minor mechanical faults, and took particular care of the rumble seat mechanism, with its leather upholstery and metal hinges. The car became both his workshop and his classroom, a place where he deepened his understanding of machinery and developed the confidence to solve problems on his own.

Alongside school and household responsibilities, Donald held several part-time jobs. Early each morning, through rain, snow, or summer dust, he delivered newspapers across Belle Fourche. He also helped gather and wash sheep's wool on local farms and in small businesses – work that demanded strength, endurance, and punctuality. Every missed delivery or careless mistake was quickly noticed.

He invested part of his earnings in spare parts and tools for his car, and part in technical books. The rest he set aside in a small savings fund – a habit that taught him discipline and foresight.

During the Christmas season, he took on a role very different from the seriousness of his other work; for the first time, he played Santa Claus for local children. It was a simple but meaningful experience, one that showed him how small gestures could bring genuine joy – a lesson in human connection that would later prove valuable in military life.

On free evenings, Donald often drove with friends to the centre of town. The dance hall, filled with live music, was the heart of Belle Fourche's social life. Swing and early jazz filled the air as couples moved across the wooden floor in practised patterns. Donald loved the music – and the dancing itself. His relaxed manner and energetic style made him popular among his peers, and his car gave him the freedom to maintain friendships beyond the town's borders.

For him, these evenings were more than recreation. They helped him build a network of friendships and strengthened his sense of belonging to a close-knit community. At the same time, he learned how to move easily among people of different temperaments – a skill that, in the diverse world of military life, would become an invaluable asset.

The years in Belle Fourche marked a gradual passage from boyhood to adulthood. Donald balanced school, work, technical training, and social life in a routine that demanded discipline. The blend of practical skill, responsibility, and social confidence gave him a sense of independence and self-assurance that would shape not only his character, but his entire path forward.

Chapter 23

First Steps into the Air

In the summer of 1934, Donald Smith was introduced – through a mutual acquaintance – to Clyde Ice, the well-known aviation pioneer of the northern Black Hills. Ice had made his name as an airmail pilot, rescue flyer, and instructor. His reputation reached far beyond South Dakota; he was known for his ability to fly in the harshest weather and to reach even the most remote communities during winter storms.

Clyde Ice's career had begun in unconventional fashion. In 1919, he traded two second-hand automobiles for a badly damaged Curtiss JN-4 'Jenny' – a discarded World War I training aircraft. With limited means but remarkable mechanical skill, he restored the plane himself and taught himself to fly. The success of that daring venture became the foundation of a small flying school in Spearfish, where he went on to train hundreds of young pilots who would later fly across the Great Plains and beyond.

For Donald, the opportunity to learn from someone with such a record was both a privilege and a challenge. He knew from the start that this would be no casual pursuit. From their first meeting, Ice made his expectations clear: dedication and persistence were essential. Lessons would continue in all kinds of weather, and the student was expected to devote serious time to study and practice.

Don's first flight instruction with Clyde Ice began when he was 16, around 1936, at a time when American aviation regulations permitted flight training but required a minimum age only for the issuance of a pilot's licence, as set out in the *Air Commerce Regulations* effective as amended in 1928.

At the kitchen table, Donald presented his wish. These were the years of the Great Depression, when every expense was carefully weighed. Flying lessons cost around $100 – a considerable sum at the time. Donald, however, had already built up savings from his newspaper route, automobile repair work, and seasonal jobs during sheep-shearing. Arthur and Laura Smith knew this dream was not a passing fancy. They remembered how, as a boy, he would spend hours watching the sky – tracing the flight of birds and the distant glimmer of passing airplanes. After discussion, they decided to contribute the remaining amount. It was a shared investment in his future.

The drive from Belle Fourche to the Spearfish airfield took about half an hour, but to Donald it felt like a journey to another world. The field consisted of a grass runway, a few wooden hangars, and the familiar silhouette of the Curtiss 'Jenny'. With its open cockpit, fabric-covered wings, and minimal instruments, the aircraft was both forgiving to beginners and demanding of anyone who wished to advance.

Ice began his instruction on the ground; an explanation of the altimeter, airspeed indicator, and compass, as well as the inspection of control surfaces, wings, and engine. He emphasised that a pilot should not rely solely on instruments, but must learn to *feel* what the airplane was doing.

The first time the Jenny lifted off from the grass field, Donald felt the wind rush across his face as the prairie fell away beneath him. Ice's brief commands cut through the roar of the engine. Every movement of the stick produced an immediate response; every correction demanded precision.

With each lesson, his confidence grew. He practised turns, learned to hold altitude steadily, and grew accustomed to sudden gusts of wind. Ice was demanding but fair – mistakes were corrected instantly, improvements recognised at once. Outside of flight hours, Donald kept meticulous notes on procedures and studied navigation charts.

These months provided more than the technical foundation of flight. They became a mental apprenticeship in discipline, decisiveness, and composure under unpredictable conditions – qualities that would prove invaluable in his later military service. What began as a local opportunity became the first step towards an aviation career, and the lessons learned in Spearfish would remain with him for the rest of his life.

Chapter 24

A Balloon in the Wind

In November 1935, Donald Smith read in a magazine about the record-breaking flight of aviation pioneers Albert W. Stevens and Orvil A. Anderson over the Black Hills of South Dakota. With a specially designed balloon, they had risen nearly twenty kilometres into the stratosphere – a feat that captured headlines across the nation. The idea that two men, through preparation and ingenuity, could push the boundaries of the known sky left a deep and lasting impression on him.

The story sparked not only his imagination but also his urge to experiment. On 23 December, 1935, Donald decided to conduct his own small test. He filled a blue helium balloon, attached a sturdy tag with his name, address, and the date, and released it from Belle Fourche at 4.30 pm. To an onlooker, it might have seemed a simple gesture, yet Donald treated it like a true flight mission. He noted the time, temperature, and estimated wind direction and strength, and carefully considered how far the balloon might travel.

Days later, an unexpected letter arrived – from Leola, South Dakota:

> Leola, S. Dak – Dec. 24, 1935
> Donald Smith, Belle Fourche, S. Dak
>
> Dear Sir,
> It was rather thrilling to find the blue balloon. It was in the spokes of the threshing machine on the east side of our farm. The air was still in it, and when I turned it loose in the house it immediately rose to the ceiling. My little girl is certainly getting a big kick out of it. I found it this A.M., 9:30, Dec. 24th. The wind yesterday was northwest, at least this morning. After displaying it at Leola, I will return it in an envelope. I live 5½ miles southwest of Leola.
>
> Write sometime.
> Yours truly,
> J.J. Guthmiller

Enclosed was a small piece of balloon fabric, still bearing Donald's printed message: 'Please return to Donald Smith, Belle Fourche, South Dakota. Sent aloft Dec. 23 at 4:30 PM.'

The distance between Belle Fourche and Leola was over 400km. The balloon had made the journey in less than seventeen hours, carried by the northwest wind. For Donald, the experiment was more than a charming curiosity. It demonstrated that even with the simplest tools, careful preparation and an understanding of conditions could send something – or someone – far beyond the limits of sight.

With Guthmiller's letter as proof of his successful experiment, Donald returned later that month to his birthplace, Whitewood. There he spent time with his sisters Grace and Dorothy, his brother George, his uncles Clarence, Harry, and William, and his grandmother Nancy. Their conversations were warm and lively, filled with stories of the past and hopes for what lay ahead.

Visits from his aunts Jessie and Flora earlier that winter had already reassured them. They had seen how well he had settled with Arthur and Laura in Belle Fourche, and how seriously he approached his studies and responsibilities. In the eyes of his family, he was no longer a boy, but a young man with purpose and direction.

The summer of 1936 marked a turning point. With his diploma from Belle Fourche High School in hand, Donald stood on the threshold of a new chapter: that autumn, he would begin his studies at South Dakota State College in Brookings. But first came the Black Hills Roundup, that proud annual celebration of Belle Fourche.

Donald volunteered eagerly, working for days to help build the arena, carry beams, assemble the grandstands, and prepare for the crowds. During the event itself, he entered a calf-roping contest, where speed, balance, and decisiveness meant the difference between success and failure.

The smell of dust and saddle oil, the rhythmic drumming of hooves, and the low hum of the crowd gave him a sense of belonging to something greater than himself. It was the sound and pulse of the West – the same frontier spirit that would one day carry him far from the plains of South Dakota, towards the boundless skies he had always watched with wonder.

Chapter 25

Brookings: Foundations of Duty (1936 – 1940)

On the morning of 14 September 1936, Donald stood in front of the house in Belle Fourche, suitcase in hand. The rising sun stretched long shadows across the yard as he prepared to leave for Brookings to begin his studies at South Dakota State College – today's South Dakota State University. At 18, he was stepping into a new phase of his life.

From the doorway, Arthur and Laura watched with quiet pride, aware that their home would feel emptier without him. After a brief embrace and one last pat for his dog, Mugs, Donald climbed into the car and headed east. His route followed US Highway 212, through small prairie towns and across the broad Missouri River at Pierre, where he spent the night before continuing on to Brookings. He arrived at dusk on the fifteenth and checked into a hotel in Brookings. That evening he wrote to Laura: 'Everything feels real now. Tomorrow before half past ten I have to report. It feels big – but I'm ready for it.'

Two days later, on 16 September, he joined hundreds of new students filing into the College Auditorium beneath the clear Dakota sky. Founded in 1881 as a land-grant institution, South Dakota State College still reflected its roots in agricultural and technical education. The Coughlin Campanile, the Administration Building, the Stock Judging Pavilion, and the Armory stood like monuments to the state's twin ideals of progress and endurance.

For Donald, this was more than the start of an education – it was the beginning of purpose. The college united three worlds that appealed to him deeply: agriculture, engineering, and military training. In the catalogue he studied courses in mechanical science, agronomy, and military organisation, seeing in them the same principles of discipline and precision that had guided his youth.

His new home on campus was East Men's Hall, built in 1921 for First World War veterans and now filled with first-year students. His third-floor room was small and spare – two beds, a desk, and a coal stove that never quite defeated the Dakota winter. Yet the building pulsed with life: the smell of polish and cigarette smoke, the hum of gramophones, and the rise and fall of voices debating politics or football late into the night. Strict curfews and inspections imposed order, but camaraderie quickly replaced constraint. Students lent each other books, pooled money for late-night suppers, and learned, as Donald later would in the Air Corps, that cooperation was survival.

He thrived in this balance of structure and freedom. The ROTC drills on the parade ground matched the discipline of dormitory life. Cadets in uniform marched in formation across the frozen campus, learning to handle the standard infantry rifle and studying tactics, organisation, and military history. Most endured the two-year requirement with resignation. Donald, however, found meaning in it. After completing the basic course, he volunteered for the advanced ROTC programme, joining the ranks of the college's most determined cadets.

The advanced course demanded more of everything – longer hours, greater responsibility, and the promise of a commission upon graduation. Leadership, map reading, operational planning, and field endurance were central to the training. Donald embraced each challenge. His dedication earned him admission to Scabbard and Blade, the honorary society for outstanding ROTC students, and regular attendance at formal military events such as the Officers' Mess.

Donald's academic focus lay in the Division of Agriculture, a discipline that combined science and practicality in equal measure. He studied plant and animal sciences, soil management, farm mechanics, and rural economics, finding in their precision the same satisfaction he once drew from repairing engines in Belle Fourche. The blend of technical skill and organised problem-solving suited him perfectly.

College life also brought moments of exuberance. On 31 October 1936, he witnessed his first Hobo Day, the university's most colourful tradition. Through the streets paraded students dressed as wanderers, led by the battered 'Bummobile', a relic of 1913 that symbolised the event. The day culminated with the Jackrabbits' American football game, the stands alive with blue and yellow, the marching band playing over the roar of the crowd. Beneath thc celebration, Donald recognised something enduring – a spirit of belonging and shared effort – a feeling he would later rediscover among bomber crews at war.

On the field, too, he made his mark. Playing centre for the Jackrabbits in the All-North Central Conference league, Donald served as the anchor of the team – responsible for coordination, timing, and the first move of every attack. Over three seasons he earned Varsity Letters, and in 1939 was named to the All-North Central Conference team, honouring him among the best players in the region.

One of his finest moments came on Hobo Day, 21 October 1939, when the Jackrabbits faced their longtime rivals, the University of North Dakota, before 8,000 spectators. The game was decided by a single extra point, made possible by Donald's decisive block. In the stands, Arthur and Laura watched with pride as their son remained calm under pressure – a quality that would define him in the years ahead.

Through those four years, Donald's days followed a demanding rhythm: classes in the morning, ROTC drills in the afternoon, football practice, and long hours of study by the dim light of the dormitory lamp. The structure suited him. It was a world where discipline, endurance, and leadership were not abstract ideals but daily habits.

On Monday evening, 3 June 1940, at 6.30pm, Donald was awarded a Bachelor of Science in Agriculture at South Dakota State College. The Coolidge Sylvan Outdoor Theatre filled with families, faculty, and students for the Class of 1940 Commencement. The State College Military Band opened with *Hildreth's Festival March*, followed by *The Traveller* and a prayer by Reverend Joseph S. Ewing. Vocalist Karl Tieman performed *Now Heaven in Fullest Glory Shines* from Haydn's *The Creation*. Then came the speeches – by administrators, professors, and representatives of the student body.

When the deans began to call the names, Arthur and Laura Smith sat close together on a wooden bench, their hands tightly clasped. They watched their son step forward, accept his diploma, and turn his head, just long enough to find their eyes in the crowd. For them, this moment was more than a ceremony – it was the culmination of years of patience and faith, the visible proof of a second beginning.

The ceremony closed with Sousa's *The Stars and Stripes Forever*. As flags rippled and the band played, the graduates marched from the amphitheatre, the evening sun on their caps and gowns. Donald Smith walked tall, aware that this was not merely the end of his college years but the beginning of a journey that would carry him from the quiet plains of South Dakota to the open skies.

When he had arrived in Brookings four years earlier, he had still been a boy in search of direction. The college had given him a sense of purpose. After the uncertainty of his early years, Brookings became the place where he could truly unfold, a community that grounded him even as it prepared him to rise.

His studies had combined science with technical skill – soil and machinery, precision and process – an ideal foundation for a future pilot. By the time he stepped from the platform that June evening, he was not simply a graduate. He was a well-rounded young man – academically trained, physically strong, and disciplined in mind and spirit. Brookings had shaped not only his education but his identity, giving him the strength to face the world that awaited beyond the horizon. After graduation, he worked for several weeks in a local garage, a natural environment for someone with mechanical aptitude.

Chapter 26

Homecoming and Preparation for the Army

It was only a few days after the graduation ceremony. Donald Smith sat at the kitchen table, the rhythmic ticking of the clock echoing in the quiet house. Mugs, his faithful dog, lay beneath the table, eyes following every small movement.

Laura asked him what was on his mind. Donald paused before saying that he wanted to tell them something. Arthur looked up from his paper, 'Go ahead, son,' he said, encouragingly. Donald told them he had decided to enlist in the United States Army Air Corps and that he was due to report to Fort Meade within the next few days. His announcement was followed by silence, before Laura finally asked him whether he was sure. 'I am,' Donald replied. 'They're looking for pilots – and that's what I've always wanted to be.' Laura nodded and said she'd known that this day would come. 'But this isn't just adventure anymore,' she added. 'The world is about to change.' Donald explained that that was why he had to do it. Arthur nodded with understanding and told his son that although they would worry, they were proud of him.

Donald reached down to pat Mugs on the head and stood up. Outside, dark clouds were gathering on the horizon. The war had not yet reached America, but for him, the moment had come. He was determined to become a pilot – something he had dreamed of since childhood.

When he enlisted, his background was recognised with occupation code 502, indicating broad mechanical experience in the automotive field. On Friday, 26 July 1940, at Fort Meade, South Dakota, he officially joined the United States Army Air Corps as an Aviation Cadet. He was 22, unmarried, and free of dependants – ready to devote himself entirely to flight training. His enlistment form carried the standard phrase 'for the Philippine Department', a routine administrative notation that applied to thousands of recruits at the time. In Donald's case, it held no special significance; his path would eventually lead him eastward – not to the Philippines, but towards a secret mission that would change history.

At the Army Recruiting Station in Fort Meade, he provided the required documents: proof of birth and citizenship, address, emergency contact, and Social Security number. Because he was over 21, he needed no parental consent. His college record and ROTC background strengthened his file. Medical records were unnecessary at this stage – his physical examination would come later.

On Saturday, 3 August 1940, he reported to Fort Meade for his medical evaluation. The examination was exhaustive. Physicians checked height, weight, and posture; vision and colour perception; hearing, reflexes, and coordination. His heart and lungs were tested for murmurs and irregularities, his teeth examined carefully – poor dental health could disqualify a candidate. Blood and urine samples were analysed for signs of infection, anaemia, or disease. Orthopaedic checks ruled out flat feet or skeletal defects, and psychological screening assessed mental steadiness under stress. Donald passed every test with ease and was issued a Certificate of Acceptability – the official confirmation that he was fit for active duty.

Like many young men from the rural Midwest, Donald Smith entered military service with practical skills shaped by his upbringing rather than by formal preparation for war. Discipline, physical endurance, and mechanical aptitude – developed through farm work and long days on the prairie – formed a natural foundation for his military training. With his entry into the cadet programme, Smith left behind the unstructured rhythm of prairie life. What he carried with him were not grand ambitions or heroic narratives, but a deeply rooted work ethic and an instinctive acceptance of responsibility – qualities that gradually acquired new form and meaning within the military.

Smith had taken his first steps in aviation at the age of 16 under the guidance of Clyde Ice, a civilian instructor who taught him the fundamentals of flying. In his subsequent army training, the emphasis lay on drill, hierarchy, and technical proficiency, through which civilian skills were transformed into operational competence. The demands of flight training introduced a new level of precision and responsibility, in which individual judgement carried immediate consequences. Instructors noted not flamboyance, but steadiness: the ability to absorb pressure, follow procedures, and persist through fatigue – qualities that had their origins in the hard, rhythmic life on the prairie and that would later characterise his conduct in combat.

Because he had applied for the Flying Cadet Program, Donald's file was sent to the Aviation Cadet Examining Board for specialised classification. This meant further testing – more rigorous standards for vision, hearing, reflexes, and intelligence. His college education exceeded the required two years of higher study, a key qualification for pilot candidates. Healthy, disciplined, and academically trained, Donald made it clear that he was not seeking an ordinary enlistment. He wanted wings.

After receiving his medical clearance, he returned home to Belle Fourche to await orders. Two weeks later, in mid-August, the telegram arrived: he was to report to San Antonio, Texas, for further testing and assignment.

Before departing, Donald returned to Fort Meade, where his travel documents were prepared – official orders, a stamped Government Transportation Request (a War Department train ticket), and a small travel allowance in cash and meal vouchers.

On 20 August 1940, he boarded the southbound train at Sturgis. The farewell on the platform was brief – no speeches, just a final lunch packet from his mother and a firm handshake from his father. Then the train lurched forward, and Donald was on his way.

The trip took nearly two days. He slept in a Pullman berth, ate simple meals in the dining car, and watched the landscape change from the open prairies of South Dakota to the dusty plains of Texas.

His next stop was the Air Corps Training Center in the San Antonio area – Randolph Field, Kelly Field, and Brooks Field – where aviation cadets were classified and tested. For five days, Donald underwent new rounds of physical, psychological, and motor-skill assessments. On 27 August, the results came in: he had been accepted for Primary Flight Training. His orders sent him west – to Oxnard, California.

On 28 August 1940, he boarded another train, heading towards the Pacific. The route passed through El Paso, Phoenix, and Los Angeles, ending near the agricultural town of Oxnard. He shared the journey with other cadets, strangers bound by the same quiet determination. The air in the sleeper car smelled of tobacco and leather; the rhythm of the train blended with the hum of anticipation.

By noon on Friday, 30 August, the train pulled into the small Southern Pacific station in Oxnard. The coastal air carried the salt of the Pacific mixed with the dry dust of harvested fields. A faded olive-green truck waited by the platform, its driver leaning on a clipboard. 'Cadet Smith?' the man called. Donald nodded. 'Climb in. We'll take you to the base.'

He hoisted his suitcase, climbed into the back of the truck, and found himself among a handful of silent young men, all staring towards the horizon. As the vehicle rattled along the dirt road, the silhouette of the airfield came into view – low hangars, antenna towers, and the distant drone of engines circling in the sun.

Only then did the realisation fully settle in. He tightened his grip on the suitcase and looked out over the shimmering California plain. He was no longer the veterinarian's son from Butte County. He was Cadet Donald Smith, US Army Air Corps – a student pilot under the bright, relentless sky of California.

The first days were not for flying but for endurance – uniform fittings, vaccinations, endless paperwork, and long lines under the sun. When the issue clerk finally handed him his flight cadet uniform, Donald held it in his hands for a moment, sensing the weight of it. It felt strange, almost unreal – yet unmistakably his.

The Air Corps Years
(1940 – 1942)

Chapter 1

The Training: Where Flying Begins

At exactly 6.00am on Monday, 2 September 1940, it truly began. The cadets stood in formation on the parade ground, the California sun still low but already merciless. The instructor barked, 'Welcome to the Air Corps. From now on, you are nothing – until you prove yourself.' Don swallowed hard. His training had begun.

The first lessons of an Aviation Cadet took place outdoors. No books, no chairs – just marching. Perfect steps, turns on command, formation drills with absolute precision. 'Forward, march!' 'Left face!' – the orders echoed for hours. The purpose was clear: discipline, rhythm, reaction. The body was drilled as much as the mind. As a farmer's son from South Dakota, Don knew what hard work meant. But this was different. Here, character itself was tested.

Only in the afternoon did they finally sit in a classroom. A blackboard waited – covered in arrows, formulas, and flight paths. The subject: aerodynamics. Lift, drag, thrust, and gravity – the four forces that held an airplane aloft. The instructor spoke fast, without pause. Then came lessons on aircraft recognition, map reading, and the first principles of navigation. Don took careful notes, his mind packed with unfamiliar terms.

Each day began with physical training: push-ups, sit-ups, sprints across the drill field. Cadets had to run two miles in formation without losing step. Anyone who faltered risked elimination. It was hard, but Don endured. His body, shaped by prairie labour, held up well. By evening, his arms trembled from exhaustion, his clothes soaked with sweat – but his mind stayed sharp.

What the cadets did not know was that they were already being judged. The instructors watched constantly. Who showed initiative? Who grasped the material? Who cracked under pressure? Don did not stand out – but he didn't falter either. He worked quietly, steadily. A calm determination that took him far.

The first week passed without a single foot set in a cockpit. And yet, Don knew: this *was* flying. Not in the air, but on the ground. Here the foundation was laid. Fail here, and you would never take off. Succeed, and one day you might earn your place in the sky.

The first ten days at the Oxnard base were more than an introduction – they were a trial. Behind the drills, theory lessons, and medical exams hid the reality: this was a secret elimination round. No one said it aloud, but the weak were quietly removed. Those who failed obedience drills, had minor medical defects, or showed frustration were dismissed without ceremony. Some left by choice; others were simply told they were 'unsuitable'. There was no farewell – just silence and an empty bunk.

Of the dozens of young men who had arrived with Don in Oxnard, a dozen were soon gone. The instructors said nothing – it was part of the process. The sky, like the service, was unforgiving. A pilot who hesitated, or whose emotions overruled his judgment, had no place in a cockpit. And above all, the US Army Air Corps – still technically in peacetime – could not afford to waste thousands of dollars on a trainee who would never fly safely. The Primary Flying School, where cadets would make their first flights in planes like the Stearman PT-17, was costly *and* dangerous. Only those found mentally, physically, and emotionally fit would proceed.

Don kept to himself – quiet, focused, methodical. No swagger, no boasting. But within him grew something the instructors *did* notice: self-control, adaptability, willpower. When he was told on the tenth day that he had been selected for the next phase, he felt no triumph – only responsibility. He knew what it meant: the right to fly had to be earned in the air, hands on the controls, not a moment of slack.

The flight school where Don began his military training lay just outside Oxnard, in Ventura County, and it wasn't a standard army base. Mira Loma Flight Academy was run by C.C. Moseley's Cal-Aero group – a civilian operator – but under strict Army Air Corps supervision. Civilian aircraft, classrooms, and instructors; military rules, discipline, and oversight. Mira Loma was one of several contract primary schools – civilian-run, but military-controlled – that began training cadets in 1940.

Over eight to ten weeks, students followed an intense schedule: daily ground instruction and multiple flight periods in Stearman primary trainers (PT-13/17 *Kaydet*) – biplanes with open cockpits, fabric-covered wings, and steel-tube frames. This was the first – and toughest – stage on the path to becoming a pilot. Only those who passed Primary could advance to Basic and beyond. Mira Loma played a key role in shaping thousands of young men, including Don.

The school itself was simple and remote: a dusty strip of grass or uneven concrete, a few hangars, and a single barracks doubling as classroom. The instructors – mostly seasoned civilian pilots or former military aviators – worked under army officers but taught in their own blunt, no-nonsense style.

The Boeing-Stearman PT-17 Kaydet was not a forgiving airplane, and that was by design: mistakes had consequences, and those consequences built character. Even climbing into the cockpit required agility. You wore a leather helmet, goggles, and a simple parachute. The wind battered your face, the engine roared without mercy. Radio communication was minimal or non-existent – orders came by hand signals or through a rubber tube linking the instructor's cockpit to that of the student.

The Primary course typically lasted eight to ten weeks, with three or four hours of ground school and two or three flight periods each day. In class, they studied the basics: aerodynamics, engine systems, emergency procedures, air regulations – and above all, discipline. But the real learning happened in the air.

Under his instructor's supervision, Don took his first true steps as a pilot: taxiing, straight-and-level flight, gentle turns, climbs and descents, recovery from stalls and spins – and, most critically, landings. These were gruelling exercises. Stall recovery was practised deliberately to sharpen reflexes. Every skill was tested – on paper, in conversation, and in flight. The instructors were strict, often curt, and could eliminate a cadet without explanation. Their mission was clear: filter the weak, forge the strong. Attrition rates were high – nearly 40 per cent washed out before finishing Primary.

Yet Don was no novice. Long before the Air Corps had put him in uniform, he had spent hours on the grass field near Spearfish, under the watchful eye of Clyde Ice – the aviation pioneer of the Dakotas. As a teenager, Don had flown with Ice in a Piper Cub, learning the basics: control, balance, altitude. Those short flights – sometimes over snowy fields, sometimes over the Black Hills – had left something behind: a feel for the air, a trust in the machine.

Now, in Oxnard, with his hands gripping the stick of a roaring Stearman, that trust returned. Not as confidence, but as calm. The instructor behind him barked orders through the speaking tube. Don felt the airplane's reactions – the way it yawed when handled roughly, the way a gentle touch on the rudder kept the nose straight. None of it was foreign – only louder, faster, more demanding.

When he banked through his first turn over the practice field, he thought back to that afternoon with Clyde – sunlight streaming through the cockpit glass, the land rolling beneath them. Clyde had said then, 'Flying isn't about showing off. It's about control. Calm. The airplane listens when you listen first.'

Those words stayed with him. While classmates panicked in stalls or trembled before their first landings, Don remained steady, focused. He knew the feeling of flight – not in this plane, not under these conditions, but in essence. The air forgave nothing, yet promised everything to those who treated it with respect.

After only eight to twelve hours of dual instruction came the decisive test: the first solo. The moment of truth. No instructor behind you – just you and the airplane. One mistake could be fatal. Some froze or crashed. Those who succeeded returned to cheering instructors – and a ritual: their shirt tail ceremoniously cut off, symbolising their first solo flight.

For Don, it was the moment when everything came together. His body tense, his mind calm. His hands found the controls instinctively, his feet the rudder pedals. The wind howled, the plane shuddered – but he felt at home. He made a flawless circuit: take-off, smooth turn over the wind sock, steady approach, flare, touchdown.

The instructors – sceptical at first of the quiet farm boy – were impressed. His technique was still raw, his radio voice unsure, but his instinct was true. With each flight, his control grew sharper; with each day, it became clearer: Don had what it took to be a pilot. Not through bravado, but through patience, discipline, and an innate feel for the machine.

Those who survived Primary advanced to Basic. Those who did not were sent home – not because they were weak, but because flying demanded everything, every single day.

In addition to Stearman flight hours, Primary included instrument instruction in the Link Trainer, known as the 'blue box'. This pneumatically operated simulator sat on a small platform connected to a plotter table, allowing the instructor to track the cadet's 'flight' in real time. Cadets practised blind flying without risk: instrument scanning, standard turns, pitch-and-power climbs and descents, timed turns, unusual-attitude recovery, and, where available, basic radio-range navigation. Sessions were short and frequent, alternating with ground school and pattern flying. The goal: to develop early instrument discipline and spatial orientation before progressing to the next phase – a standardised requirement across all contract schools like Mira Loma, operating under Army Air Corps supervision.

Chapter 2

Basic Flying School – From Young Student to True Pilot

Don had passed through Primary Flying School with ease – and his instructors quickly noticed he possessed something beyond the ordinary. During his first solo flight, he stayed calm when crosswinds pushed him off line, and there was a natural balance in his turns that couldn't be taught in ten flying hours. 'You've flown before,' one instructor remarked, not accusingly but with quiet respect. Don nodded, hesitant but honest. He hadn't broadcast it, yet it was true. Clyde Ice had taught him to trust what you feel. No official flight hours, but real experience. And it showed in the air.

After completing his course in Oxnard, Don was transferred to a military flying school near San Jose, on the wide expanse of Moffett Field. Here began the next phase: Basic Flying School. What had felt like an introduction in Oxnard was now a disciplined military regimen. No more civilian instructors, no room for flexibility. Everything ran by the clock, under a strict chain of command. Checkpoints, concrete runways, radio discipline, and uniformed precision defined the rhythm of the day. It felt as though the war was drawing closer.

Don was assigned to the Vultee BT-13 Valiant, a rugged and notoriously temperamental trainer nicknamed the 'Vibrator' for its violent shaking in flight. The plane was heavier, faster, and far less forgiving than the Stearman. Its enclosed cockpit limited visibility, and its controls demanded both strength and finesse. Here, cadets didn't just *learn* to fly – they learned to perform under pressure, to act within seconds, and to decide when the margin for error vanished.

Days began at sunrise. Morning classes covered instrument flight, radio communication, formation flying, and emergency procedures – recovery from stalls, engine failure, control failure. After that came the flying itself: sometimes in tight formation, sometimes in rough crosswinds, sometimes at night. Night flights were the hardest. The only visual reference was a narrow strip of light surrounded by black emptiness. One wrong judgment, one moment of panic, could end it all.

Yet Don felt at home. What others learned from manuals, he understood instinctively. His time with Clyde Ice had given him something rare: confidence without arrogance. He knew the quiet of the cockpit, the instinct to react before thinking, the feel of the air around the wings. Instructors described him as 'steady, alert, and naturally correct'. Fellow cadets noticed that he never boasted – but never failed, either.

Still, not everyone made it. Some lost control on landings; others spun out of turns and never recovered. Don seldom mentioned it in letters home, but between the lines it was clear: every flight could be the last. Those who pressed on grew close. They shared more than lessons – they shared exhaustion, pressure, hope, and fear.

Don was slowly becoming one of the best in his class. His radio work was crisp, his landings precise, his demeanour calm and disciplined. He didn't fly to impress – he flew because he understood there was no room for anything less.

Chapter 3

Advanced Flying School – The Final Test

In November 1940, Donald Smith entered the third and most demanding stage of his pilot training: Advanced Flying School. He was assigned to Kelly Field, a sprawling Air Corps base just outside San Antonio, Texas. Together with nearby Brooks Field and Randolph Field, it formed the core of the Army's advanced flight training system – known collectively as 'The West Point of the Air'. The nickname was no exaggeration. Everything there revolved around precision, discipline, and performance.

Don noticed the difference immediately. The military structure was sharper than ever. Days began before sunrise with roll call, physical training, and inspection. Then came advanced classes in aerodynamics, navigation, meteorology, radio operations, and aircraft mechanics. Theory and practice alternated in a relentless schedule.

His new trainer was the North American AT-6 Texan – no longer a simple trainer, but a bridge to the real thing: a high-performance monoplane with a retractable landing gear, powerful engine, and a full instrument panel. 'The AT-6 isn't a trainer anymore,' Don wrote home. 'It's a step towards war.'

At Kelly Field, he learned formation flying, instrument navigation, and blind-flight procedures. At nearby Brooks Field, he practised advanced manoeuvres: stall recovery, precision landings, dives, and steep turns. The instructors – men hardened by years of experience – tolerated no carelessness. Every flight was analysed in detail, every error dissected.

Brooks Field, Texas
5 March, 1941

Dear Folks,

I received your letter this morning and suddenly realised that I had failed to write over the weekend. Probably because I had to fly Saturday afternoon and again that night. I had my last night cross-country then – three hours in the air. Working all day Saturday didn't make it feel much like a weekend, and on Sunday I had to catch up on sleep.

I have 42 hours now, and probably two more days of flying before we finish. I've completed everything except my instrument work and will get a couple more trips before earning my instrument rating.

We've been having our final medical checks – X-rays, blood tests, and probably another eye exam before graduation. The weather here has been unpredictable: one day so hot a man in San Antonio had heat stroke, today it's cold and raining. I hope it clears by graduation day; we're supposed to fly a formation review at 4:15. They've done it before, and I guess it's to become standard now.

The mileage is starting to build up on my car. I hope I can drive it home – it's nicely broken in. I'm glad gas and oil are cheap here on the field – 17¢ for gas, 6¢ for the best bulk oil. In town it's 20¢ or more, though you can find 16½¢ downtown.

Not much more news around here, so I'll close for now.

As ever, love,
Don

Despite the pressure, camaraderie flourished among the cadets. They learned to rely on one another – in the air and on the ground. Don shared his notes, helped others with navigation calculations, and in return received support during the tougher flights.

But the training also took its toll. Accidents happened. Every cadet knew that a single lapse could be fatal. 'We're not learning to fly without fear,' Don wrote, 'we're learning to turn that fear into focus.'

And he did. His earlier lessons with Clyde Ice had given him an edge, but he knew he had to earn everything anew. Each successful flight brought him one step closer to his goal – the silver wings that marked a man as a pilot of the United States Army Air Corps.

Chapter 4

Salary

During his training at the Primary Flying School in Oxnard, California, Donald received a monthly allowance of $75 – the standard pay for Aviation Cadets in the US Army Air Corps in 1941. It wasn't much, but for young men like Don – raised in modest circumstances and living on their own for the first time – it meant a great deal. It was his first official wage: tangible proof that he was building a future as a military pilot in service of his country.

This allowance covered personal expenses: toiletries, postage, haircuts, snacks, recreation. Uniforms, meals, lodging, and medical care were provided by the government. Yet every cadet was expected to learn financial discipline – to save, plan, and make choices. For some, it was an exercise in restraint; for others, a test of maturity. Don, raised on the frugality of the prairie, spent little. Every dollar felt earned – and every purchase was deliberate.

Everything changed once he completed his flight training. The day he received his pilot's wings, along with the rank of second lieutenant, was more than ceremonial. It marked the official beginning of his career as an officer and operational pilot – and that was reflected in his pay slip.

From that moment, Don earned roughly $245 per month, composed of:

- $125 base pay as a second lieutenant
- $62.50 flight pay (a 50 per cent supplement for all pilots on active flying status)
- $57.50 or more in variable allowances, depending on assignment, location, and conditions (such as quarters allowance, subsistence, or temporary duty pay – TDY pay)

Compared to the average annual income of an American worker in 1941 – about $1,500 – this was generous, especially for a man in his twenties with no dependants. But with higher income came higher expectations. Don was now required to present himself as an officer: to purchase his own uniforms, maintain proper appearance, behave appropriately in social settings, and – above all – perform his duties as an Air Corps pilot with dedication and discipline.

The transition from cadet to officer was not merely financial or symbolic. It also meant that he was now eligible for operational assignments. His wings granted him both the right and the duty to lead crews, fly bombers, and – if called upon – carry out missions in a world edging towards total war. Every decision mattered; every mistake could cost lives.

For Don, it felt like the final step into adulthood. His pay was not just a reward, but a measure of trust. And he was determined to honour that trust – in the air, where it truly counted.

Chapter 5

A Dance Night in San Antonio

After meeting a few young women in San Antonio who encouraged him to dance, Donald began seriously considering taking dance lessons. Dancing wasn't entirely new to him – back in Belle Fourche he had often danced with friends at local gatherings – but he had never been a particularly skilled dancer.

The girls took his awkward steps in their stride, smiling even when he accidentally stepped on their toes. Their kindness gave him the confidence to let go of his self-consciousness and enjoy the music. Still, in a letter home, he mentioned his plan to take lessons – hoping to make a better impression at the formal events that often accompanied military life.

That plan, however, quickly changed when one of his fellow cadets made another suggestion: 'I know a young lady,' he said. 'Why don't you go on a blind date?'

Curious about where that might lead, Don agreed. That was how, in mid-February 1941, he met Minnie Marie Rauh, a young woman from San Antonio, Texas. Her warmth and charm put him instantly at ease. Dance lessons suddenly seemed unnecessary – their connection made every clumsy step irrelevant.

The meeting with Minnie Marie would prove to be a turning point. Though she was still a student at Thomas Jefferson High School in San Antonio, and just a little younger than Don, something about her struck him deeply. Her kind disposition and natural grace made him feel comfortable in a way he hadn't expected. What began as a casual introduction soon grew into something meaningful.

Marie was born Minnie Marie Rauh on 5 October 1920, in Dallas, Texas – two years after Don. Her father, Leon Rauh, worked as a telegraph operator, a respected profession in an era when the telegraph was the lifeline of communication. But tragedy struck early: Leon died in 1927, when Marie was only 6 years old. His death left a deep mark on her childhood and meant that she grew up without a father's presence.

After his passing, Marie was taken in by relatives. She first lived with her uncle, William E. Rauh, and his wife, Sophia, who provided a loving and stable home. Later, she moved in with her grandfather, Ben Rauh, a successful cotton merchant and proud immigrant from Bavaria, Germany. He gave her a warm household and instilled in her enduring values: hard work, self-respect, and perseverance.

When Marie's mother, Deluca Stubbs, remarried Walter Crouch, the family relocated to San Antonio. Walter, a salesman specialising in hotel supplies, became her stepfather and took an active role in raising her. Through this marriage, Marie took on the Crouch surname. Alongside her younger sister Monette Crouch, she grew up in a reorganised but caring household. The renewed sense of family – her bond with her sister and her supportive stepfather – helped her regain stability and strength after a childhood marked by change.

Their meeting, almost accidental, would alter the course of both their lives. What began as a simple dance in San Antonio became a bond that grew against the backdrop of military discipline and a world moving towards war. In the months that followed, Don's training carried him from base to base, and their connection continued through letters – brief moments of warmth amid the growing demands of duty. It was a wartime affection, sincere and unassuming, cut short by the events that would soon claim his life.

During his training, Donald purchased a Ford – a practical decision that greatly improved his life as a cadet. Having his own car gave him mobility and a rare sense of independence amid the rigid structure of military life. It allowed him to travel off base during short breaks, to escape the discipline and noise of the flight line, and to find brief moments of calm in the midst of constant instruction. For Don, the car represented more than convenience; it was freedom, a small but meaningful outlet during the demanding months of his training.

Chapter 6

Choice of Assignment

In a letter dated 23 January 1941, written from Brooks Field, Don offered a revealing look into his thoughts and ambitions during this critical phase of his training. He explained that the cadets were asked to list their preferences for both the type of aircraft they wished to fly and the stations where they hoped to serve after graduation.

Like all aviation cadets, Don had the opportunity to request an aircraft specialisation. He chose bombardment – a decision driven by his interest in teamwork, formation flying, and the strategic importance of bomber operations. The Air Corps valued such motivation: in early 1941, bomber crews were in higher demand than fighter pilots, increasing the likelihood that Don's preference would be honoured.

Though cadets could express their wishes, the final decision always rested with Air Corps command. Assignments were determined by a combination of flying ability, physical suitability, and – above all – operational needs.

In his letter, Don also listed the three domestic bases where he most hoped to be stationed following graduation:

1. Lowry Field, Denver, Colorado – his first choice.
2. McChord Field, Washington.
3. Muroc Field, California – an isolated desert base known for its experimental flight work.

While some of his fellow cadets volunteered for foreign duty, Don remained cautious. 'A few of the boys asked for foreign duty,' he wrote. 'I had thought I would rather stay in US for a while at least.'

He also noted that each cadet was required to list three Chinese stations among their preferences – a striking indication that the Air Corps was already preparing for possible deployment in Asia, months before Pearl Harbor.

The letter, clear and thoughtful, revealed a young man balancing ambition with realism. With 160 flight hours completed and about fifty remaining before earning his wings, Don was already thinking ahead – about where he might serve, what kind of pilot he wanted to become, and what responsibilities awaited him.

His letters to his parents, Arthur and Laura, offer an intimate record of that transformation – physical, mental, and emotional. In an earlier letter, he described Brooks Field with admiration and awe: 'Brooks Field is impressive. The aircraft here move like birds in a flock, and the cadets are like ants, always in motion. Everything here breathes discipline and determination. It feels like I have to prove all over again that I belong here – but that only drives me more.'

That sense of purpose remained his constant fuel. Despite uncertainty and the weight of training, Don grew with every flight – both as a pilot in the air and as a man on the ground.

Chapter 7

Pilot Wings

After eight weeks of intense training, countless flight hours, and rigorous evaluations, the long-awaited moment finally arrived in March 1941: Don Smith received his silver pilot wings. The ceremony took place at Kelly Field, Texas, one of the oldest training centres of the US Army Air Corps and, at that time, the beating heart of advanced flight instruction

Brooks Field, Texas
12 March, 1941

Dear Folks,

I didn't hear from you this morning but expect a letter soon. We've been taking it very easy this week, with a couple of practice review formations, and tomorrow will be the final showing. We graduate Friday morning and will be busy moving in the afternoon. I'm not sure what my address in town will be, but you can still send letters here, as I have to report once a day until my orders arrive and I move to a new station.

We had inspection on our new uniforms, and mine passed all right. I think these are a little snappier than the ones we wore at school. I heard that Dr Foley has been called for a year's active duty, as well as Merraugh and Simminson, so that's going to leave the department short-handed. One of the men on the farm was also drafted, so it looks like everyone's going to be in the Army for a year or so.

There isn't even a good rumour about where we'll be sent. We all applied for ten days' leave after graduation, but I suppose it'll go the same way as the last class – no leave granted.

> The weather has been nice lately, and yesterday afternoon, after flying, we went on a picnic in the hills west of San Antonio. It's beautiful country up there – a little higher than this side – and we found a clear stream to eat lunch by.
>
> Not much happening here; the days just drag by until graduation. Lots of visitors and friends are arriving for the big day. I just hope the weather holds so the folks from up north won't think it always rains down here.
>
> Will close for now and write again once I'm settled in my new home.
>
> As ever, your loving son,
> Don

After months of flying, studying, waiting, and persevering, Don had reached the end of his formal flight training at Brooks Field, near San Antonio, Texas. In the weeks leading up to graduation, he had spent endless hours in the air – by day and night, in formation, under instruments. He had practised navigation, altitude control, discipline – and trust. Not only in his aircraft, but in himself.

On Friday, 14 March 1941, Don's graduating class assembled in full military dress on the parade ground of Kelly Field, the neighbouring base where the official graduation ceremony – the Wings Parade – took place. It was the day they would receive their long-awaited pilot insignia: the silver wings of the US Army Air Corps.

The ceremony marked the completion of their training and their transformation from cadets into officers. The event was conducted with full military formality. Cadets stood in perfect formation – boots polished, caps aligned. In attendance were senior officers, instructors, and invited guests – sometimes including family members or dignitaries from nearby commands.

Following the flag parade and the playing of the *Army Air Corps March*, the commanding officer delivered an address on the core virtues of military aviation: duty, discipline, courage, and perseverance. Then, one by one, the cadets were called forward to receive their insignia – usually accompanied by a firm handshake and a quiet 'congratulations'.

From that moment, each was no longer a cadet, but a second lieutenant – a commissioned pilot, ready to serve in the expanding Air Corps.

The evening of the day Don received his pilot's insignia he attended the graduation dance held in the large Recreation Hall at Kelly Field – a spacious, high-ceilinged hall designed for cadet entertainment and relaxation. The room was decorated with flags and festive lights; the floor gleamed with wax, and a small dance orchestra played the popular tunes of the day, from Glenn Miller to Tommy Dorsey. Folding chairs and tables lined the walls, while the broad dance floor filled with dozens of newly commissioned officers in their crisp uniforms and guests from San Antonio.

For Don the evening meant more than mere ceremony. His dance partner was Marie Crouch, the young woman from San Antonio, whom he had met only a few weeks earlier through a blind date – a common practice among young flyers, who often spent their weekends at dances and social gatherings in town. Don had found her kind and graceful, and decided to invite her personally to the ball.

In a letter home written a few days after the ceremony, Don noted: 'Our dance went over very nice, and everyone seemed to have had a good time.'

By then, Don and Marie were already making tentative plans for a future together. They talked about a wedding in early summer, though new assignments and military duties would soon postpone their hopes. Still, that dance in the Recreation Hall at Kelly Field remained their first tangible chapter – the moment when a young pilot and a young woman found each other on the eve of a world in turmoil.

Chapter 8

Transition to Active Duty

After earning his pilot's wings on 14 March 1941, at Kelly Field, Don entered a brief transitional period before receiving official orders for his next assignment. While awaiting his posting, he and two fellow pilots decided to rent an apartment in San Antonio. For the first time in months of intense training, there was room for rest, reflection, and friendship.

The days in San Antonio formed a rare pause between the rigid discipline of flight school and the weight of active service. The shared apartment offered more than practical housing; it became a place of camaraderie. The young pilots laughed, debated, reminisced about their training, and discussed their futures in a world on the brink of war.

For Don, this period meant more than relaxation. It allowed him to deepen his relationship with Marie. They saw each other often, talked about their dreams and hopes, and came to understand one another more fully. Marie understood the nature of military life – constant movement, few certainties – yet she was willing to follow him wherever duty would lead. That choice strengthened their bond even more.

During those weeks of transition, Don also maintained close contact with home. He wrote letters to his brother and sisters, to relatives in Kingsbury County, and to friends in Belle Fourche. His words carried pride but also a quiet longing. His connection to his roots remained strong, even as he prepared for a life in uniform.

When his orders for McChord Field, near Tacoma, Washington, finally arrived, Donald knew the next chapter of his life was beginning. The transition brought mixed emotions. He looked forward to the new stage of his career, but it also meant saying goodbye to a place and people who had become dear to him. He and Marie parted for the time being, promising to see each other again soon.

Donald prepared himself mentally and physically for departure. Together with Marie, he began making plans to rent another apartment in

Tacoma, so that despite the uncertainty of military life, they could still build a shared home. The prospect gave him strength, stability, and motivation.

When he shared the news with his roommates, they all realised their paths would soon diverge. Their time in San Antonio had been short but intense. They had forged friendships and readied themselves for the responsibilities that lay ahead. Don left with confidence.

Before his transfer to McChord Field in Washington, Don planned an important stopover – a visit to his parents in Belle Fourche. He wanted not only to see them again after the intense months of training at Oxnard, Randolph, Brooks, and Kelly Field, but also to introduce them to the woman who had gradually captured his heart: Marie.

Throughout his training, Donald had kept his parents informed through regular letters. Although there is no evidence that he visited them in person during this period, his correspondence reveals deep gratitude and enduring affection. To Don, Arthur and Laura Smith remained a steady source of moral support, even from afar, as his military career took shape.

The visit to Belle Fourche meant a great deal to him. The familiar house, the comforting presence of his parents, and even their dog Mugs offered a rare moment of peace amid a life full of change. Arthur and Laura were visibly proud of his achievements, though they could not hide their concern about the uncertain times ahead. Their conversations turned to his ambitions, his dedication to flying, and the awareness that the path before him would not be without risks.

During this visit, Donald spoke openly with his parents about Marie for the first time. He told them that their relationship had grown deeper and that he was even thinking about marriage. Arthur and Laura listened closely. Although surprised by his frankness, they could sense the sincerity of his feelings. His words brought hope and joy to what was otherwise an emotional farewell.

The short stay in Belle Fourche gave Don not only the strength that comes from family but also a tangible sense of his personal future. His parents realised that he had truly become an adult – a young officer with responsibilities, dreams, and a woman ready to stand by his side. They knew that, whatever the future might hold, Don would continue to carry their values with him – in uniform, in the air, and perhaps someday as a husband.

With renewed strength and a warm heart, Don departed for Washington. The farewell was difficult, but it gave him one last anchor before he fully stepped into a life of service to his country.

Chapter 9

Washington

After completing his pilot training, Don was assigned to McChord Field, located in Pierce County, Washington. Since 1940, the base had been part of the Northwest Air District within the GHQ Air Force and had grown into an important centre for air defence in the northwestern United States.

From McChord Field, pilots conducted air patrols along the Pacific coast and trained in bombing runs, reconnaissance, and aerial combat tactics across California, Oregon, and Washington. The threat of war hung palpably in the skies, and the base took on an increasingly vital role in preparing for possible attack. McChord Field became a crucial link in the nation's growing network of military readiness.

Don was assigned to the 89th Reconnaissance Squadron, a specialised unit within the 17th Bombardment Group (Medium). The squadron's duties included:

- Tactical reconnaissance flights along the Pacific coast;
- Gathering intelligence on enemy shipping and coastal defences;
- Transition training on the new B-25 Mitchell, and later participation in anti-submarine patrols following the attack on Pearl Harbor.

By this time, Don had logged countless training hours and earned a solid reputation as a dependable pilot. What the future held, he could not yet know – but one thing was certain: the war had caught up with him, and now it was his turn to fly.

Tacoma, Washington – May–June 1941

During his training period at McChord Field, Don Smith temporarily rented an apartment at 523 South G Street in Tacoma. The red-brick building, erected in 1925, was typical of the neighbourhood – three stories tall, with white shutters and a graceful arched entrance reached by a split staircase. A black iron fire escape ran down the façade, and two neatly trimmed bushes flanked the doorway. The building housed several young officers who, like Don, were awaiting permanent assignment.

He shared the place with other pilots and crew members who were training on bombers such as the B-18 Bolo and the newly arrived B-25 Mitchell. The rooms were simple but sufficient. There was little time to settle in – by day they were in the air or on the base; by evening, they studied procedures and prepared for the next day's briefings.

Although his stay in Tacoma was temporary, Don was already thinking ahead. Together with Marie, he dreamed of renting an apartment in Spokane after their marriage – closer to Felts Field, where he was frequently assigned. The thought of a shared home gave their plans a sense of reality, even amid the uncertainty of military life.

McChord Field, Washington – 14 May 1941

The early morning sun cast long shadows across the airfield as Don packed his bag. In two days, he would depart for Felts Field in Spokane. McChord had become familiar ground, but the army seldom allowed a pilot to stay in one place for long. His next assignment awaited.

With his orders in hand, he looked one last time at the line of aircraft shimmering in the light. Soon he would have to prove himself again, in a new environment, with new instructors and a new rhythm. Yet one thing remained constant – the drive to improve, to react faster, to land perfectly every time.

Felts Field, Spokane – 17 May 1941

The flight to Spokane had been rough. Turbulence had shaken the aircraft violently, but once the wheels touched the runway, a new phase of training began.

Each morning started with a briefing. The officers reviewed precision bombing techniques, rapid take-offs, emergency procedures, and formation flying. The days were tightly structured and left no room for error. Felts Field was no place for leisure – here they trained to survive.

Within days, Don received his first practice flights in the B-25 Mitchell. The cockpit was cramped, the control levers heavy, but the sky felt like freedom. The Mitchell was new, fast, and powerful – just like he aspired to be. Each flight brought him closer to the mastery expected of a bomber pilot.

Felts Field, Spokane – 25 May 1941

The days passed quickly, like the aircraft that roared skyward in tight formations.

'Today we'll simulate an attack on a bridge,' the instructor announced during the morning briefing. 'You'll fly at low altitude and release your bombs within three seconds.' Don nodded. Every second counted.

They took off in groups of four, each with a co-pilot and bombardier aboard. Flying barely 100 metres above the ground, they approached the target. Don gripped the controls tightly. Three seconds. Release. Pull up.

A dull thud followed. A small plume of smoke rose from where the sand-filled practice bomb had struck. Bull's-eye.

McChord Field, Washington – 3 June 1941

After two weeks of training, Don briefly returned to McChord. But there was no time for rest. Housing was scarce; he kept his belongings in his car, as did several other officers without permanent quarters.

His days were filled with flying, maintenance, and classroom instruction on the theories of air warfare. His car became a temporary home. He learned to sleep wherever he could, to wait when he must, and to be ready the instant an order came through.

Felts Field, Spokane – Return, around 18 June 1941

By mid-June, Don received new orders: he was to report back to Felts Field. The B-25 training programme was entering a more intense phase. More aircraft were arriving, and crews were expanding. Everything pointed to something larger on the horizon.

The 17th Bombardment Group was split between McChord and Felts Field due to capacity limits – a sign that preparations were accelerating.

Chapter 10

The Marriage of Donald Smith and Marie Crouch

On 21 June, 1941, at five o'clock in the afternoon, Donald Smith and Marie Crouch stood side by side in a small, unadorned room in King County, Washington. The ceremony was intimate; only a handful of people were present. While the marriage was officially recorded in King County, Washington, the marriage license was issued in Pierce County, where Don was stationed at McChord Field. In his letters, Don referred to the location simply as Seattle, reflecting common contemporary usage.

Marie's parents had travelled from Texas to Washington to be with her on this special day, accompanying their daughter as she prepared to begin a new life far from home. Don's parents, Arthur and Laura Smith, were unable to make the long journey from South Dakota, their health and the hardships of travel keeping them close to home. Yet Don and Marie were resolute – they knew that their love was stronger than the uncertainties ahead.

In the weeks before their marriage, the couple had already decided to rent an apartment in Spokane, where Don expected to be stationed for part of his upcoming assignment. They imagined building their first home together there, even as the war loomed ever closer.

The Justice of the Peace, Chas. R. Oakes, stood before them and gave a short but solemn address. He spoke of the power of love and commitment, of standing together through difficult times. Don glanced at Marie, who held his hands tightly in hers. Her eyes shone despite the strain of the previous weeks. They knew that Don could be reassigned at any moment, but rather than wait, they had chosen to meet fate halfway.

When it came time for the vows, Marie took a deep breath: 'Donald, I promise you loyalty and support, wherever we may go. I know your path is unpredictable, but I will always be your home.'

Donald gently squeezed her hands and replied: 'Marie, I promise to love and protect you, wherever life may take us. We don't know what tomorrow will bring, but as long as we're together, we can face anything.'

With a warm smile and a nod from the judge, the rings were exchanged. Marie's parents, standing a few steps away, held hands – proud of their daughter and of the man she had chosen.

When the Justice pronounced the final words – 'I now declare you husband and wife.' – Don and Marie looked at each other and lingered for a moment before sharing a soft, genuine kiss. There was no grand celebration, no lavish feast – only a simple, unforgettable moment of union.

A little after five o'clock, their marriage was complete. It was officially recorded on 8 July, 1941, but that formality meant little to them. Their life together had already begun.

> 25 June, 1941
>
> Dear Folks,
>
> I received your letter today, and while we are right in the middle of another move, I wanted to write you. We are driving to Pendleton tomorrow to draw some armament equipment and then go on to Felts Field at Spokane and act as officer of the guard for about ten days until the rest of the squadron moves over from Pendleton.
>
> We were married last Saturday evening at Seattle, and had three days off from work to get our apartment fixed up here. We had a lot of things like dishes and silverware to get, and that along with the rest of the things took up most of our time off. We were just nicely settled here, and now it is time to move again, but we expect to find some apartment at Spokane and have until the middle of September before we are moved again.
>
> It would be nice if we could get enough time off to get to Belle, but until this sojourn at Felts Field is finished and the move back to Pendleton accomplished there is little hope of doing so.
>
> Thursday morning – will have to close and hurry on. I will write you as soon as we get to Felts Field, which by the

way will be my new address, the same as when I was there before.

I just wanted to write a note before the weekend.

As ever, love,
Don

In the summer of 1941, Don Smith and his new bride Marie moved into an apartment at 125 West Sixth Avenue, Spokane, Washington – a stylish brick building that had only recently been renamed the Seymour Apartments, after its owner, Seymour Birch. Yet until shortly before the couple's arrival, the building had carried another, striking name: The Tokyo Apartments. With hindsight, that name feels almost prophetic.

Only a few months later, Don would take off from the deck of an aircraft carrier as one of the pilots in the famed Doolittle Raid, bound for Japan. His assigned target was the port city of Kobe, part of a daring American retaliation for the attack on Pearl Harbor. Though Don did not fly over Tokyo itself, that city was the symbolic heart of the mission. In that light, the name of his former residence gains an uncanny resonance.

Those echoes from the past would emerge much later, when an archivist reconstructed the address from Don's surviving letters. It was purely by chance that I came across this archivist, named Larkin (as in the Doolittle Raider, Larkin), by coincidence, another Doolittle flyer bore the surname Birch, just like the Spokane landlord. A chain of seemingly random, yet intriguing, connections.

The five-storey complex, built in a Japanese-inspired style, was considered one of Spokane's most modern apartment houses. It offered both furnished and unfurnished units with gas stoves, refrigerators, and compact kitchenettes, renting for $25 to $50 per month. Nestled on a quiet, tree-lined street near the city centre, it became Don and Marie's first true home together.

Felts Field, Spokane – 24 June, 1941

The sun beat down on the airfield as Major General John F. Curry, commanding officer of the Second Air Force, conducted his inspection. More than 600 enlisted men and eighty-six officers of the 17th

Bombardment Group, including Don Smith, stood in formation. The camp was immaculate: over 150 tents, a mobile radio unit, a field kitchen, and even a fire truck stood neatly arranged for review.

According to the *Spokane Chronicle* of 24 June 1941, twenty-three newly commissioned second lieutenants arrived that day at Felts Field – fresh from Stockton and Kelly Field. Though Don had already been stationed at the base earlier that spring, the arrival of so many new officers reflected the rapid expansion of the US Army Air Corps. Across the nation, new squadrons were forming, airfields were multiplying, and what had begun as a modest training program was transforming into the framework of a wartime air force.

The following day, 25 June, the *Spokane Chronicle* published a photograph titled 'Big Bombers Spectacular Sight at Felts Field'. It showed rows of gleaming B-25 Mitchells, and the accompanying article announced that by late summer, sixty-nine Mitchells would be stationed at the field. The 17th Bombardment Group was growing rapidly, preparing for its eventual transfer to Pendleton, Oregon – one more step in the Air Corps' steady march towards war.

Pendleton, Oregon – 26 June, 1941

Pendleton was a dusty cow town, unremarkable at first glance. Yet for the Army Air Corps it offered exactly what was needed: wide open plains, little civilian air traffic, and a strategic position close to training ranges.

Don spent only a few days there, collecting equipment and paperwork. He knew his stay would be short – the new base was not yet fully operational. Until then, the men shuttled between locations, living out of their duffel bags and flight gear.

Felts Field, Spokane – 18 July, 1941

The summer heat hung heavy over the tents as Don returned to Spokane. The shift from the warmth of Marie's presence to the strict rhythm of military life was abrupt. But there was no room for sentiment.

On one of the few free afternoons, he joined fellow pilots at a lake outside the city. The sun blazed high, and the water shimmered like liquid gold. For a brief moment he felt like any young man again – not a pilot in training for war.

That night he returned to the crowded field. There weren't enough beds for everyone. Don was assigned to the motor pool – an improvised sleeping area among the trucks. He lay in the back of a transport vehicle, his leather flight jacket serving as a blanket. Above him, the stars stretched across the dark Washington sky.

It wasn't luxury, but it was part of the job. Pilots had to learn to adapt – to sleep when they could, to wait when they must, and to be ready when the next order came. And that order would come soon.

By July 1941, the 89th Reconnaissance Squadron was gradually being transferred from McChord Field to Pendleton Field, Oregon.

Although the first detachments – including Don's – had briefly stayed in Pendleton in late June, the unit only began full-scale training there after 21 July. At Pendleton they received the new B-25B Mitchell bombers and began intensive training in preparation for future operations.

From that point on, Pendleton became the central base of the 17th Bombardment Group's activities – the starting point of a path that would eventually lead them to Columbia Army Air Base, South Carolina, in early 1942.

The months at Felts Field marked more than a routine training phase – they reflected the rapid transformation of the US Army Air Corps into a modern air force. Here, the 17th Bombardment Group became one of the first units to master the new B-25 Mitchell, honing tactics that would soon prove invaluable. This early familiarity with the aircraft, combined with the group's growing reputation for precision and discipline, would later make the 17th the natural choice for a mission unlike any before – the daring strike on Japan that would become known as the Doolittle Raid.

Spokane, Washington – August 1941

Amid Don's demanding flight schedules, technical courses, and constant transfers along the West Coast, he and Marie still found moments of calm – and even small domestic milestones.

In a letter dated 24 August 1941, written from Spokane during a short pause in his training, Don described a simple yet revealing moment:

Above: The Streeter family, 1900. Back row left to right: Flora Streeter, Clarence Streeter, Harry Streeter, William Streeter. Front row: George Streeter (father), Eva Streeter (mother of Donald G. Smith), Nancy Streeter and Jessie Streeter. (© Janice Evans. Used with permission)

Below: The Streeter family, 1912. Back row left to right: Eva Streeter, Jessie Streeter, Nancy Streeter (mother of the six children) and Flora Streeter. Front row: William Streeter, Harry Streeter, George Streeter (father) and Clarence Streeter. (© Janice Evans. Used with permission)

Left: Eva Streeter and Charles "Chas" Gregory, parents of Donald Gregory. (© Janice Evans. Used with permission)

Below: Newborn Donald Owen Gregory (right)**,** son of Eva Streeter, pictured with his cousin, Ruth Streeter (left), daughter of Harry Streeter, in 1918. Donald was a strong baby. (© Janice Evans. Used with permission)

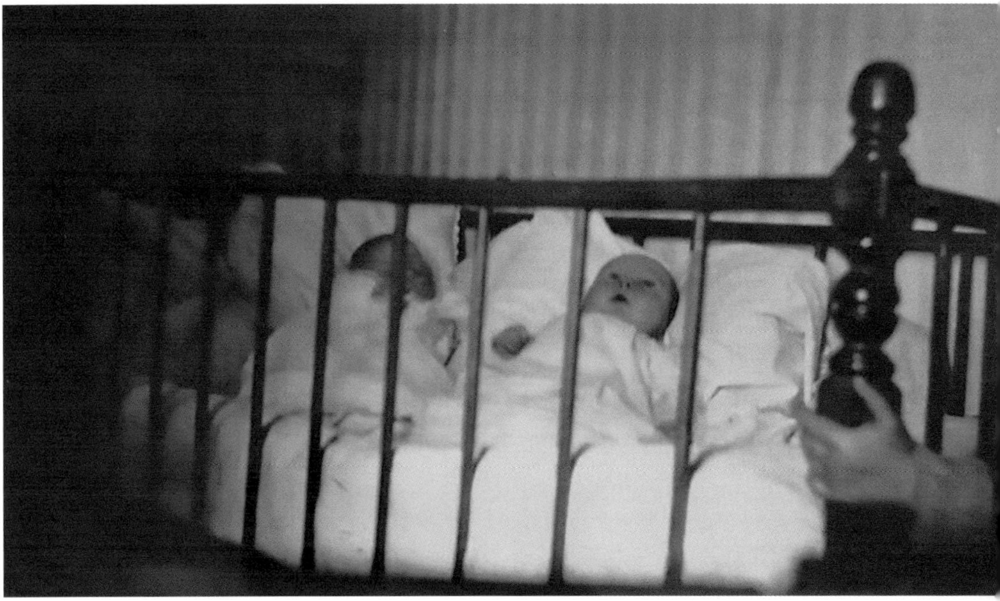

Above left: Laura Bolte, stepmother of Donald Gregory Smith. (© Janice Evans. Used with permission)

Above right: Dr. Arthur Smith, stepfather of Donald Gregory Smith. (© Janice Evans. Used with permission)

Below left: Donald Gregory Smith after his adoption by Arthur and Laura Smith, aged 7. (© Janice Evans. Used with permission)

Below right: House on 823 Day Street, Belle Fourche, South Dakota. Sitting on the porch. Left to right: Family member; Laura Bolte, stepmother of Donald; family member; Donald Smith; Ruth Streeter; sitting in the highest position is Fern Streeter, sister of Ruth Streeter.

Above left: The Jackrabbits, the American football team of South Dakota State College in Brookings, 1939. No. 26 is Donald Smith. (© Janice Evans. Used with permission)

Above right: Donald Smith, playing American football with the Jackrabbits of the South Dakota State College in Brookings. (© Janice Evans. Used with permission)

Left: Donald Smith and his stepmother, Laura Bolte. (© Janice Evans. Used with permission)

Right: Captain Donald Smith, pilot crew 15 during the Doolittle Raid. (© Janice Evans. Used with permission)

Below: First row, Donald Smith, standing at the right with eight other Doolittle Raiders on 18 June 1942, in Washington after the award ceremony for the Doolittle Raiders at Bolling Field.

Above left: Donald Smith sitting between his step-parents, Laura Bolte and Arthur Smith, at the Belle Fourche roundup on 4 July 1942. (© Janice Evans. Used with permission)

Above right: Donna Marie Smith, daughter of Don and Marie. (© Janice Evans. Used with permission)

Below: After Don made a water landing near Tantoushan Island, part of Xiangshan County in Ningbo, Zhejiang, about 800 meters off the coast, Ma Liangshui and his wife Zhao Xiaobao took care of Don and the other members of Crew 15, providing them with shelter and assistance. They protected the airmen from falling into the hands of the Japanese occupation forces.

The Tokyo appartments in Spokane, Washington where Donald and his wife Marie lived during 1942. (© Public Library Spokane. Used with permission)

Donald Smith and his Crew 15 on board of the USS Hornet steaming towards Tokyo for the daring Doolittle Raid. Smith standing left on the front row. Picture taken on 17 April 1942. (Public domain photograph, courtesy of the U.S. National Archives and Records Administration (NARA))

Above: The pigstee where Crew 15 hid after the waterlanding on the East Chinese Sea in front of Tantou Island, China. Hiding for the Japanese forces after the Doolittle Raid. (© Tri State museum, Belle Fourche. Used with permission)

Left: The grave of Donald Smith on the Pine Slope cemetery in Belle Fourche, South Dakota. (© Janice Evans. Used with permission)

Right: Donald Smith before entering the USAAF – picture June 1942. (© Janice Evans. Used with permission)

Below: The Children's Home Orphanage, Sioux Falls, South Dakota, circa 1890. Donald and his sister, Grace Gregory, were placed here in 1924 following their mother's death. (Public domain image. Courtesy of the South Dakota State Historical Society)

Above: Don Smith with Crew 15 in China, April 1942, shortly after the Doolittle Raid. Don is seated in the middle of the front row. (Public domain photograph, courtesy of the US National Archives and Records Administration (NARA))

Left: Donald Smith at the Belle Fourche Roundup on 4 July 1942. As a Doolittle Raider, he was an honoured guest at that year's event. Having lived in Belle Fourche, he received an intensely warm welcome following the Doolittle Raid. (© Janice Evans. Used with permission)

Above left: Mae and Hazel Streeter, nieces of Donald Gregory Smith. Mae (right) is pictured as a teacher and Hazel (left) as a student at the University of South Dakota in Madison, South Dakota. During a school visit to the Children's Home orphanage in Sioux Falls in January 1925, they found Donald and his younger sister, Grace. Both sisters later taught at the one-room Streeter School in Whitewood Township.

Above right: The Smith family home on 823 Day Street, Belle Fourche, South Dakota as it stands today. The house retains its original façade, front steps, and window layout visible in the early 1930s photograph of Donald Smith with his family. (Private collection of Janice Evans)

Below: Lieutenant Colonel James H. "Jimmy" Doolittle (Crew No. 1) takes off from the deck of the USS *Hornet* at the start of the daring Doolittle Raid on Japan, 18 April 1942. This was the first time medium bombers had ever launched from an aircraft carrier. (Public domain, US Navy / National Archives)

THEY BOMBED JAPAN

Lt. Donald G. Smith, left, outstanding Belle Fourche high school and State college athlete, manned one of the bombers led by Brig. Gen. James H. Doolittle, right, on the flight in which Tokyo was bombed.

Lt. Donald G. Smith (left) of Belle Fourche, South Dakota, and Brig. Gen. James H. Doolittle (right). Newspaper clipping, 1942, announcing the Tokyo Raid. (Public domain)

B-25 Mitchell bomber at Eglin Field, Florida, during training for the Doolittle Raid, March 1942. (Public domain photograph, US National Archives and Records Administration (NARA))

Above: Doolittle Raiders Sergeant Edward Saylor, Lieutenant Thomas R. White, Lieutenant Donald G. Smith, Lieutenant Griffith P. Williams, and Lieutenant Howard A. Sessler with residents of Sanmen County, Zhejiang Province, China, 23 April 1942. (Public domain photograph, US National Archives and Records Administration (NARA))

Below: A Martin B-26B "Marauder," a fast but unforgiving twin-engine medium bomber introduced in 1942. Captain Don Smith was flying an aircraft of this type when he crashed in England. Known to its crews as the "Widowmaker" for its high stall speed and demanding handling characteristics, the B-26 served in the Pacific, Mediterranean, and Northwest Europe theaters until the end of the war. (Public domain photograph, US Air Force / NARA)

Lieutenant Donald Gregory Smith in his US Army Air Corps officer's service uniform, circa 1941–1942. The photograph shows him wearing the pilot's wings and the Sam Browne belt, a distinctive feature of pre-1943 Army officer dress. (Private collection of Janice Evans)

Donald G. Smith with his dog "Mugs," Belle Fourche, South Dakota, circa 1936. Then about 18 years old, Donald was attending high school and spending his free time outdoors near his hometown. (Private collection of Janice Evans)

The fields near Wild Goose Leys Cottage, Abbots Ripton, UK where Captain Don Smith's B-26 Marauder *Snafu* (41-17751) most likely crashed. In the background lies the runway of RAF Alconbury, where Smith was attempting an emergency landing. *(*Photo © Niels Rottiers, used with permission)

Right: The Wild Goose Leys Cottage in Abbots Ripton, Cambridgeshire. (Photo © Niels Rottiers, used with permission)

Below: The former control tower at RAF Attlebridge, from where Captain Donald Smith took off on his final flight. The observation dome has since been removed. (Photo © Niels Rottiers, used with permission)

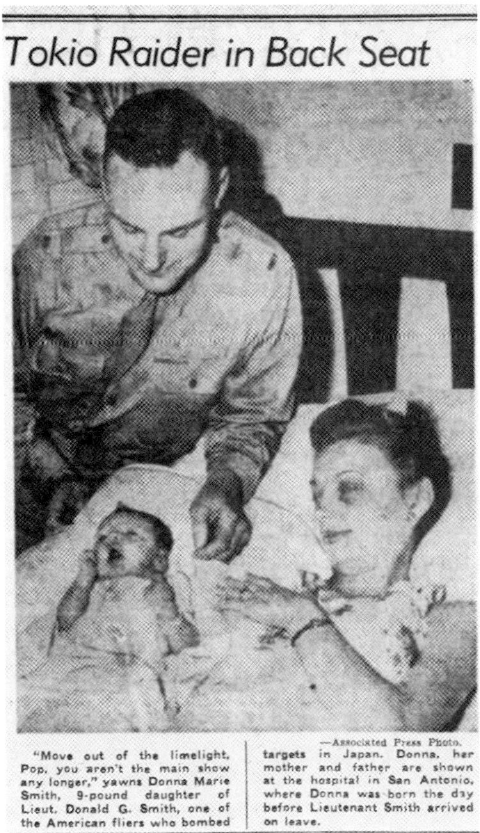

Tokio Raider in Back Seat

—Associated Press Photo.

"Move out of the limelight, Pop, you aren't the main show any longer," yawns Donna Marie Smith, 9-pound daughter of Lieut. Donald G. Smith, one of the American fliers who bombed targets in Japan. Donna, her mother and father are shown at the hospital in San Antonio, where Donna was born the day before Lieutenant Smith arrived on leave.

Above: A surviving Nissen hut at RAF Attlebridge, where aircrews lived, trained, and were briefed on enemy operations. At RAF Attlebridge Captain Donald Smith took off on his final flight. (Photo © Niels Rottiers, used with permission)

Left: Lieutenant Donald G. Smith with his wife Marie and their newborn daughter Donna Marie Smith. Doolittle Raider Smith had just returned on leave and met his daughter for the first time, only a day after her birth. His daughter, Donna Marie, had been born on 6 July 1942, at Brooke General Hospital, Fort Sam Houston in San Antonio. (AP Wirephoto)

Because Don was a Doolittle Raider and had gained national recognition in the United States, a reporter humorously wrote that his newborn daughter was saying: "Daddy, step out of the spotlight for a while — it's my turn now, I've just been born." This article and photo appeared in several newspapers across the United States.

'Sunday afternoon, and while Marie is driving us around for her daily lesson I will write you a short note…'

Marie was learning to drive, with Don sitting beside her in the passenger seat, writing letters to his family as she practised. It was a quiet snapshot of their life in transition – not only geographically, from one field to another, but also personally, as a young couple navigating the shifting realities of wartime life.

The driving lessons were more than a practical skill for Marie; they symbolised her growing independence and her determination to follow Don wherever duty sent him – from Washington to Colorado, Texas, and eventually to the Deep South. What seemed like an ordinary moment captured the delicate balance between domesticity and mobilisation that so many wartime couples experienced.

In the second half of November 1941, while Don and Marie Smith were living in their apartment at 125 West Sixth Avenue in Spokane, Marie shared unexpected news: she was pregnant with their first child.

Don, returning home from a long day of flight training, reacted with genuine joy. The announcement brought happiness, but also an undercurrent of worry. International tensions were rising, and American newspapers spoke more urgently than ever about a possible war with Japan.

Marie confided her fears about the uncertain future as she prepared for motherhood in an increasingly unstable world. Don reassured her, promising that whatever happened, he would take care of her and the baby. It was a promise that would soon be tested.

Just weeks later, on 7 December 1941, Japan attacked Pearl Harbor – and the United States entered the war.

Despite the constant threat of new orders and the unpredictability of military life, Don and Marie's time in Spokane still held moments of peace. They visited local diners, walked through the tree-lined streets, and met other young officers and their families. The Seymour Apartments became a small wartime community – a temporary haven where new families began their lives even as the world around them edged towards chaos.

Don and his pregnant wife remained in Spokane until early 1942, when he received new orders transferring him to Columbia Army Air Base, South Carolina.

Those months in Spokane marked a quiet, domestic chapter in an otherwise turbulent time – a brief interlude of stability before the storm.

Chapter 11

Don, The Pilot Who Never Lost Sight of Marie

For Don, Marie was never an afterthought. In his letters – no matter how technical or military in tone – her name appears often. Not in sweeping declarations of love, but in the quiet, natural rhythm of someone who lives and thinks with her in mind. She was his steady point of calm, even when he was thousands of feet above the ground.

Don was not a man of many emotional words, yet his devotion is unmistakable in the way he includes her in everything. When she took a train trip to Savannah, he arranged sleeping berths for her along the way. When she was learning to drive, he sat beside her – writing letters while she practised behind the wheel. When he bought a car, he made sure the insurance was in order so she could drive safely. Small gestures, but each carried deep meaning.

He spoke of her with respect – never as an accessory to his life, but as a partner in it. He admired her independence, her humour, and her ability to adapt to constant change without complaint. And when she wasn't with him, he missed her deeply. Between the lines of his letters runs a quiet current of longing – not dramatic or poetic, but a steady sense of *us* in everything he did.

Marie's voice does not appear directly in Don's letters, yet her presence is everywhere. She is not a shadow or a background figure, but a capable young woman carving out her own place in a world of uniforms, orders, and unfamiliar towns.

She followed Don from base to base – sometimes by train, sometimes by bus, sometimes in the company of another officer's wife, and sometimes entirely on her own. She lived in rented rooms, hotels, or shared apartments with other women whose lives mirrored hers. She learned to drive. She made friends. She wrote to Don's parents, handled their correspondence, and took care of the countless practical details that kept their young marriage functioning.

Marie moved easily between the domestic and the military worlds. She adapted without losing herself. Her decision to follow Don – not once, but again and again – spoke of courage. She was not merely following a man; she was choosing to share a life defined by duty, distance, and risk.

Though Marie's own letters have not survived, she is present in every page of Don's. Between his sentences, she exists – as a steady heartbeat behind the noise of engines and orders. Marie: his wife, his travelling companion, his anchor and quiet strength. Wherever Don went, she followed – not always physically, but always in spirit.

Throughout 1941 and early 1942, Marie travelled repeatedly to be near Don. While he flew from field to field in bombers and transports, she packed her suitcase and boarded trains or took the car herself. In August 1941, she joined him in Spokane, Washington, and later in Pendleton, Oregon. In October, she took the train alone to Savannah, Georgia, travelling via El Paso – armed only with a hotel reservation and the hope of meeting his unit upon arrival. It was an impressive feat for a young woman in an age when such travel was anything but simple.

Her most remarkable journey came earlier that autumn. When Don arrived at Ellington Field, near Houston, Texas, Marie refused to stay behind. From Spokane, she set out with another officer's wife, driving more than 1,800 miles south – across mountains, plains, and deserts – without modern highways, navigation systems, or reliable communication. Don recorded her departure in his letter of 29 September 1941: 'Marie left Spokane by car with the wife of another officer and is heading south. They expect to be in Houston in a few days.' It was a daring undertaking – one that revealed her determination, initiative, and loyalty.

Marie also built her own community. In Augusta, Georgia, she shared an apartment with other officers' wives. She cooked, managed household details, and tried to keep life as normal as possible while the men were flying. In November 1941, she took a day trip to Atlanta with two friends while Don was on duty – small moments of normalcy in a world increasingly ruled by uncertainty.

Marie was no background figure. She was a woman in motion – independent, devoted, and unafraid to meet the world on her own terms.

Chapter 12

Don's Movements (April 1941 – March 1942)

With the prospect of an extended and uncertain assignment ahead, Don and Marie made a difficult but practical decision. Marie, now several months pregnant, would return to her family in San Antonio, Texas, to spend the remainder of her pregnancy in the care of her mother and her younger sister, Monette – a return to familiarity, warmth, and safety.

When Don received orders to report to Columbia Army Air Base in early 1942, their separation became inevitable. His demanding schedule and constant relocations made their time together scarce, yet they managed to see each other whenever circumstances allowed – brief reunions that carried the weight of tenderness and farewell in equal measure.

San Antonio – the city where Marie had grown up and where her mother and sister still lived – became her refuge as she prepared for the birth of their child. For Don, stationed hundreds of miles away, her safety and the promise of their child became his source of strength amid the uncertainties ahead.

The parting was painful, but both knew it was the right choice. While Don prepared for the unknown future of wartime service, Marie found peace and support among her family. Despite the distance, their bond remained unbroken – sustained by letters, faith, and the shared hope of reunion once the war was over.

Don began his active military service in the spring of 1941 at McChord Field, Washington. His first surviving letters from there date to 14 April 1941, describing the routines of training flights over the Pacific Northwest and the growing pace of Air Corps activity as the nation prepared for war.

On 8 August 1941, he was temporarily assigned to Lowry Field in Denver, Colorado, where he attended a technical course at the Air Corps Technical School. His stay was brief but intensive, including several flights to California. By the end of August, he returned to the Northwest via Spokane, Washington, and Felts Field, where he was reunited with Marie.

In early September 1941, Don was transferred to Pendleton Air Base, Oregon, reporting there on 2 September. At the time, the 17th Bombardment Group was awaiting delivery of new aircraft from the factory. The weeks that followed were filled with preparation for large-scale manoeuvres and the forming of bomber crews. His stay in Pendleton lasted until late September.

On 17 September, Don stayed briefly at the Hollywood Plaza Hotel, on the corner of Hollywood Boulevard and Vine Street in Los Angeles. It was a well-known and stylish hotel, popular among travellers and film industry guests. Don wrote a letter home on the hotel's official stationery, featuring the building's illustration and address at the top. His stay there was likely short – part of a military transfer between Pendleton and Spokane.

On 25 September he departed again, this time flying in formation with his crew to Ellington Field, near Houston, Texas. The cross-country flight from Oregon to Texas marked a milestone in his training. He remained there through early October, focusing on formation flying and precision bombing practice.

Around 3 October, Don flew on to New Orleans, Louisiana, and shortly afterwards arrived in Savannah, Georgia, where, on 13 October, he was reunited with Marie, who had followed him there by train. Together they explored the coastal city whenever Don's demanding night-flight schedule allowed.

On 6 November Don was reassigned to Daniel Field in Augusta, Georgia, where he participated in large-scale nighttime manoeuvres with searchlights and coordinated bomber formations. Marie lived nearby in a rented apartment shared with other officers' wives. Don was weary from the constant relocations, but remained composed and professional. In a letter dated 20 November, he mentioned that Marie had even taken a day trip to Atlanta with two other wives – a small glimpse of normal life amid the military routine.

By late November, another transfer followed – this time to Maxwell Field, Montgomery, Alabama, where Don reported on 3 December.

Just four days later, the world changed.

On the morning of 7 December 1941, the Imperial Japanese Navy attacked Pearl Harbor, Hawaii. The assault destroyed much of the US Pacific Fleet and brought the United States fully into the Second World War.

When the news reached Maxwell Field, Don was among those stunned by the enormity of it. In letters written days later, his tone shifted from routine to readiness. The easy rhythm of training life was gone; war had arrived.

Within a week, he was ordered back to the Northwest. The transition from peacetime preparation to active defence was abrupt. What had once been a cycle of drills and transfers now carried real urgency.

The attack on Pearl Harbor prompted an immediate reorganisation of military priorities. The 89th Reconnaissance Squadron, previously focused on training and mapping missions, was now assigned to coastal patrol duties. Fears of a Japanese strike against the American mainland ran high, and the squadron began flying reconnaissance and anti-submarine patrols along the Pacific coast.

At the time, Don was serving with the 17th Bombardment Group. On 24 December 1941, B-25 Mitchell medium bombers of the group, flying anti-submarine patrols near the mouth of the Columbia River, reported engaging a Japanese submarine. Initial accounts claimed a successful attack.

Later investigations, however, cast doubt on the claim – no wreckage was ever found, and some suggested it may have been a mistaken sighting, perhaps even a whale. Within the squadron, the story became a source of dark humour, but it reflected the tense atmosphere of those early weeks after the attack.

Notably, Don was stationed at Pendleton Field around the same time. Although he was not directly involved in the incident, he likely shared the same tense environment as the crews who participated in the mission – a climate of vigilance and unease that gripped every airman on the coast.

After weeks of training, cold weather, and heightened alert along the West Coast, Don received new transfer orders in February 1942. In a letter dated 11 February he was still at Pendleton Field, but on 19 February he wrote from Columbia, South Carolina, noting that he had 'arrived yesterday'. His arrival can thus be placed on 18 February 1942.

He almost certainly travelled by train – a journey of roughly 2,500 miles (4,000km) that would have taken four to five days. Don had endured countless relocations by that point, but this time there was no complaint. Perhaps he had grown used to the rhythm, or perhaps the gravity of the war left him silent.

Upon arrival at Columbia Army Air Base (then known as Lexington County Airport), Don was assigned to a simple canvas tent, shared with another officer. He quickly resumed flight training under austere conditions. His only comment on the food was typically understated: 'It's warm, anyway'. The remark revealed no frustration, only a kind of weary acceptance – the humour of a man who knew that complaining was pointless.

By mid-February 1942, the 89th Reconnaissance Squadron was permanently based at Columbia Army Air Base, its mission shifting towards anti-submarine operations along the southeastern coast and the Gulf of Mexico, now threatened by German U-boats. Coordination with the US Navy intensified.

In late February 1942, while the 17th Bombardment Group was still stationed at Columbia Army Air Base in South Carolina, Group Commander Lieutenant Colonel William C. Mills received a discreet message from Washington: several experienced B-25 crews were to be selected for a 'special, highly dangerous mission – volunteers only'. No further explanation was given. The only words that circulated through the camp were 'extremely hazardous' and 'from the highest authority'. Even the squadron commanders had no idea what was happening. Officers moved quietly from tent to tent, asking men if they would volunteer for a mission of extraordinary difficulty – without knowing where, why, or for what purpose. No one truly knew what lay ahead; they could only speculate.

> Lexington County Air Port
> Columbia, S.C.
> Spring, 1942
>
> Dear Folks,
>
> Just received your letter this morning, and as I have a few spare minutes before going to dinner I will write you a few lines and hope you get it by Sunday. Glad to hear you finally

got the car home, and can understand the trouble you had getting parts, as priorities have tied up nearly everything up.

The rest of the Squadron arrived a couple of days after I did, and now we have settled down to some concentrated training. I have another flight this afternoon, but that is the way I like it, something to keep me busy. Marie was going to come over here for a couple of weeks some time around the middle of March, but now I have been put on a crew to go on a mission, and will be leaving this station in a few days, so don't know if I will get to see her again or not. We have everything arranged in San Antonio, and the army was so busy that we had to make plans with a civilian doctor. In normal times, we are provided army medical care, but now it was just out of the question, as they are swamped with their own work, and as there are so many officers' wives staying in San Antonio, the army arranged with a specialist to handle the officers' wives. So everything is working out all right.

They call this the sunny south, but I am inclined to believe differently, as they have us quartered in tents, and it is really cold in there. We have stoves, but they don't burn all night, so in the morning it is really a task to get up and build a fire. But we should kick, the food is good, and it will be getting warmer as the time goes on. This field is a brand new one, and they just finished putting the pilot landing lights last night, and in a few weeks I'll be able to do a little night work.

They selected five ships from each sqdn. and we are going out to a new field to carry out a special mission for a few weeks, and then we are going on to the coast, so it will prove rather interesting to say the least. We are limited to 20 pounds of baggage, which doesn't leave much room when we are taking a couple changes of uniforms and a few toilet articles.

Well folks, must close for now and hurry over to the mess hall, as we have a flight scheduled in 30 minutes, and we have to keep 'em flying. Goodbye for now, will try and find a few spare moments some time to write a more coherent letter, but this one was really a rush job. Hope you all are feeling well again, and everything is all right.

As ever, your loving son,
Don

His final known transfer during this period was to Eglin Field, Florida, where on 5 March 1942, he wrote of the warm climate and the start of intensive new training – the prelude to a mission that would change his life forever.

Against this backdrop, in late February and early March, selection began within the 17th Bombardment Group for a top-secret and exceptionally dangerous mission. Few details were given; the volunteers knew only that it came from the highest level of command.

Don Smith was among those approached.

What had begun in Spokane as a routine training assignment would soon lead him into one of the most daring aerial operations of the Second World War – the Doolittle Raid.

Chapter 13

The Doolittle Raid

In early 1942, at Columbia Army Air Base in South Carolina, several crews from the 17th Bombardment Group were unexpectedly called aside. Without any explanation, they were told that volunteers were being sought for a secret and dangerous mission. What the operation involved was not disclosed – secrecy was paramount. Only crews with prior experience on the B-25 Mitchell were eligible.

Within each squadron, five crews were selected based on their flying skill, teamwork, and reliability. The preparations moved quickly: they were given only a few days' notice and allowed no more than 20lb of personal gear. It was clear that this was no routine transfer.

Don Smith was among those chosen. In his letter home, he mentioned that he had been assigned to a 'special mission' and would be leaving soon. His tone was restrained, but the message unmistakable: he had received an assignment of unknown purpose – and that alone made it extraordinary. The selection at Columbia would prove to be the beginning of something much larger. For Don, it marked a turning point in his military career.

Don had been selected for one of the most secret and daring operations of the war: the Doolittle Raid. Conceived as retaliation for the attack on Pearl Harbor, the plan called for American B-25 bombers to be launched from an aircraft carrier to strike the Japanese homeland – Tokyo, Yokohama, and Nagoya among the targets – and then continue on to China. The military impact would be limited, but the psychological effect immense: it would show that Japan was not untouchable and give the American public a much-needed surge of hope.

In early 1942, Don entered a period of intense training and secrecy. From Columbia Army Air Base, he and a group of selected pilots and crews were transferred to Eglin Field, Florida. There, deep within the pine forests of the Florida Panhandle, they began a series of unorthodox exercises: taking off from extremely short runways, flying low over water and terrain, and practising precision bombing at minimal altitude. Little was explained, but it was obvious that this was no ordinary preparation. Everything pointed to a mission of exceptional demands. Still, one crucial element was missing: the actual aircraft they would use on their secret mission.

Those planes were far to the north, in Minneapolis, where technicians from Mid-Continent Airlines were modifying a carefully chosen group of B-25s. Each aircraft was being adapted for a task it had never been designed to perform: a long-range flight over open ocean, without escort, with limited defensive armament. Extra fuel tanks filled the bomb bays, unnecessary guns were removed, and some of the remaining machine guns were replaced with wooden decoys to save weight. Every change served a single purpose – maximum range, speed, and one-time precision.

Only later, when the modified aircraft were assigned to the men, would the pieces begin to fall into place.

A Letter from Eglin Field

In the midst of his training and preparation, Don was given the chance to fly a training mission to Houston, Texas. In a letter dated 18 March 1942, he told his parents that he had been able to see Marie there. Her parents had driven her to Houston, where they met Don for only a few minutes that day. They stayed one night in the city before Don returned to Eglin. His tone was matter-of-fact, almost detached – but between the lines, the significance of that moment is clear.

At first glance, the flight appears to have been a routine training assignment – one of many such missions flown during the Eglin period. Yet in light of what we now know, it carried a deeper weight. On 6 July 1942, just four months later, Marie gave birth to their child. That Don had been allowed to see her at such a critical time – on the eve of a secret and perilous mission – speaks volumes. Given the tight discipline and secrecy at Eglin Field, it is unlikely that this meeting happened by chance. More probably, Don received special permission to see her – a rare exception to rigid military protocol, prompted by personal circumstances.

For Marie, too, it was no small effort: together with her parents, she travelled roughly 200 miles (320km) from San Antonio to Houston – a journey of four to five hours in those days – just to see Don for a brief moment. What takes only a few lines in his letter was, in truth, a precious moment of closeness: a quiet, unspoken farewell under the pressure of time.

The flight to Houston was therefore not an ordinary training mission. It was a journey laden with double meaning – both military and personal. A brief meeting on the edge of history, in the shadow of a mission from which Don may already have sensed he might not return. And at the same time, a wordless acknowledgment of the life that was on its way – unborn, yet already present in his choices, his silence, and his resolve.

In the same letter, Don mentions in passing the series of vaccinations he and his comrades received. It was a familiar ritual in wartime preparation: a sequence of injections against typhoid, tetanus, diphtheria, and other tropical diseases. Such details, often noted with a touch of humour, reveal the scope of medical preparation for an overseas mission whose destination remained officially unknown. Don's remark is one of the few tangible clues that his group was being readied for a dangerous and distant operation – far beyond the borders of the United States.

EGLIN FIELD
FLORIDA

18 March, 1942

Dear Folks,

I just rushed over from dinner, so I could find time to write you a few lines; and also so I could use the typewriter in the office, as it makes writing much easier. I received your letter last Saturday, after it had been forwarded from Columbia, and you said you didn't expect me to receive it, well I guess we were lucky, as I will be able to hear from you at least once more before we leave. Right now it looks like we will get out of here next week, as we have everything taken care of and the planes all have been repaired. We are finishing the necessary work on the planes, along with some flying.

Last week I took a trip to Houston, Texas, and I called Marie before I left, and her folks brought her over to Houston, and we were able to see her for a few minutes, we stayed over night, and I flew back here the next day.

They are still shooting us with vaccine, and by the time they finish with us, I don't expect to have any blood left, just a mixture of serum.

Well folks, I must close and run along, as the men are all getting back for work, and we are getting ready for another mission, so will close for now. Just wanted to let you know everything was all right, though awful busy.

As Ever, your Son,
Don

In the spring of 1942, while the world was still reeling from the Japanese attack on Pearl Harbor, a small group of American pilots was secretly preparing for a mission that would change history. At Eglin Field, hidden among the pine forests and training ranges of northwestern Florida, more than twenty B-25 Mitchell crews were being readied for an operation whose final objective was known to only a handful of men. In the end, only sixteen crews would depart aboard the aircraft carrier USS *Hornet*, bound for their place in history – the Doolittle Raid.

Don was among those men and would go on to command Crew No. 15 in the attack on Kobe, Japan. But why was *he* chosen, when others were not? Why his crew, and not the many others who trained beside them? The answer lay in a careful balance of skill, teamwork, discipline, and character – qualities that were constantly measured and quietly judged on the airfields of Eglin.

The assignment was brutally demanding: they had to master take-offs in heavily modified aircraft from a runway less than 500ft long – built to resemble the deck of an aircraft carrier – fly at treetop level, navigate without radar or radio contact, and drop bombs using only the simplest optical sights. Above all, they had to survive. The selection for the mission was deliberate, methodical – and unforgiving.

The criteria were strict but never written down. Veterans and historians have since reconstructed the process along the following lines:

1. Technical flying skill – Pilots had to handle a fully loaded B-25 flawlessly and lift off within the short, simulated carrier runway. Those who were too slow, unsteady, or hesitant in the air were sent home.
2. Crew coordination – The mission demanded absolute cooperation between pilot, copilot, navigator, bombardier, and gunner. Crews that lacked cohesion, or showed friction under pressure, were disqualified. The aircraft had to function as one organism.
3. Physical and mental endurance – Training was relentless, often conducted under fatigue and stress. Crews were kept on standby through long nights, flying with little sleep, expected to remain sharp, steady, and composed.
4. Discretion and discipline – The entire operation was top secret. Even within the group, few knew the destination. Every man was judged on his reliability, obedience, and ability to keep silent. There was no room for egos – or loose talk.
5. No medical or mechanical liabilities – Some crews were ruled out due to illness, injury, or mechanical issues with their aircraft. These practical factors also shaped the final composition.

Within this demanding environment, Don distinguished himself. His performance was remarkable; he managed to lift his fully loaded B-25 off the ground in just 87m or (285ft) Multiple sources later confirmed the feat, which impressed both instructors and fellow airmen.

His letters and later recollections reveal a man who never bragged or sought attention – quiet, thoughtful, and utterly focused. During earlier phases of training he had already impressed instructors with his technical grasp of the B-25, his composure in the cockpit, and his ability to think clearly under pressure.

He also shared a strong, stable bond with his crew, which remained intact throughout the entire training program. This was notable – many other crews experienced changes or replacements during the process. The fact that Smith's team stayed together suggests a high level of cohesion and mutual trust, key requirements for the mission ahead.

Equally important was his discipline and discretion. His letters from Florida are strikingly vague, revealing almost nothing about his location or activities – a clear sign of loyalty to the strict confidentiality he was sworn to uphold.

For all these reasons – skill, steadiness, teamwork, and reliability – Don Smith and his men earned their place among the chosen sixteen who would carry out one of the most audacious missions of the Second World War.

Lieutenant Donald Smith was appointed pilot and aircraft commander of Crew No. 15. With his men – copilot Lieutenant Griffith P. Williams, navigator Lieutenant Howard A. Sessler, engineer-gunner Sergeant Edward J. Saylor, and gunner Lieutenant Thomas R. White – he would, on 18 April 1942, lift off from the deck of the aircraft carrier USS *Hornet*, bound for Kobe, Japan.

Chapter 14

Notes on Crew 15

The crew's nicknames were Smitty, Griff, Sess, Doc, and Ed. The nickname 'Doc' referred to Lieutenant Thomas R. White, who served as the crew's gunner but was a physician by training. 'Doc' White had first volunteered for the secret mission in the hope that his medical background might be of use, but was told that no physicians would be included. Determined to go anyway, he reapplied as a gunner – a combat position for which he had no formal training. During the intensive course at Eglin Field, however, White quickly proved his worth: in gunnery and proficiency tests he achieved the second-highest score of all participating airmen. On the strength of that performance, he was assigned to Crew No. 15 under Lieutenant Smith's command. White earned his place not through his medical credentials, but through pure skill and perseverance – as a soldier, not a doctor. In the aftermath of the Doolittle Raid, 'Doc' White would again play a vital role.

The numbering of the sixteen Doolittle Raid crews was not random but reflected the order of take-off and the geographic sequence of their targets. The first aircraft were assigned to strike the Tokyo area, while the later crews aimed further west, at cities such as Yokosuka, Nagoya, and Kobe. As pilot of Crew No. 15, Don Smith was tasked with bombing industrial objectives in the port city of Kobe – not Tokyo, as is often mistakenly assumed.

Crew 15 was a composite unit. Both the aircraft and its two pilots – Smith and Williams – came from the 89th Reconnaissance Squadron. During the reorganisation at Eglin Field they were temporarily attached to the 34th Bombardment Squadron, which would exercise formal operational control during the raid. The other crewmen – Lieutenant White, Lieutenant Sessler, and Sergeant Saylor – were already members of the 34th. The result was a blended team: an aircraft and two pilots from the 89th working seamlessly with three men from the 34th – a practical reflection of how necessity forged flexibility in the Doolittle project.

In late March 1942, Don Smith and the other crews said their farewells to Eglin Field. The transfer from Eglin to McClellan Field, a major US Army Air Depot near Sacramento, California, took place between 23 and 27 March, depending on the crew. This marked the end of their secret training and the beginning of the final phase of preparations for the mission. Flying in small groups of two or three, the B-25s crossed the continent westward towards McClellan Field.

At McClellan, the aircraft were thoroughly inspected and fine-tuned. The major modifications – extra fuel tanks, stripped armament, and weight reductions – had already been completed, but final adjustments were now made. Medical kits, ammunition, maps, and emergency rations were loaded aboard. As mechanics worked over the planes, the crews waited in silence, sensing that something momentous was near. No one yet knew the true destination – only that it was serious, and imminent.

Then, after days of waiting, a coded message arrived: 'Tell Jimmy to get on his horse.'

The signal had been given. The next flight would take them to Alameda Naval Air Station. Beyond that lay the unknown.

The flight from McClellan Field to the naval base at Alameda, California, on 31 March, was short but filled with anticipation. This was where everything would come together. As the bombers arrived one by one over the edge of San Francisco Bay, they were drained of fuel, hoisted by massive dockside cranes, and carefully placed onto the deck of the USS *Hornet* (CV-8).

Don Smith was given a rare honour during this leg of the journey: Lieutenant Colonel James H. Doolittle himself rode as his passenger. It was a mark of confidence – an unspoken gesture of trust that did not go unnoticed among the men. On the deck of the *Hornet*, preparations continued with military precision as the ship readied for its westward crossing – and for war.

Young, restless, and fully aware of the gravity that lay ahead – but still living in the calm before the storm – many of the raiders gave in to youthful exuberance during the ferry flights from Eglin to Sacramento and on to Alameda. Perhaps they saw the journey itself as an extension of training – or perhaps Doolittle, with a knowing smile, had allowed them some freedom before the unknown.

Over towns and farms they thundered at treetop height; chickens scattered, children screamed and ran indoors. Some crews even flew beneath telephone wires or low bridges – one, a wooden traffic bridge somewhere in the South – purely for the thrill. At stopover airfields they performed 'buzz jobs', roaring low over control towers and tents at full throttle. Upon arrival in Alameda, several aircraft swept low across the harbour, startling dockworkers who instinctively dived for cover.

At least one pilot – and perhaps more – dared to fly under the span of the Golden Gate Bridge, a final act of defiance before the lines were cast off.

They flew recklessly, but not carelessly. Their low-level precision had been honed to perfection at Eglin, and now they handled their heavy B-25s like fighters. These were their last days of freedom – days when the war still seemed distant, when young men flew as if the sky belonged only to them.

One of the most memorable moments came from Captain Robert Gray, who flew directly over his hometown of Killeen, Texas, in his B-25 *Whiskey Pete*. He dropped to rooftop level above the main street; workers flung themselves flat as windows rattled in their frames. Banking sharply over Killeen High School, his alma mater, he seemed to bid farewell to the town that had shaped him – and to the memory of his childhood pony, the namesake of his plane. The editor of the *Killeen Herald* later wrote that 'it could have been no one else but Bob Gray' who had shaken the sky over town that day. It would be the last time the people of Killeen saw him alive.

Chapter 15

Destination: Tokyo

Only after departure in San Francisco on 2 April 1942 did they receive final instructions confirming their true objective: the Japanese homeland. Each man was issued a silk escape map, a Chinese 'blood chit' promising reward for aid to downed airmen, and basic survival guidance for what might follow the raid. Another Task Force left Pearl Harbor on 10 April 1942.

During the seventeen-day voyage across the Pacific, the eighty men of the Doolittle Raiders – pilots, copilots, navigators, engineers, and gunners divided among sixteen crews – filled their days with discipline, repetition, and silent anticipation.

1. Training and Procedures
   Because the B-25 Mitchell had never before operated from an aircraft carrier, the pilots constantly reviewed short-take-off techniques in their minds, rehearsing every movement and decision. They practised emergency drills, crew communication, bombing procedures, open-sea navigation, and fuel-consumption calculations for the long flight to the Chinese mainland.
2. Physical Inspection of Aircraft
   Each crew inspected its own bomber down to the smallest detail. They checked weapon systems, fuel lines, and bomb racks, adjusted control cables, and verified the fastening of every chain and tie-down on the deck. The B-25s could not be moved; they remained lashed in two tight rows on the *Hornet*'s flight deck. On 17 April – one day before the scheduled strike – they were positioned precisely in take-off order.
3. Route Planning and Target Study
   Every crew received aerial photographs and maps of its assigned target – Tokyo, Yokosuka, Nagoya, Kobe, and other cities.

Navigators worked with compass headings, time-distance-speed tables, and instructions for the southwest course towards the Chinese coast after the attack.

4. Mental Preparation
   The men spent long hours together: writing letters, reading, exercising lightly, or simply trying to keep their nerves under control. Some practised makeshift gunnery drills on deck; others memorised the silhouettes of Japanese ships and aircraft.
5. Security and Discipline
   Strict secrecy remained in force. Even most of the *Hornet*'s own crew had no idea why sixteen army bombers stood chained to the deck. The raiders were quartered separately, under the discreet supervision of Jimmy Doolittle himself.

Unlike naval aircraft, these land-based bombers could not be stored below deck. Several practical and technical reasons made this impossible:

1. The hangar deck was already full of carrier aircraft.
   The *Hornet*'s hangar deck was almost completely filled with its own air group – scout planes, torpedo bombers, and fighter aircraft – all essential to the ship's defence. Except for a few aircraft kept on the flight deck, nearly all of the carrier's planes were stored below. As a result, there was no available space to accommodate the B-25s in the hangar deck.
2. The elevators were too small and too weak.
   The B-25 was a twin-engine medium bomber designed for land operations. Fully loaded, it weighed over 15,000kg (33,000lb), with a wingspan of nearly 20m (67ft) and a fuselage too large for the *Hornet*'s elevator openings. The carrier's lifts were both too narrow and not strong enough to hoist an aircraft of that size.
3. The bombers were permanently secured to the deck.
   Because of these limitations, all sixteen B-25s were lashed down on the flight deck in two rows. From the moment they were hoisted aboard at Alameda, California, the aircraft were firmly chained to the deck to withstand the ship's motion at sea. They could not be moved or stored elsewhere. The aircrews thus became, quite literally, passengers on the ship – unable to fly until the moment of the attack.

4. The airmen lived as part of the deck crew.
   The sixteen pilots and their crews, including Lieutenant Donald Smith, had been aboard since the *Hornet*'s departure on 2 April 1942. There was no way back: their bombers stood ready above them, prepared for a one-way mission. Some airmen later recalled strapping themselves down to sleep during rough seas as the ship rolled violently. They lived in cramped quarters among the carrier's sailors, with their only way off the ship waiting just above – the deck and their aircraft.

These logistical and technical constraints underscore the daring and unprecedented nature of the Doolittle Raid. Never before had an aircraft carrier transported land-based bombers so close to enemy territory – with no possibility of resupply, regrouping, or return.

For the eighty raiders, life aboard the USS *Hornet* was an exercise in patience, discipline, and preparation under extreme conditions. They slept in improvised quarters – stretchers, hammocks, or bunks squeezed between sailors – amid the constant noise, vibration, and smell of fuel and machinery.

Their days blended into a steady routine of mental rehearsal and technical inspection: repeating take-off sequences, checking navigation charts, and reviewing emergency plans – all without ever leaving the ship. Gunners practised with dummy weapons; navigators spread their maps on the deck, tracing imaginary routes over enemy territory.

The tension on the USS *Hornet* grew with every passing day. Beneath the shadows of their silent B-25s, the men waited – knowing that their next flight would not be a drill, but a one-way mission deep into enemy territory.

Alongside the 16 flight crews, roughly 130 support specialists sailed with the raiders. This group included mechanics, armorers, ordnance officers, instrument technicians, fuel experts, and other specialists. Their role was critical: they maintained the aircraft daily, checked engines and electrical systems, loaded bombs, and carried out repairs – often exposed to the elements on the open deck.

On the morning of the attack, these men stood ready beside each aircraft to ensure it was fully armed and airworthy. They would not fly in the mission, yet without their skill and discipline, not a single B-25 could have taken off safely. After the bombers launched, these technicians remained aboard the *Hornet* and returned to the United States with the ship.

In addition to the core sixteen, several reserve crewmen – pilots, copilots, navigators, and gunners – had been designated as stand-bys in case of illness or last-minute replacement. Though they ultimately did not take part in the raid itself, they played a vital part. Some assisted in preparing the aircraft, helped load bombs, or provided technical aid where needed. Others simply offered moral support to their comrades – a word, a nod, a shared silence before the leap into the unknown.

Their presence was a reminder that every mission depends not only on those who fly, but also on those who remain behind to make flight possible.

Both task forces were scheduled to rendezvous at sea on 13 April 1942, slightly later than initially planned. Admiral William F. Halsey experienced delays returning to Pearl Harbor due to poor weather following his last conference with Navy officials in San Francisco, which postponed his departure by several days.

The actual meeting took place on 13 April 1942, at coordinates 38°00′00″ N, 180°00′00″ E, near the International Date Line. The combined force now numbered roughly 10,000 sailors. Once merged, the two formations continued as Task Force 16, under Halsey's overall command.

On 17 April, the ships of Task Force 16 were refuelled by two accompanying oilers. After refuelling, the oilers detached and returned to Pearl Harbor, while the two aircraft carriers and their remaining escorts of destroyers and cruisers continued westward towards Tokyo at an average speed of 20 to 25 knots.

Immediately after the launch of the sixteen B-25 bombers, the task force reversed course and made its return voyage to Pearl Harbor.

All details concerning the composition, movements, and coordination of both task forces are drawn from the official Halsey–Doolittle mission report, dated 28 April 1942.

Letter from the USS *Hornet*:

15 April, 1942

Dear Folks,

We have been authorised to write letters, as long as we are careful what we say, and if the censor pass it.

We left in such a hurry, I didn't get a chance to write you after we were ordered away. I was lucky enough to get into San Antonio one night on the way, and while we were restricted from writing, I told Marie the next time she wrote you, she could mention I had been there. We are still on the move, so cannot give you any address where you might write me, but just as soon as possible I will write you again and give you my address.

When we left, we were supposed to be back in two months, but am afraid it will be a little longer. I suppose Marie wrote I had received my promotion the day we left. It was dated back to February 1st, it was almost two months catching up with me.

[censored part] we will have to pick it up on the return journey. Now we are [censored part] ahead of your time. This letter may be quite a while reaching States, but it will surely make it back to you.

I wrote Marie a note also, and just wanted to let you know everything is all right. A lot of new experiences to tell about when I get back.

Will close for now, and until you hear from me again, don't worry about me.

Your loving Son,
Don

On 17 April, 1942, as the USS *Hornet* continued westward through the Pacific, the sixteen B-25 crews gathered briefly on the open deck. The attack on Japan was imminent. In the fading light, Lieutenant Colonel James H. Doolittle held a small metal box containing a Japanese medal – once presented to the United States years earlier as a gesture of goodwill during a period of formal friendship.

Doolittle spoke briefly. His message was simple: the medal, once accepted in peace, would now be returned in war. The airmen attached it – along with a few other decorations retrieved from government archives – to one or more bombs that would be dropped over Japan the next day.

It was a small but powerful act; not revenge, but symbolism. The gesture transformed a token of friendship into a message of resolve, echoing the memory of Pearl Harbor, the attack that had drawn America into the conflict.

When the brief ceremony ended, the men dispersed in silence. The briefings were complete, the aircraft ready. All that remained was the mission itself.

That same day, each of the crews posed for a formal photograph beside their B-25 on the deck of the *Hornet*. These images – sixteen in total – remain today the defining portraits of courage and duty before one of the most daring operations of the Second World War.

At dawn on 18 April 1942, the *Hornet* task force – then about 1,000km from Japan – was sighted by a Japanese patrol vessel, the *Nittō Maru*. Although the ship was quickly sunk by gunfire from the cruiser *Nashville*, it had almost certainly managed to send a radio warning. The Americans assumed they had been detected.

Fearing a counterattack from Japanese aircraft or naval forces, Doolittle made the critical decision to launch immediately – more than 370 km and thirteen hours earlier than planned.

The order echoed through the ship's loudspeakers: 'Army pilots, man your planes.'

Each crew took their position aboard their B-25 Mitchell. The premature launch meant that the aircraft were now dangerously far from their intended recovery zones in China, with barely enough fuel to reach the mainland. But there was no turning back.

At 08.20, the first bomber thundered down the deck and lifted off – the first time in history that medium bombers had launched from a carrier in wartime. One by one, the sixteen aircraft rolled down the short, pitching deck and rose into the headwind.

Lieutenant Donald G. Smith took off from the USS *Hornet* on 18 April 1942 at 09.15. He flew the B-25 Mitchell serial number 40-2267, known by the crew as 'TNT'. After more than five hours of flight, Crew 15 finally sighted the coastline of Honshu, Japan's main island. Below them lay the approaches to Kobe, shrouded in a thin morning haze that shimmered above the sea. Their B-25 flew at an altitude so low that the crew could see waves breaking against the shore and fishing boats rocking in their wake. For long stretches, Smith kept the bomber barely 200ft (60m) above the water, sometimes even less. The low flight helped them evade detection, but it also demanded absolute concentration; one lapse could have sent them crashing into the sea.

Before sighting the Japanese coast, the crew of TNT picked up a local radio broadcast drifting faintly through the static – light music, cheerful and ordinary, a strange sound after five hours of silence over the open Pacific. The signal grew stronger as they approached the islands, and for nearly an hour the men listened in silence, each aware of what it meant: they were closing in on Japan. Then, without warning, the music stopped. A sequence of alarms blared – sharp tones lasting perhaps forty-five seconds each – followed by a man's voice shouting three urgent words. The pattern repeated again and again, nearly ten times, before the transmission cut off entirely.

A few minutes later, the coast of Honshu appeared through the haze. TNT had come in slightly north of its intended route, making landfall at approximately 13.50 hours. Smith adjusted course southward, flying low over Tokyo Bay and then Nagoya Bay, both dotted with small fishing boats whose crews looked up in confusion as the American bomber roared past at wave-top height. Ahead lay the city of Kobe – their target.

Inside the vibrating fuselage, the men worked in silence. Lieutenant Howard A. Sessler, the navigator, bent over his chart table, confirming their position by comparing the coastline's shape to his pre-war maps. Ahead, he recognised a distinctive oval landmark that broke through the haze – Koshien Stadium in Nishinomiya, the enormous national baseball arena built in 1924. Sessler pointed it out to Smith, calling it their visual cue to begin the attack run.

For the Americans aboard TNT, that stadium carried an echo of memory. Only eight years earlier, in November 1934, the same field had hosted Babe Ruth, Lou Gehrig, and a team of American all-stars who had toured Japan in a celebrated goodwill series. Japanese newspapers at the time had called it a bridge between East and West, a symbol of sportsmanship and friendship. Now, that same arena served as a marker for war. Where cheers and laughter had once filled the stands, the low, rising thunder of American bombers rolled in from the sea.

Don levelled the aircraft and lined up for his bombing approach. As TNT descended over Kobe Bay, he increased power and climbed briefly to about 450m – just enough altitude for the bombs to arm properly before release. Below them, the waterfront spread out in a patchwork of docks, warehouses, and industrial yards. Sessler called out the final heading. 'Steady… steady… bombs away!'

Four 500lb (227kg) incendiary bombs fell from the open bay doors, whistling towards their targets: the Uyenoshita Steel Works, the Kawasaki Dry Dock, and nearby oil depots and machine shops. Seconds later, the waterfront erupted in fire and smoke. The crew felt the concussion even from the air as black columns of smoke billowed upward.

Almost immediately, Japanese anti-aircraft batteries opened fire. Type 88 75-mm guns and machine guns from rooftops, ships, and warehouses filled the air with bursting shells. But the attack's unorthodox altitude confused the gunners. Their heavy weapons, built to hit high-flying targets, could not depress far enough to track the low B-25s. Shells exploded chaotically across rooftops and streets; fragments clattered off factory walls. Inside TNT, the crew could hear the sharp metallic ping of shrapnel striking the fuselage.

'Keep it low, Don – keep it low!' shouted copilot Lieutenant Griffith 'Griff' Williams over the interphone. Smith pushed the throttles forward, the engines roaring as the bomber skimmed above the rooftops.

The danger intensified when several A6M Zero fighters scrambled from a nearby airfield to intercept. Their silver wings flashed in the sunlight as they closed in from the east. Smith immediately dived towards the smoke drifting from the burning docks, weaving between the industrial stacks to break visual contact. Lieutenant Thomas R. 'Doc' White, manning the tail position, watched the enemy fighters overshoot. His twin 'guns' were only black-painted wooden decoys, but in the confusion, the Japanese pilots appeared to believe they were real. After a brief pursuit, the Zeros broke off.

With their bombing run complete, Crew 15 cleared the airspace above Kobe and turned southwest, climbing gradually as they left the burning city behind. Through the side window, Sessler caught a final glimpse of the harbour – the cranes, the ships, the rising black smoke. It was their proof that the mission had succeeded. But as the coastline faded into the mist, a new concern replaced triumph: their fuel gauges were falling dangerously low.

As TNT cleared the burning docks after its bombing run and roared towards the coastline, the crew caught sight of the beaches below. Smoke drifted inland from the harbour, curling over the sand. Along the shore, people had gathered – men, women, even children – staring upward at the low-flying bomber. Some waved at first, perhaps thinking it was one of their own planes returning from patrol. Others simply pointed or shouted, the sound lost beneath the engines' thunder.

Lieutenant Griffith 'Griff' Williams later recalled that TNT flew so low they could see faces clearly – people shielding their eyes, children standing ankle-deep in the surf. As realisation set in, a few youngsters picked up stones and hurled them skyward, harmless gestures of defiance that somehow captured the confusion of the moment.

This very scene would later be immortalised in a cartoon by Captain Richard 'Dick' Kirschbaum, an American war artist stationed in China, who wryly noted that 'the only resistance pilot Don Smith and his crew met over Japan came from stone-throwing kids'.

Kirschbaum was a journalist and illustrator who had gained recognition before the war at the *Newark Evening News* for his aviation-themed cartoons and his illustrated collection 'Fifty Famous Flyers' (1941). After being called to active duty in April 1942, he became Public Relations Officer with the 14th Air Force, formerly the Flying Tigers command under General Claire Chennault. From his post in Chungking, China's wartime capital, Kirschbaum chronicled the lives of American pilots in the China–Burma–India theatre – including the recently returned Doolittle Raiders.

Known for his quick wit and keen eye for human detail, Kirschbaum often portrayed the lighter side of war: caricatures of airmen, humorous cockpit sketches, and satirical glimpses of chaos amid courage. His cartoon depicting Don Smith's encounter with stone-throwing children over Japan captured that same mix of irony and empathy – a reminder that even in the midst of destruction, fragments of innocence could still intrude upon the machinery of war.

With the coastline behind them, TNT banked southwest and climbed gradually into the haze, leaving Kobe receding under a rising column of smoke. Ahead stretched only ocean – the long, perilous route towards China.

Inside the aircraft, the mood was tense but disciplined. The men spoke little. Lieutenant Howard A. Sessler, the navigator, sat over his chart table, red pencil in hand, recalculating headings and drift angles. His task was grimly precise: steer a straight course towards China with almost no margin for error. He used dead reckoning, the compass, and whatever fleeting glimpses of the sun pierced through the grey sky.

Each minute mattered; every degree off course could mean death by fuel starvation somewhere over the sea.

Sergeant Edward J. Saylor, bombardier and flight engineer, monitored the engines and fuel gauges from the nose compartment. It didn't take long for him to notice trouble: the right engine was consuming fuel faster than the left. He reported the discrepancy through the interphone – calm, factual, but urgent.

Pilot Don Smith responded immediately. 'Throttle back the right engine. Let's even her out.' Lieutenant Griffith 'Griff' Williams, the copilot, made the adjustments, carefully trimming the mixture to stretch every remaining gallon. The B-25's speed dropped slightly, but it was the only way to survive the crossing.

Hours passed. The vibration of the engines filled the fuselage like a steady heartbeat. Rain squalls drifted across their path, forcing occasional course corrections. Sessler estimated that, with luck and a favourable tailwind, they might reach the Chinese coast just before nightfall – but only if the winds held steady. He underlined the figure twice in his notebook: two hours of fuel left – no reserve.

As daylight faded, the sea turned slate grey and indistinguishable from the sky. The crew moved in near silence, each man lost in his own thoughts. Lieutenant Thomas R. 'Doc' White, stationed near the rear, kept watch through the side windows, scanning for ships or land. He had treated wounded men before, but never faced the creeping dread of a fuel gauge sinking towards empty over an endless ocean.

A faint tailwind gave them hope. For nearly an hour, TNT surged westward, driven by the unseen hand of the monsoon. But the reprieve didn't last. As dusk deepened, Saylor's voice crackled through the interphone: 'Don – we've got maybe twenty minutes of fuel left.'

There was no panic, just the quiet shifting of men tightening harnesses and checking their gear. Moments later, Sessler looked up from his maps. 'Land ahead – I think I see it!'

Through the mist, faint shapes appeared – dark against the dying light. Was it the mainland? An island? The contours were uncertain, but it was their only chance. Don made the decision without hesitation. 'Prepare for ditching. Check chutes, secure loose gear.'

The men moved quickly, working by instinct. Their mission was complete, but their survival now depended entirely on skill, luck, and the sea.

By nightfall, the weather had worsened. Heavy rain swept in sheets across the windshield, blurring visibility to almost nothing. The coastline ahead was not what they'd hoped for – jagged cliffs and crashing surf rather than the flat fields of eastern China. Sessler identified it as a small offshore island, uninhabited and hostile. There was no chance of a landing on solid ground.

Fuel gauges hovered near zero. Smith knew the aircraft would soon lose power. He brought TNT down to wave-top height, scanning for a patch of relatively calm water. The crew braced themselves. 'Stand by for impact,' Don ordered.

At 19.30, with engines sputtering, the bomber struck the sea. The impact was brutal – a wall of water engulfed the cockpit, and the fuselage shuddered from nose to tail. Miraculously, TNT held together and stayed afloat, rocking violently in the swells. 'Everybody out!' Don shouted. 'She won't last long!'

The crew scrambled to their escape stations. Following procedure, they donned their Mae West life vests but didn't inflate them yet, to avoid being trapped inside the sinking plane. Saylor pulled the release handle for the life raft, but it snagged on a metal bracket, tearing a small puncture along one side. Air hissed out – a fatal flaw – but the raft still held enough buoyancy to serve.

The sea was cold, the rain relentless. The men slid into the water one by one, clutching the half-inflated raft as waves slammed them apart and together again.

Amid the chaos, Doc White realised he had left the medical kit aboard. Ignoring shouted warnings, he fought his way back through the surf towards the sinking aircraft. For a few moments he vanished in the darkness – then reappeared, clutching the small green case above his head. He dragged himself to the raft, gasping for breath.

As they regrouped, someone called out for Lieutenant Howard Sessler. No answer. He had been seen near the wing only moments earlier, but now he was gone – swept away into the blackness. The four remaining men shouted his name into the wind, but the sea gave nothing back. Don Smith took command. 'We head for shore. Together.'

With the wreck sinking behind them, the survivors began the agonising swim towards the island. The current was strong, the waves breaking over their heads. They clung to the crippled raft for support, kicking against the drag of their soaked uniforms. The rain fell harder, mingling with seawater and sweat. Each man moved by sheer willpower – survival reduced to rhythm, stroke by stroke.

At last, through the gloom, they glimpsed white water and rocks. Crawling, stumbling, and half-dragged by the surf, they reached the narrow strip of beach at the base of a cliff. Exhausted, they collapsed in silence, the surf breaking around them. The mission that had begun aboard a carrier in the Pacific had ended here, on an unknown shore in the dark.

That same night, far above the storm-tossed beach, a small fishing village clung to the Chinese coastline. Inside a mud-walled hut, Zhao Xiaobao, an 18-year-old bride, sat playing cards with her husband Ma Liangshui and a few friends. Rain pattered on the thatched roof; the oil lamp flickered in the draft.

Suddenly, a thunderous roar broke the quiet – the unmistakable sound of engines, followed by a distant crash that rolled like thunder across the bay. The dogs outside began barking furiously. Startled, the villagers exchanged fearful looks. In Japanese-occupied China, sudden noise meant danger – bandits, air raids, or worse. Ma's father-in-law grabbed a lantern, but before he could open the door, Xiaobao whispered, 'It's not thunder. It's something else.'

Panic rippled through the house. The villagers fled into the rain, climbing the rocky slope behind the village to hide among the trees. For an hour they huddled there, listening to the wind and the pounding surf below. No shouts, no gunfire – only the storm.

Finally, Ma's father-in-law volunteered to return and investigate. He disappeared down the path, his lantern bobbing through the darkness. When he reappeared, his voice trembled with astonishment.

'No bandits,' he said. 'No soldiers. Foreigners – with big noses. I saw them on the beach!' The others stared at him in disbelief. Foreigners? On this isolated stretch of coast, deep inside occupied territory? It was unthinkable.

Hearing this, the villagers decided to return home. Slowly, they made their way down from the hills towards their houses, still uncertain but driven by curiosity. Ma Liangshui, his young wife Zhao Xiaobao, and several neighbours carried bamboo poles and lanterns as they walked through the wet fields and narrow paths.

Back in the village, everything seemed quiet. The boats were still on the beach, the nets hung where they had been left, and the air smelled of salt and smoke. Wanting to be sure everything was safe, Ma and a few men began to search the area around their huts. When Ma checked the pigsty behind his house, he suddenly stopped.

Inside the shadowed stall, among scattered hay and broken boards, lay four strange men – soaked to the skin, their flight suits torn, their faces pale with exhaustion. Their boots and uniforms were unlike anything the villagers had ever seen. Ma hesitated, heart pounding, then called softly to the others.

The fishermen gathered around the doorway, peering in. The men inside did not move aggressively; they were clearly spent, shivering with cold. Donald Smith slowly raised his hand, palm open, and said something in English that none of the villagers understood. His tone, however, was calm and imploring rather than hostile.

After a moment's whispered discussion, Ma and the others realised these were not Japanese soldiers. Their features, their voices, even their smell of salt and engine oil – everything about them was foreign. The villagers watched cautiously as one of the strangers reached into a pocket and drew out several coins, offering them with a faint, apologetic smile. The gesture was unmistakable: not a threat, but a plea for help.

Still uncertain, Ma's father-in-law fetched a young schoolgirl from the neighbouring hut – a bright child known for her curiosity, and her old schoolbook filled with illustrations of world flags. The girl knelt beside the strangers and opened the book. Page after page of coloured banners passed under trembling fingers until Don stopped her and pressed his finger firmly on the Stars and Stripes.

For a long moment no one spoke. Then the old man's face lit with recognition. He pointed at the flag, then at the sky, miming a plane swooping down. The villagers murmured to one another – rumours had already spread that American planes had bombed Japan the previous day. It was suddenly clear who these men were.

A current of understanding passed between them. Whatever else they were – soldiers, foreigners, intruders – these drenched, exhausted men were enemies of the Japanese, and therefore friends.

The decision was made quickly. Ma gestured for them to follow, helping the weakest to his feet. The villagers brought the airmen into a nearby storage hut and wrapped them in dry blankets. They shared bowls of rice porridge and weak tea, their hospitality cautious but sincere.

Through gestures and halting words, the Americans learned where they had come ashore: Tantoushan Island, a small, sparsely inhabited island off the coast of Zhejiang Province – Japanese-occupied territory, yet still dotted with loyal Chinese fishing villages.

According to local records from Zhejiang Province, the airmen of Crew 15 from the Doolittle Raid came ashore near Dawanggong Village (大王宫村) on Tantoushan Island (檀头山岛), part of Xiangshan County in Ningbo, Zhejiang.

The four airmen were suffering from hypothermia, exhaustion, and physical fatigue. Ma's wife, Zhao Xiaobao, took the initiative in providing care. Clothing was dried near a simple hearth, and food was prepared – eggs and dried shrimp – meagre provisions, yet enough for the men of Crew 15 to regain some strength.

Their physical condition gradually improved. No immediate medical intervention was required. The villagers provided basic care without notifying the Japanese authorities – a risk they were clearly willing to take.

The dedication of the local community during this phase was crucial to the crew's survival. Their actions reflected courage and humanity, despite the grave danger of aiding American military personnel under Japanese occupation.

Later that evening, after the first phase of recovery and shelter, Lieutenant Donald Smith informed the local fishermen about his crew's composition. Through gestures and simplified English, he made it clear that his full crew consisted of five men, but one member – navigator Lieutenant Howard Sessler – had been missing since the water landing.

Smith explained that four of them had reached the life raft, but Sessler had likely been swept away by the strong current. He had not been seen since. The Chinese fishermen understood the gravity of the situation. At dawn, they agreed to begin a search along the coastline and surrounding terrain.

Reports had already circulated of Japanese troop movements near Tantou Mountain. The fishermen warned that Japanese occupation patrols were active in the area. Despite the risk, they decided to proceed. A small group, composed of local fishermen and two members of Crew 15 led by Don, set out shortly afterward.

While exploring the rugged coastal terrain – moving cautiously among rocks and thickets – they heard a faint voice in the distance.

The patrol immediately stopped and located the source of the sound. Moments later, they found Lieutenant Sessler. He was exhausted, hypothermic, and barely able to move. Though physically weakened, he remained conscious and coherent.

The Chinese villagers and Smith provided immediate first aid and stabilised his condition. With the help of local fishermen, Sessler was carefully evacuated and brought back to a temporary shelter in the village. The mission was completed without incident.

Upon returning to the village, Lieutenant Sessler was given dry clothes, warm food, and shelter. Despite his exhaustion, he was able to communicate and recover steadily. The reunion restored Crew 15's integrity.

The moral effect was profound. The entire crew was now relatively safe, though still deep in enemy-held territory. The role of the villagers had been decisive. Their decision to aid the Americans – despite the threat of Japanese reprisals – was crucial for the survival of the unit. In the following hours, it was agreed that their stay on the island should remain temporary. Plans were made to leave the area and establish contact with Chinese resistance groups or Nationalist forces inland.

After a careful assessment of the tactical situation and the increasing activity of Japanese patrols in the waters around Tantou Mountain Island, it became clear that Crew 15's continued presence posed an immediate danger. The likelihood of discovery or capture grew with every hour. In coordination with local village elders, guerrilla units, and resistance members, it was decided to evacuate the Americans.

The chosen plan called for a clandestine transfer to Nantian Island – a larger and more strategically favourable island southwest of their landing site. From there, further extraction to mainland China could be organised and secured.

Responsibility for the operation rested entirely with the local villagers. Village leader Ma Liangshui and his wife, Zhao Xiaobao, took charge of the coordination. In the hours before evacuation, the five Americans were hidden separately in safe houses throughout the village. Camouflage was meticulous: tracks to the huts were erased, fires extinguished, and homes left to appear deserted.

Through her contacts in neighbouring villages, Zhao obtained cotton fishermen's jackets to disguise the crew. Food and rations were discreetly collected and packed into small bundles. Ma arranged for a sampan and scheduled the departure for the night of 19/20 April 1942, using fog, darkness, and cloud cover to evade Japanese coastal patrols and aerial observation.

In the early hours of the night, Crew 15 prepared silently. Final coordination was carried out with Ma and the fishermen, who provided the men with dry clothes, simple rations, and instructions for behaviour in case of enemy contact. Around 02.30am, the sampan set out, heading southwest. Ma personally guided the vessel, steering through the dark waters. The danger became real when Japanese patrol boats approached. Searchlights cut through the mist, and the rumble of engines carried over the water. On Ma's command, the Americans lay motionless on the bottom of the boat. Thanks to the cover of weather and the calm composure of their Chinese guides, detection was avoided. The sampan reached Nantian Island undetected, where a guerrilla unit received the crew and guided them onward.

Once on Nantian Island, contact was made with the same resistance group that had earlier rescued Crew 7. This guerrilla unit had already gained experience in assisting and moving downed American airmen. During a brief exchange, the fighters confirmed that Lieutenant Ted Lawson and his men had been safely evacuated through their network. Donald Smith expressed his gratitude, to which a young resistance fighter replied, 'You Americans never give up. We respect that.' Mutual respect was established, forming the basis for continued cooperation.

Despite the successful crossing, danger remained constant. Japanese patrols were active and had already found unusual footprints, suggesting the presence of foreigners. At one point, Crew 15 and their Chinese allies took refuge in a Buddhist temple. When Japanese troops approached, the monks hid the Americans in a cave behind the sanctuary. The temple was thoroughly searched, and one monk was beaten, but he revealed nothing. His silence saved the airmen's lives.

After the Japanese departed, the group resumed their journey, moving partly on foot – sometimes barefoot – guided by their Chinese escorts. The resistance network supporting them was well-organised, with safe routes, shelters, and supplies. Don later acknowledged their indispensable help: 'Without them, we would have been nowhere.'

The transfer of Crew 15 to Nantian Island marked a pivotal step in the wider escape network that enabled the Doolittle Raiders to evade capture after the Japan raid. The collaboration between Chinese fishermen, villagers, and guerrilla fighters demonstrated the vital importance of civilian support in occupied territory. Their bravery meant the difference between imprisonment and survival – and remains today a symbol of solidarity and shared resistance in the common fight against Japan.

The final leg of the journey – the crossing from Nantian Island to the Chinese mainland near Shipu – took place under extreme tension. Before sunrise, the five Americans departed Nantian Island in a low sampan, manned by local fishermen and guided by Chinese guerrilla fighters. The small craft moved silently through the dark, veiled by thick mist, as every stroke of the oars carried them further from Japanese patrol waters and closer to the uncertain safety of the mainland.

Midway through the passage, the deep hum of a Japanese patrol vessel broke the quiet. The rowers pushed harder, straining to reach the coast before detection. Once ashore, the Americans were quickly led into a narrow creek, where they took cover among reeds and mud along the bank. Lying flat, they listened as the patrol's engines drew closer – it seemed the Japanese might land at any moment to search the area. The tension was unbearable; the men exchanged silent glances, their hearts pounding in the stillness. Minutes stretched endlessly until, at last, the sound of engines faded away and the coast fell quiet again. Only then did they dare to rise. Guided by their Chinese allies, they began their dangerous trek inland. The memory of that morning – lying in the wet earth, aware that discovery was only a few steps away – would remain forever etched in their minds.

Upon his return from the Doolittle Raid, Don recounted this story at several gatherings held in his honour. During homecoming celebrations, he spoke modestly of the harrowing escape from China, always emphasising the courage and compassion of the Chinese villagers who had saved his crew

Shortly after reaching the Chinese mainland, the men of Crew 15 received troubling news about their fellow airmen from Crew 7. Their aircraft, The Ruptured Duck, had crash-landed heavily. Pilot Lieutenant Ted Lawson and three of his crewmen were severely injured and had been taken to a hospital in Linhai, where they were being treated by Chinese doctors and members of the resistance.

Lieutenant Thomas R. 'Doc' White, the gunner of Crew 15, was not a typical airman. As noted, before joining the Army Air Corps he had trained and worked as a physician. When he heard of Lawson's condition, he immediately sought out Donald Smith. White had managed to salvage part of his medical kit from the waterlogged B-25 and felt a professional and moral duty to act. 'Don, we've got to get to Linhai,' he said. 'Lawson and the others are in bad shape. I can help.' Don was hesitant because he knew the Japanese were patrolling the area and that there was a good chance they would be caught. 'Doc' White was insistent; he was the only one with medical training and knew his skills would be needed. Don turned to one of the Chinese guides. 'Is there a safe route to Linhai?' The man thought for a moment, then nodded. 'It's dangerous,' he said quietly, 'but possible.' Smith gave a single nod. 'Then we go.'

And so began a new phase of their perilous journey – no longer merely a struggle for survival, but an act of compassion and duty.

Chapter 16

The Enze Hospital in Linhai

Upon arriving at the hospital in Linhai, Donald Smith and 'Doc' White found their fellow Raiders of Crew 7 in a grave condition – especially Pilot Lieutenant Ted Lawson. 'Doc' White used his medical knowledge and the few remaining supplies he had to assist in treating their injuries. Working closely with the Chinese doctors, he helped stabilise the wounded men as best he could under the desperate circumstances.

The combined efforts of 'Doc' White, the local Chinese physicians, and the tireless resistance workers proved invaluable during those dark days, when Americans and Chinese alike risked their lives to help one another against their common enemy.

Yet despite every effort, Ted Lawson's left leg could not be saved. Infection had set in, rapidly progressing to gangrene. Lawson's condition was critical. The amputation was carried out jointly by 'Doc' White and the Chinese physician, Dr Chen, using improvised instruments and minimal anaesthesia.

In addition to surgery, White resorted to emergency blood transfusions. He was aware of the blood types of each of the raiders and was therefore able to determine which men could safely donate blood. Under field conditions and with no proper equipment, he drew blood from members of Crew 15, from fellow survivors of Crew 7, and from himself, administering it to Lawson as a last, life-saving measure based on medical judgement and necessity.

For their actions in aiding wounded members of Crew 7, Sergeant David Thatcher and Lieutenant Thomas R. 'Doc' White crew were awarded the Silver Star Medal for gallantry, in recognition of their courage and for going well beyond what was required of them under the circumstances.

As Japanese occupation forces advanced towards Linhai, the hospital became increasingly unsafe. Orders soon came for evacuation. Don was instructed to lead his Crew 15 – together with the slightly wounded Sergeant David Thatcher of Crew 7, Ruptured Duck – on an immediate withdrawal to Quzhou, where they would regroup with other surviving raiders and avoid capture.

It should be noted that these orders came directly from Lieutenant Colonel James H. Doolittle in Chongqing. Recognising the desperate situation at Linhai, Doolittle authorised 'Doc' White to remain behind and assist the wounded men of Crew 7, particularly the gravely injured Lawson. White's medical skills were urgently needed, and his presence gave the wounded a fighting chance of survival.

After days of hardship and danger, Don and his surviving crewmates – together with Sergeant David Thatcher of Crew 7 – found temporary refuge in the small village of Houtang, part of the Genglou subdistrict near Quzhou. There, under the protection of local villagers, they recovered from exhaustion and malnutrition.

During their stay, the raiders experienced an extraordinary moment of humanity. Students from Houtang Middle School, curious and excited about the foreigners in their midst, challenged the Americans to a basketball game on the school's small concrete court. Word spread quickly. By the time the improvised match began, more than 1,000 villagers had gathered around the court, cheering loudly.

As the game started, the language barrier dissolved. Laughter, gestures, and the rhythm of the game replaced words. Don – still lean and weary from his ordeal – played with intensity and good humour, diving for rebounds and encouraging his men. The Chinese students, younger and faster, matched the Americans play for play. After a hard-fought match, the Houtang team narrowly won, 42–40.

The crowd erupted in applause. Though the raiders had lost, smiles and laughter filled the air. Standing among the players, Don grinned broadly, clapped one of the boys on the shoulder, and said in broken English, 'You very good – very fast! Next time, we win!' The boy laughed and replied, 'No next time – you go home, America!'

Smith looked at his crew, and for a moment, the war seemed far away. In that small Chinese village, under the same sky that had seen so much destruction, young men from opposite sides of the world had shared something simple – a game, a smile, and the fragile warmth of peace.

For Don and his men it became an unforgettable moment of humanity, a brief pause in the chaos of war. It symbolised the deep bond that had formed between the Doolittle Raiders and the Chinese people who risked everything to help them.

Many of the raiders, including Don Smith and his crew, never intended to reach Quzhou on foot – it was never part of the original plan. Quzhou had been designated as one of five prepared landing fields in China, meant to provide fuel and safe haven after the attack.

However, because the raid had launched thirteen hours earlier than scheduled, the bombers reached the Chinese coast well before the airfields were ready. The ground crews, fuel supplies, and radio operators had not yet arrived, and poor weather obscured the runways.

With their fuel exhausted, most crews were forced to bail out or crash-land across eastern China. Once on the ground, the survivors knew only one thing: Quzhou was the nearest location where they might find help from friendly Chinese forces or American contacts. Guided by villagers and resistance fighters, they began the long and perilous journey inland – not by design, but by necessity – driven by the faint hope that Quzhou still awaited them.

Upon reaching Quzhou, the Doolittle Raiders received direct orders to continue their journey westward to Chongqing, then the wartime capital of China. The city, deep in the interior and under Chinese Nationalist control, offered the first true sanctuary from Japanese patrols and the chaos of occupied territory. From there, the raiders were to regroup, receive medical care, and coordinate with American and Chinese authorities for their eventual evacuation.

Chapter 17

Chongqing: Gateway to Survival

During the Second World War, Chongqing served as the central hub for American military, diplomatic, and intelligence operations in China. The US Embassy, led by Ambassador Clarence E. Gauss, coordinated political and military assistance to the Chinese government. It was in Chongqing that critical strategic discussions took place, diplomatic missions were organised, and plans for cooperation against Japan were refined.

Despite its distance from the front, Chongqing was one of the most heavily bombed cities in China during the war. Japanese air raids had transformed the surrounding hillsides into vast networks of tunnels and shelters, and the sound of sirens and anti-aircraft fire remained a constant presence even during the Raiders' brief respite.

The headquarters of the China–Burma–India (CBI) Theatre, commanded by General Joseph W. Stilwell, was also located in Chongqing. Stilwell held a dual role: commander of Allied forces in the CBI region and chief of staff to Generalissimo Chiang Kai-shek. From Chongqing, he directed joint operations, oversaw the training of Chinese troops, and coordinated Allied offensives across Southeast Asia.

The Office of Strategic Services (OSS) – the forerunner of the CIA – operated extensively in Chongqing as well. OSS agents conducted intelligence gathering, sabotage missions, and provided support to Chinese resistance movements within Japanese-occupied territory. Their cooperation with Chinese military and intelligence units proved crucial in undermining Japanese control throughout eastern and central China.

Meanwhile, the American Volunteer Group (AVG), better known as the Flying Tigers, maintained close ties with Chongqing, even though their main base was in Kunming. Under the command of General Claire L. Chennault, they carried out air raids on Japanese targets and provided air support for Chinese ground forces, strengthening the defence of China's wartime capital.

In addition, American military advisory groups were stationed in the city, helping to modernise the Chinese army through instruction in tactics, logistics, and weapons handling.

For the Doolittle Raiders, Chongqing represented the first true point of safety after their perilous escape through Japanese-occupied China. Upon arrival, they received food, clothing, and medical attention – their first real rest since the raid on Tokyo. American and Chinese officials greeted them as heroes, arranging a formal ceremony in which Madame Chiang Kai-shek, the wife of China's leader, personally presented medals and gifts to the airmen. The event symbolised the deep respect and shared sacrifice between the United States and China in their common struggle against Japan.

At the time, Chongqing – then China's temporary capital – lay deep in the interior, far from the Japanese front lines. For the exhausted Raiders, it was a refuge. They were housed in simple quarters, offered hot meals, and given time to recover from weeks of hardship.

Don was one of the men who spent several days recuperating. They shared accounts of their ordeal, drank tea on balconies overlooking the hazy city, and reflected on the Chinese civilians and resistance fighters who had risked their lives to bring them to safety. Smith would later express his deep gratitude for their courage and compassion, both in official reports and in post-war interviews.

For China, the Doolittle Raid carried a significance that went beyond its limited military impact. Since 1937, the country had endured relentless Japanese aggression, bombardment, and occupation with little visible retaliation. The raid on Tokyo was therefore received as a powerful symbolic act: an enemy that had long inflicted suffering on China had, at last, been struck in return. The arrival of the Doolittle Raiders in Chongqing was greeted with genuine pride, not merely as an Allied success, but as a moment of shared vindication in a war that China had been fighting largely alone for years.

On 29 June 1942, Madame Chiang Kai-shek, the wife of Chiang Kai-shek, China's wartime leader, personally presented medals and gifts to the Doolittle Raiders during a formal reception in Chongqing, in the presence of her husband. Fluent in English and deeply involved in Sino-American relations, her presence carried particular symbolic weight, expressing China's gratitude while quietly underscoring the immense sacrifices the country continued to endure. American diplomats and military officers based in Chongqing coordinated the Raiders' onward evacuation.

The pride felt in Chongqing was tempered by an emerging awareness of the price China would pay for the raid. In the weeks following the Doolittle operation, Japanese forces launched brutal reprisals against civilian populations in eastern China, particularly in Zhejiang and Jiangxi. Villages suspected of having aided the American airmen were destroyed, and thousands of civilians were killed. For Chinese officials and citizens alike, the success of the raid was thus inseparable from the suffering that followed – a reality well understood in Chongqing, where the burden of the war had long been borne by the civilian population.

After several weeks of recovery and debriefing in Chongqing, Don and the other surviving Doolittle Raiders received orders to begin their long journey home. Their first leg took them by military transport from Chongqing to Kunming, the key Allied air base in Yunnan Province and the eastern terminus of the famous aerial supply route known as 'the Hump'.

Flying aboard US Army Air Forces C-47 transport aircraft, Don and his men crossed rugged mountain terrain that had claimed many aircraft before them. From Kunming, they continued westward across the Himalayas to Dinjan and Chabua in Assam, India, then on to Delhi, Karachi, Baghdad, and Cairo, before proceeding through Nigeria, Brazil, and the Caribbean to reach the United States. This route – spanning three continents – marked the end of their perilous odyssey, which had begun on the deck of the USS *Hornet* seven weeks earlier. For Donald Smith, the departure from Chongqing symbolised not only survival, but the long-awaited return from one of the most daring missions of the war.

Route taken by the first group of returning Raiders, including Don Smith:

- 27–29 May – Kunming, China
- 1–2 June – Dinjan/Chabua, India
- 3–4 June – Delhi/Agra, India
- 5–7 June – Karachi (then part of British India)
- 8–9 June – Baghdad, Iraq
- 9–10 June – Cairo, Egypt
- 13 June – Nigeria
- 14 June – Belém, Brazil
- 15 June – Trinidad and Puerto Rico

16 June – Bolling Field, Washington, D.C., USA.

On 18 June 1942, a formal welcome ceremony was held at Bolling Field in Washington, D.C., where the raiders were honoured as national heroes. General Henry 'Hap' Arnold, commanding general of the US Army Air Forces, praised their bravery and determination, declaring: 'In the name of the President and the American people, I salute your courage, devotion, and success.'

He emphasised that while the raid had been limited in its physical damage, its psychological impact was immense – boosting American morale at a dark time and proving that Japan itself was not beyond reach.

After the ceremony, the surviving crews travelled on to their hometowns for emotional reunions with family and friends. Though celebrated as heroes, men like Don carried with them the haunting memories of their ordeal – and the heavy knowledge of the price the Chinese people had paid for their survival.

In later years, memories of Donald Smith's flying during the Doolittle Raid itself took on an almost legendary quality among his crewmates. In a post-war account published in *YANKS* magazine and recorded by historian Stan Cohen, Ed Saylor of Crew 15 recalled Smith's exceptional low-level flying on the mission to Japan. Saylor remembered Smith flying so close to the ocean that spray from the waves struck the aircraft, leaving the taste of salt on his lips. To Saylor, the moment epitomised Smith's confidence and mastery at the controls – calm, precise, and unflinching in one of the most exposed phases of the raid. These recollections reflect personal memory rather than formal mission records, but they underscore the extraordinary flying demanded by, and displayed during, the Doolittle Raid itself.

Chapter 18

Two Homes Awaiting

After their return to the United States in June 1942, public interest in the Doolittle Raiders grew at lightning speed. Although most details of the mission and their dramatic escape from China remained classified, newspapers, radio broadcasts, and magazine features turned the airmen into instant national heroes. *Life* magazine devoted prominent coverage to the raiders in its issue of 1 June 1942 – featuring several of them, including Lieutenant Donald Smith, whose portrait soon became a treasured collector's image. Across the country, parades, receptions, and public ceremonies celebrated their courage. Letters of gratitude poured in, and citizens sent invitations, gifts, and messages of admiration to the men who had carried the war to Japan's doorstep. Recognising the wave of patriotic enthusiasm, the US government enlisted several of the raiders – among them Donald Smith – to take part in nationwide war bond drives, where their presence inspired citizens to invest in the war effort. Standing before large crowds in auditoriums, factories, and train stations, Don and his fellow aviators embodied resilience and hope at a time when America needed it most.

During his return journey to his hometown of Belle Fourche, South Dakota, following the official ceremony at Bolling Field on 18 June 1942, Don was repeatedly recognised by fellow passengers as he travelled by train across the country. Strangers approached him in stations and railcars – some shyly, others with heartfelt emotion – wanting to shake his hand, thank him, or ask for his autograph. For many Americans still reeling from the shock of Pearl Harbor, Don and the other raiders personified the nation's fighting spirit and determination to strike back.

Before he went back home to Belle Fourche, Smith visited South Dakota State College in Brookings, where he had once studied and played on the Jackrabbits football team. His arrival was warmly celebrated by faculty, former classmates, and local residents, who saw in him both a friend and a symbol of courage. At a small gathering in the Student Union, Don spoke modestly about his training, the raid, and the values that had sustained him – discipline, teamwork, and perseverance – qualities he said were first shaped during his college years.

In keeping with a long-standing campus tradition, Smith was invited to carve his name into the wooden wall of the college cafeteria, alongside those of other alumni who had brought honour to the school. It was a simple yet enduring tribute to his journey from prairie student to wartime hero.

The Rotary Club of Brookings hosted a luncheon in his honour at the Dudley Hotel. Local business leaders, veterans, and townspeople gathered to hear him recount the raid – from the tense take-off on the USS *Hornet* to the perilous escape across China. Smith answered their questions with humility and gratitude, emphasising the bravery of the Chinese civilians who had risked their lives to save him and his crew.

At the end of the event, elderly veterans of the First World War rose to shake his hand, recognising in the young airman the continuation of their own struggle for freedom. For Don, the gesture carried deep meaning – it was not just a welcome home, but a bridge between generations of service.

On his way to Belle Fourche, Don's train finally arrived in Rapid City on the morning of 2 July 1942. Waiting on the platform were his parents, Arthur and Laura Smith, accompanied by members of the Belle Fourche Welcome Home Committee. His mother wept with relief; his father simply said, 'We're proud of you, son.'

As Don stepped off the train, others in the crowd recognised him as one of the Doolittle Raiders. The station fell momentarily silent, until the conductor – his voice steady but filled with emotion – called out 'Welcome home, hero'. Applause broke out across the platform, echoing long after the train pulled away. For Don, it was the culmination of an extraordinary journey – from a windswept carrier deck in the Pacific, across enemy skies, through the mountains of China, and finally home to the quiet streets of South Dakota.

On the evening of 2 July 1942, Lieutenant Donald Smith arrived in Belle Fourche, together with his parents. The train from Rapid City was met by a large crowd gathered at the station. Hundreds of townspeople – friends, neighbours, former teachers, and childhood companions – stood beneath red, white, and blue banners as the American flag waved proudly above the platform. A local Boy Scout troop formed an honour guard.

As Don stepped down from the train, the town band struck up the national anthem. Mayor Walter J. O'Donnell officially welcomed him on behalf of the city, expressing his pride in Smith's role in the Doolittle Raid. Smith's response was modest and heartfelt: 'I'm just glad to be home.' It was not a formal military ceremony, but rather a spontaneous, deeply sincere outpouring of affection from a community honouring one of its own. Smith recognised familiar faces in the crowd; some wept openly, others waved flags or shouted his name.

When the reception ended, Smith walked home with his parents through the quiet evening streets. His mother held his hand; his father placed a silent, reassuring arm around his shoulders. For a moment, the war felt distant. At home, one old friend was waiting. As Don opened the door, Mugs, the family's cocker spaniel, leapt towards him, barking and wagging his tail furiously. The dog had waited by the door all day. Don knelt, smiling, and embraced him – a simple, joyful reunion after months of danger and uncertainty.

That night, his mother prepared a simple home-cooked meal, the familiar scents of which must have brought back memories of childhood. The next morning, 3 July, the *Belle Fourche Post* ran a front-page story titled 'Local Hero Welcomed Home by Entire Town'. The accompanying photograph showed Don on the train platform with his parents, surrounded by a sea of flags and smiling faces.

Later that day, Don attended a community brunch at the Don Pratt Hotel, organised by the Belle Fourche Welcome Committee under Lon Newell. Dozens of residents attended, including local business owners, veterans, and family friends. During the event, Laura Smith, Donald's mother, was invited to speak. Her words were brief but powerful: 'Thousands of South Dakota boys are fighting overseas. We must think of them – and of the mothers who have watched their sons go.'

Her message was met with heartfelt applause. Then Don spoke. Calm and composed, he described the Doolittle Raid – its training, the take-off from the USS *Hornet*, and the harrowing escape over enemy territory. He praised the bravery of his crewmates and the unbreakable bond that had held them together through danger and exhaustion.

What deeply moved the audience was his acknowledgment of the Chinese civilians who had helped the raiders and suffered brutal reprisals afterwards. Smith spoke plainly about the heavy cost paid by those who had risked everything to save American airmen. His words left the room in reflective silence.

Local reporters captured every detail for publication in newspapers across the region. During the Q&A that followed, Smith answered questions modestly and without embellishment – speaking not just as a soldier, but as a hometown boy who had never forgotten where he came from.

For the people of Belle Fourche, the evening was more than a civic celebration. It was the homecoming of a familiar face – a neighbour who had written history, and who, for one quiet summer evening, had come back home.

The greatest spectacle awaiting Lieutenant Donald Smith was yet to come. The Belle Fourche Commercial Club had established a special Welcome Home Committee in his honour, ensuring that he would be received as guest of honour at the town's most cherished tradition – the Black Hills Roundup. And fittingly, the celebration would take place on 4 July – Independence Day.

For Don, the Roundup was part of his own story, woven into the fabric of his youth – the dust, the smell of leather, the sound of hooves and cheering crowds. After months of war, uncertainty, and exhaustion, this return to familiar sounds and scents felt almost unreal, a fleeting moment of peace after so much chaos. Yet this time, everything was different. He was no longer one of the onlookers. He was the man everyone had come to see.

Because of wartime travel restrictions, the usual number of out-of-state contestants had been reduced, and local riders filled the roster. Several national reporters, their usual assignments cancelled due to the war, came to Belle Fourche instead – unaware that among the spectators that day sat one of Jimmy Doolittle's Raiders, soon to be honoured before a crowd of thousands.

As the grandstands filled with nearly 4,000 people, the hum of the audience gave way to a hush. The announcer's voice echoed over the loudspeakers: 'Lieutenant Donald Smith, veteran of the Doolittle Raid, is here among us today.'

At that moment, Don – in uniform – entered the stands with his parents. The crowd rose to its feet in a wave of applause. Flags waved, cheers rang out, and the music swelled as the town of Belle Fourche welcomed home its native son. His parents stood proudly beside him, beaming with quiet dignity.

Reporters were momentarily stunned. Rodeos had grown scarce during wartime, and few expected to encounter a national hero at such a local gathering. For many, Donald Smith had been merely a name in a newspaper article about the raid on Tokyo. Now, seeing him in person – a tall, modest man standing beside his family – gave the story a new and human dimension. Within days, papers across the country carried reports of the 'small-town hero welcomed home on the Fourth of July'.

As the applause faded, Don took in the scene – the familiar hills, the faces from his youth, the simple warmth of home. Yet even in that moment, his thoughts drifted far from the cheering crowd.

He thought of Marie, who could give birth at any moment. The thought filled him with both joy and unease. Would he make it home in time? Would he be able to hold his baby in his arms? As the applause continued, his thoughts drifted away from the crowd and the noise of celebration. For a moment, he was no longer the war hero everyone had come to cheer, but simply a young man longing to return home – to his wife, and to the life that was waiting for him.

The following morning, 5 July, he said goodbye to his parents. The farewell was simple and restrained in the quiet, practical manner of the Smith family, yet it carried an unspoken emotional weight. Mugs, his loyal cocker spaniel, lingered nearby, sensing the unease of departure as Don bent down to give him a final pat before leaving.

That same morning, he began his long journey south to San Antonio, Texas, where Marie, was expecting their first child. He took a train to Denver, hoping to secure a military flight from Lowry Field to Texas. When no transport was available, he continued by long-distance bus – a slow, exhausting trip that left him anxious and pressed for time. His greatest fear was missing the birth.

When Don finally arrived in San Antonio on 7 July, he was one day too late. His daughter, Donna Marie, had been born on 6 July 1942, at Brooke General Hospital, Fort Sam Houston in San Antonio. The name had been chosen in advance – a blend of 'Don' and 'Marie'.

Don spent the following days at the hospital with his wife and newborn daughter, cherishing the quiet hours together – a rare, intimate pause in an otherwise demanding military career.

A few days later, a photograph of the young family appeared in newspapers across the country, distributed by AP Wirephoto. The black-and-white image showed Don in uniform beside Marie and the baby in bed. The caption read, with gentle humour: '"Move out of the limelight, Pop – you aren't the main show any longer," yawns Donna Marie Smith, nine-pound daughter of Lieutenant Donald Smith.'

For a brief moment, the public's fascination with the Doolittle Raiders reached into Don's private life, turning a simple family scene into a symbol of hope and renewal – the calm after the storm of war.

Upon arriving in San Antonio, shortly after the birth of his daughter, Don made his first stop – not at home, but at the telegraph office. He wanted his parents in South Dakota to hear the news directly from him – and without delay. In the warm, airless room, he dictated his message to the clerk with military precision: 'Daughter born. Name: Donna Marie Smith. Mother and child doing fine. Regards, Donald.'

The message was transmitted promptly – though not quite as intended. When Arthur and Laura Smith received the telegram in Belle Fourche, they noticed something odd. Their son's brief but joyful announcement had arrived with a small but curious error: the baby's name was written as Dianna Marie instead of Donna Marie.

Arthur raised an eyebrow and handed the note to his wife. 'Must've been a long day at the telegraph office,' he said. Laura smiled faintly. Whatever the spelling, it was still their first grandchild – and that was reason enough to celebrate.

A few days later, a letter from Don cleared up the confusion. 'Her name is Donna Marie,' he wrote, 'a combination of mine and Marie's – we thought it fitting.' The name, simple yet deeply personal, symbolised the bond between husband and wife in a world where nothing seemed certain anymore.

After completing his thirty-day leave, Don received new orders. Instead of returning to his old post at McChord Field in Washington, he was instructed to report directly to Kelly Field, Texas – a decision that reflected both practicality and a touch of compassion from the army. With his wife recovering from childbirth and their newborn daughter in San Antonio, the reassignment kept him close to home while still putting his combat experience to good use.

Kelly Field, one of the US Army Air Forces' principal training bases, became Smith's new post. There he was assigned a dual role: instructor and tactical adviser. He trained young pilots in formation flying, navigation, and emergency procedures – skills he himself had learned under fire during the Doolittle Raid. His calm authority and modesty earned him the respect of both cadets and fellow officers. There was no bravado, no embellishment – only steady professionalism.

For the first time since the beginning of the war, duty and family were within reach of each other. Marie, recovering from the birth, was discharged from Brooke General Hospital at Fort Sam Houston a few days later, and the young family found temporary lodging with her parents in San Antonio.

Don made the most of those brief weeks. He balanced early-morning flight briefings with late-night feedings, the noise of engines with the quiet breathing of his newborn daughter. But he also knew it could not last. The war was moving fast, and men with combat experience were in short supply. Within weeks, his name appeared on a new roster – this time for overseas deployment with the 319th Bombardment Group (Medium).

As one of his colleagues later put it, 'The army gave him a little time to catch his breath – and to hold his daughter. Then it was back to work.'

Chapter 19

The Last Flight of the B-26 Marauder 41-17751 'SNAFU'

The Birth of the 319th Bombardment Group (Medium) Barksdale Field, Summer 1942

Amid a war that was spreading rapidly across continents, a brand-new unit of the US Army Air Forces was activated on 26 June 1942, at Barksdale Field, Louisiana: the 319th Bombardment Group (Medium). The group was to become part of the growing offensive arsenal of the USAAF, built, trained, and readied for combat in record time for deployment to the European and later North African theatres of war.

The group consisted of four squadrons:

437th Bombardment Squadron (Medium)
438th Bombardment Squadron (Medium)
439th Bombardment Squadron (Medium)
440th Bombardment Squadron (Medium)

Command of the new unit was entrusted to Major Alvord R. Rutherford, an officer known for his firm leadership and clear vision. His deputy was Major Robert A. Zaiser, appointed as the Group's Executive Officer. Each of the four squadrons received its own commander:

Lieutenant Raymond H. Lipscomb – 437th Squadron
Lieutenant Donald L. Gilbert – 438th Squadron
Lieutenant Frank M. Tuttle – 439th Squadron
Major David J. Jones – 440th Squadron

The backbone of the group was formed by seasoned airmen from the experienced 17th Bombardment Group, from which the famous Doolittle

Raiders had originated only months earlier. Additional personnel were drawn from the 405th Squadron of the 38th Bomb Group, and further reinforced by a large influx of newly graduated officers and recently trained enlisted men from stateside training bases. Within just a few weeks, this blend of experience and inexperience had to be forged into a cohesive and operational combat unit.

The 319th was equipped with the brand-new Martin B-26 Marauder, a twin-engine medium bomber with a mixed reputation. The B-26 was known in military circles as a fast, powerful, yet 'tricky' aircraft. Its short wings, high landing speed, and sharp climb performance made it notorious among pilots and crews. The bomber demanded discipline, precision, and skill. New pilots trained under experienced instructors, while maintenance crews immersed themselves in the complex technical systems of this advanced aircraft. Although initially met with caution and scepticism, confidence in the B-26 grew steadily as training progressed, and it came to be regarded as an effective and reliable combat platform.

The first weeks of training were not without mishaps. On 16 July 1942, a B-26 from the 437th Squadron crashed only a few miles south of Barksdale Field. The aircraft was piloted by Lieutenant Raymond H. Lipscomb, commander of the 437th Squadron. One gunner was killed, and the remaining crew members were injured. Lipscomb himself survived but was forced to step down from command. He was succeeded by Lieutenant Ellis R. Arnold, who would lead the squadron for the remainder of the training period.

On 29 July 1942, the 319th Bomb Group suddenly gained national attention. Five officers who had taken part in the daring Doolittle Raid on Tokyo on 18 April, 1942, were officially assigned to the unit:

Major David M. Jones, pilot of Crew 5
Lieutenant Donald G. Smith, pilot of Crew 15
Lieutenant Griffith P. Williams, copilot of Crew 3
Lieutenant Richard E. Miller, navigator of Crew 6
Lieutenant Thomas C. Griffin, navigator of Crew 9
(Ranks as of 29 July 1942.)

After returning from China, the surviving raiders were given a choice: they could remain in the United States as instructors – their combat experience being invaluable in training new aircrews – or volunteer for further combat duty. Several, including David Jones, Donald Smith, and Griffith Williams, chose to return to operational service. High command deliberately placed them with the newly formed 319th Bomb Group, where they would serve not only as experienced combat pilots but also as symbols of courage and determination. Their presence lent the unit prestige, inspiration, and a tangible connection to the Tokyo Raid – a blend of personal choice and strategic placement.

Within the group, these men were admired as heroes, embodiments of bravery, perseverance, and success at a time when America desperately needed victories. Few could have foreseen that within a year, their stories would take tragic turns – some would crash, others would become prisoners of war in Europe, and some would not survive later missions. But at that moment, they radiated pride and purpose, standing among the young and inexperienced airmen of the 319th, ready to share their hard-won knowledge and experience.

David Jones was appointed commander of the 438th Squadron, and the integration of these heroic veterans – men who had bombed Tokyo less than a year earlier – provided the 319th with a strong moral foundation. Most of the group's personnel had never flown a combat mission before; suddenly, they were being trained by pilots who had struck the Japanese homeland itself.

On 6 August, the group began an intensive training phase at Harding Field, near Baton Rouge, Louisiana, with ground and flight exercises continuing day and night. Everything was focused on rapid readiness for front-line deployment. But once again, tragedy struck. On 21 August, a B-26 from the 439th Squadron crashed shortly after take-off, piloted by Lieutenants Dorer and Latz. All on board were killed. That same day, the group received formal notice that it would soon be deployed overseas. Only two days later, on 23 August, another aircraft, this time from the 440th Squadron, went down near Slaughter, Louisiana. Lieutenant Farnsworth survived with serious injuries, but his crew perished instantly. Despite these losses, training advanced at a relentless pace.

Captain Donald G. Smith had likely been informed of the formation of the 319th Bombardment Group shortly after returning from the Doolittle Raid, around late May or early June 1942. The group had been officially activated on 26 June, and given the importance of Don's combat experience, it is logical that his assignment was discussed around that time. His presence in the unit carried deep symbolic meaning – he was living proof that a small, determined team could turn an impossible mission into success. For the young recruits of the 319th, he was a mentor, a guide, and a source of inspiration.

Yet Don did not join the group immediately. Upon returning from the Doolittle Raid, he became a father, and out of humane consideration, he was temporarily reassigned to Kelly Field, San Antonio, Texas, after the birth of his daughter on 6 July 1942.

Behind the scenes, Don was already contributing to the early organisation of the 319th Bombardment Group, maintaining contact with the staff at Barksdale Field and providing input on training goals, crew selection, and operational procedures for the B-26 Marauder. His experience in flying under pressure and navigating unfamiliar terrain made him uniquely suited to help shape the new unit.

Those weeks at Kelly Field offered a rare moment of peace and family life. Don balanced his duties with fatherhood, spending as much time as possible with his wife and newborn daughter. But the war waited for no one. The world kept burning, and deep down Lieutenant (soon to be Captain) Donald Smith knew his respite was only temporary. Duty would call again – and this time, he would leave not only as a pilot, but as a father.

On Sunday, 19 July 1942, Don travelled to Austin, spending the night at the Driskill Hotel. The trip was deliberate – he sought a brief retreat from the bustle of San Antonio to complete administrative work and prepare for his assignment to the newly formed 319th. As an experienced combat pilot, he had a specific role to play in shaping the group and used his quiet time in Austin to finalise paperwork, order baby announcements, and to write home. He expected to leave for Tampa, Florida, on Tuesday 21 July, to report to the Third Air Force Headquarters, but at the last moment, his transfer was postponed on higher instruction – likely for logistical or organisational reasons. Don immediately returned to San Antonio, spending two more precious days with Marie and baby Donna Marie.

On Thursday, 23 July 1942, Don finally departed for Tampa, where he was to report for further duty. He was flown there – a logical decision given the distance from Kelly Field and the urgency of his orders. In Tampa, he received his official assignment to the 439th Bombardment Squadron of the new 319th Bombardment Group, marking the start of a new phase in his military career. Shortly before this transfer, he had been promoted to captain.

He didn't remain in Florida for long. After just one day, he was ordered to travel by bus to Louisiana – an exhausting two-day journey across the Deep South, likely via Mobile, Alabama, through Mississippi, and onward to Shreveport. It was midsummer on the Gulf Coast: buses were overcrowded, rest stops brief, and sleep scarce.

Finally, on Sunday afternoon, 26 July 1942, Don reached Barksdale Field, near Shreveport, where he was assigned to the 439th Bombardment Squadron of the newly formed 319th.

> BARKSDALE FIELD, LOUISIANA
> 28 July, 1942
>
> Dear Folks,
>
> I suppose you had begun to wonder what had happened to me. Since I left San Antonio last Thursday, I've been to Tampa, Florida, checked in, and was reassigned here to Barksdale Field – to the 439th Bomb Squadron. I arrived Sunday afternoon after two long days on the bus, and they put me straight to work Monday morning. I've switched to another type of medium bomber, so it's taken me these past two days to get used to the difference. Tomorrow, I'll start as an instructor pilot, teaching the young pilots how to handle the ship. We work from 7:30 in the morning until 6:00 at night, and some nights we have flying until 11:00 p.m. So you can see how busy we are. I don't even have time to go to the club for lunch – just grab a sandwich at the PX.
>
> I hope you received the pictures and that short note I wrote last week. Even though it was my leave, I still had plenty to do, helping Marie and Donna. I talked to Marie tonight, and she said the baby is gaining nicely – she'll soon weigh ten pounds. Marie is up and about again, going out shopping, and in a few weeks, I hope to have her come here with the baby for as long as we remain in this country. We're forming a new squadron; I'm the second-ranking officer, and there are only three of us with much experience at all. The rest of the men are fresh out of training school.

I had a wonderful time on my leave – busy, but a real change. Donna Marie received so many gifts before I left, and Marie said tonight that more are still coming. I imagine she'll tell you all about them next time she writes. Mother, will you please tell Marie the proper way to address Mrs. Roberts and Babe's thank-you note for the lovely pin they gave her? She wasn't sure whether to write 'Mrs. Dan Roberts' or not. Just include it in your next letter – we're trying to get everything taken care of, busy as we are.

Must ring off for now, as I still have to write an exam tonight, and a short note to Marie. I've been typing so fast that this typewriter is beginning to smoke.

Your loving son,
Don

In the summer of 1942, at Barksdale Field, Louisiana, the 439th Bomb Squadron began to take shape – one of four units within the newly created 319th Bombardment Group. The squadron's establishment was part of a wider mobilisation of the US Army Air Forces following the attack on Pearl Harbor. The need for new, well-trained bombardment units was urgent. The 439th was assembled at high speed, marking the beginning of an intensive period of training and formation.

In its early stage, the squadron consisted mainly of young, freshly graduated pilots and crewmen. Only three pilots had any operational flying experience; the rest were at the very start of their active service. The Martin B-26 Marauder, the aircraft they were assigned to, was known for its technical complexity and notorious difficulty. This medium bomber demanded exceptional precision, discipline, and aeronautical skill – qualities most of the young men still had to acquire.

At Barksdale Field, Don Smith joined the core team responsible for organising and building the new 439th Bomb Squadron as second-in-command. His role was extensive: he not only helped lead the formation of the unit but also took an active part in training, evaluating, and preparing personnel. He was well aware of the responsibility he carried. His own combat experience from the Doolittle Raid gave him authority but also placed a heavy moral burden on him. He knew that the survival of these young recruits would depend, in part, on the quality of their training and preparation.

The process began with the recruitment and selection of crews. Young cadets and mechanics were assigned to the unit, joined by a handful of experienced instructors. Don personally oversaw the screening of new recruits. He focused not only on technical ability but also on character, mental resilience, and teamwork. He believed that a cohesive crew was more valuable than individual skill.

Once selected, the crews entered an accelerated training programme. They studied formation flying, navigation, bombing techniques, radio communication, and aircraft maintenance. Special emphasis was placed on mastering the unique handling characteristics of the B-26 Marauder. The aircraft demanded precision from both pilots and engineers – any mistake could prove fatal.

After this theoretical foundation, practical training followed. The crews practised take-offs, landings, navigation, and formation flying. They carried out bombing runs under varying conditions. Every flight was analysed. Smith earned a reputation for being thorough and demanding. He was sharp in his evaluations and set the bar high. Mistakes were identified, discussed, and corrected repeatedly until the crew got it right. His style was strict, but focused on building the skills needed for survival.

Alongside technical instruction, combat simulations were introduced. Crews learned to react to enemy fire, engine failures, onboard fires, and crash landings. These realistic scenarios were meant to prepare them for the conditions they would face over Europe. Don supervised these exercises with relentless dedication. From personal experience, he knew that lack of preparation could mean death. For him, there was no room for complacency – every session counted.

Beyond the operational and technical side, Don placed great emphasis on team spirit. He believed that mutual trust was essential for success in the air. A united crew, he maintained, could better withstand the mental strain of combat. Smith worked actively to build camaraderie within the squadron. He organised joint briefings, encouraged open communication, and made himself approachable to his men. His leadership was not distant – he listened, advised, and gave confidence in return.

Still, the training period was harsh. The B-26 had already earned a grim nickname – the 'Widowmaker'. Its short wings, high landing speed, and sensitive controls made it unforgiving to inexperience. Accidents were frequent. Smith felt the tension among his men. He saw their doubts but refused to yield to fear. His task was not only to train them but also to strengthen their resolve. Again and again, he reminded them that mastery of the aircraft, trust in one another, and relentless practice were what separated life from death.

On 1 August 1942, before the initial phase at Barksdale Field had even concluded, the 319th Bomb Group received notice of an upcoming European deployment. Five days later, on 6 August, the official transfer orders arrived. The entire unit moved to Harding Field, near Baton Rouge, Louisiana, marking the beginning of a second and more intense training stage.

The move took place under pressure and with incomplete resources. At departure, the group possessed only thirty-one B-26 Marauders, less than half of the intended sixty-five, and its personnel was also short – about sixty officers instead of eighty-one, and 500 enlisted men instead of 600. Despite these shortages, the tempo did not slow.

Harding Field offered little comfort. Whereas Barksdale still had solid infrastructure, Harding consisted mostly of tents for the enlisted men and temporary wooden barracks for officers. Life there was rough, hot, and demanding. The airfield lay near the Mississippi River and had three runways – two diagonal and one parallel to the river – surfaced with smooth black tar. The longest runway was 4,600ft (1,400m). There were no fixed schedules or leisurely classes anymore; the B-26s flew almost continuously. Pilots and crews were subjected to a strict and accelerated programme – the final preparation for the unknown front ahead.

Each pilot had to log an impressive number of hours in a short time: on average 100 hours in the Marauder, plus ten hours 'under the hood' – a term used for instrument flying, with full visibility blocked. During this second phase, skill, responsibility and maturity grew within the unit. The young men who had arrived as cadets at the start of the summer were now becoming combat-ready. Formations tightened, coordination improved, and discipline strengthened. Don Smith watched his men grow – as pilots, as teams, as soldiers. Yet he knew no simulation could truly prepare them for what was coming: the fire, the chaos, and the losses that awaited them in war.

Don himself had served barely ten days at Barksdale Field when, in early August, he too received transfer orders. He refers to the move to

Harding Field in a letter of 5 August to his parents. He mentions that the new base 'wasn't very large', but that he knew it would be busy and demanding.

Between 5 and 15 August 1942, much changed for Don. His letter of the 5th was written in Barksdale, where he was hoping to find a furnished apartment and to have Marie join him soon. That weekend, her parents were to drive her to Houston, from where she would continue by Pullman sleeper train. Ten days later, on 15 August, Don wrote again – this time from Harding Field – saying that everything had gone well. Marie and their baby Donna had arrived safely on Monday, 10 August, and he had indeed found an apartment ready for them to move into. The family was together again, at least for a while.

Under the sweltering heat of the Deep South, Don and Marie found a brief moment of peace. A small room, a few shared meals, a handful of days and nights together – fleeting moments they cherished, knowing that fate was closing in.

During this short period of regrouping and preparation, Don and his men balanced between two worlds: the fading traces of family life and the looming shadow of war. That sense of transition hung over Harding Field like a haze – everything pointed towards the next step, one that would be final.

Training continued without mercy. Between early August and the end of September, four fatal crashes occurred on the base. The causes were never fully determined – fatigue, mechanical issues, or inexperience may all have played a part. For Don and his fellow officers, it was a painful reminder that even training for war could be deadly. The airfield meant not only preparation – but also loss.

As the day of departure drew closer, Don felt the weight of his responsibility deepen. He had done his best to prepare his men, technically and mentally. Now he would have to let them go. Still, one thought stayed with him – that the trust, camaraderie, and careful preparation they had built together might just be enough to make the difference.

And somewhere deep inside, he held onto one last hope: that not only would they fight, they would also return.

During the summer of 1942, Don Smith felt the growing pressure of his military responsibilities, combined with the emotional burden of a likely transfer to Europe. He knew a posting to England was inevitable and that he would have to leave Marie and their newborn daughter behind. The parting weighed heavily on him.

Despite the intensity of his training schedule, Don remained closely involved in his family's well-being.

Harding Field, Louisiana
15 August, 1942

Dear Folks,

Just a few minutes to spare this evening before I start night flying, so I thought I'd drop you a quick line to say the picture you sent has arrived – and yes, I'm still holding together just fine.

The family is back together again now. Marie and little Donna arrived last Monday afternoon by Pullman, and thankfully I already had an apartment lined up and ready for us to move into. Donna has grown so much – twelve pounds already! – and I barely recognised her at first. Her hair gets a bit lighter each day, starting to turn sandy around the edges now, even though it was quite dark when she was born. She's growing fast.

We're working hard here, trying to whip the outfit into shape. There's a mountain of work, especially for us older pilots. I wrote from Barksdale last week – hope you got that letter all right. Marie's been busy too, hasn't had much time to write either you or her folks, but things are settling a little now. Hopefully, she'll be able to catch up soon.

As for me, I have to leave the house at six each morning to make it to work on time, and when I'm flying at night, I don't get home until after midnight – so you can imagine, there's not much sleep happening these days.

How are things back home? It feels like forever since I've heard anything – the days are crawling by. I did hear from Eldon, though. He said they're still doing drills, waiting anxiously for flight training to begin. I sure hope he gets going soon and makes the grade.

That's all I can manage for now. I'll write again soon, especially once Marie has time to add a few lines of her own. Donna sends her love to her grandparents.

As ever,
Your loving son,
Don

The formation of the 439th Bomb Squadron demanded substantial effort. Don's days were filled with technical briefings, flight planning, and tactical consultations. Yet after duty hours he remained a husband and father, drawing moral strength from the brief span of family life.

439th Bomb Squadron, Harding Field, La.
22 August, 1942

Dear Folks,

I received both of your letters this past week, along with the photo – thank you! Marie and the baby are doing well, and just two days ago, Marie's mother arrived. With word that we might be shipping out soon, she decided to come be with Marie and the baby, and to accompany them back to San Antonio once I leave. I only get into town about every other day, and even then, I need to be back at the base by 10:30 p.m., except for one night off each week. So I don't get to see my family nearly as much as I'd like. Still, every time I do, our little girl seems to have grown again.

I sent you a telegram this morning – I didn't want you to worry. A couple of planes went down yesterday, and although the papers didn't print the names, I imagine the news spread quickly across the country. I heard that parents everywhere were calling their sons all day. I'm glad I got ahead of that with my message to you.

Last night I was lucky to be home. We had a wonderful dinner, and Marie and I did some shopping downtown. She spent the evening with Donna and had such a lovely time holding her. We're planning to take more pictures of the baby in the coming days, and I'll send them to you once we've picked out the best ones. And by the way – it's now Captain Smith, not part of the Horse Marines, and certainly no Pocahontas!

If it turns out I'm no longer in the USA a few months from now, Marie is planning to visit you with the baby. That way, she can stay with you for a while, and you'll get to meet your granddaughter. I think it will do her good, and break the routine of staying home alone.

No big news from down here in Louisiana otherwise. I'll be waiting to hear back from you soon, and I expect I'll be shipped out any day now. Once I go, Marie will keep writing to you from here, and I'll write again once I'm settled and know where I'll be.

As always,
Your loving son,
Don

By mid-August 1942, confirmation arrived that Don's squadron would be transferred to Europe. Don told Marie himself. The conversation was simple, on a hot evening in their small apartment, while Donna slept peacefully in her crib. The news hit like a hammer. They had both seen it coming, but the reality was heavier than the expectation. Don spoke calmly, as he always did, but Marie could see it in his eyes. They said little that night. The silence was charged, full of questions without answers. They both understood this was no ordinary move. The war was no longer approaching – it now stood between them.

Don, Marie, and Donna Marie lived together in Baton Rouge for a short period of about two-and-a-half weeks, from 10 to 29 August 1942. On 29 August, Marie and her mother left for San Antonio. Her mother had come to Baton Rouge a few days earlier, to help pack the apartment.

At the Missouri Pacific station, Don helped load the luggage. Donna Marie lay half asleep in Marie's arms. Don took her for a moment, held her gently, then handed her back. There was little to say. Marie's mother waited discreetly at a distance while he held his family one last time – a private moment of deep meaning, despite the discipline his rank required.

As the train pulled away, Don stood watching, eyes fixed on the receding car. Only later would it become clear this was the last time he would see his wife and child.

The days after their departure passed in a blur. Don returned to his routine at Harding Field, but the apartment was empty, and the silence struck harder than before. Focus shifted quickly. From 7 September 1942, the 439th Bomb Squadron, to which Don belonged, was officially transferred to Baer Field, Fort Wayne, Indiana, where the final preparations for the transatlantic crossing would be made.

The unit readied itself for departure: men assembled their gear, maps were studied, engines tested. Don spoke less than usual, his attention fixed on what lay ahead. The moment of departure was drawing near – this time into the unknown. On 7 September Don wrote another letter to his parents.

> 439th Bombardment Squadron (Medium),
> Army Air Forces,
> Harding Field, Louisiana
> 7 September, 1942
>
> Dear Folks,
>
> I received your letter this morning, and since I have a few minutes tonight before heading to the office, I'll write you a short reply using the government typewriter. I also wanted to thank you for sending that newspaper clipping. Lieutenant Lien, our engineering officer here, graduated from the same state school as I did, the same year too, and he showed it to me a few days ago. We've been having fun reminiscing and keeping track of the rest of the boys from school. I'll return your copy of the article with this letter – much appreciated.
>
> Last Saturday morning, I flew over to Columbia to retrieve some luggage I had stored there. I honestly thought I'd never get to see it again. It had been left behind last winter when we were rerouted, so I was glad to pick it up and bring it back. The place has changed a lot since I was last there

in the spring – many new hangars, planes, and people. The base has really expanded. By the way, how's the bomber base at Rapid City progressing? I don't think we'll be moved there unless it's finished within the next few weeks.

Our little daughter is growing noticeably every day. Marie said you could probably see the difference just from the latest photo. Her grandparents are doting on her constantly, and she's getting used to playing with them all the time. When she was just with Marie, she hated being alone for even a minute. Marie and I would often have to be in the same room just to keep her content.

Yes, Mother – the 'Gp' in my unit stands for 'Group.' I'm in the 319th Bomb Group, 439th Bomb Squadron. Each group has four squadrons, much like a company in a battalion. I've been assigned additional responsibilities as Engineering Officer and now have to stay on top of everything. If I want to eventually earn a promotion, I need to keep working hard every day.

Marie took a new photo of herself and Donna and is sending it soon. I've asked her to send extra copies too, so you'll have some on hand. I miss them a lot – not a minute goes by without thoughts of them. That way I can at least feel like I'm staying in touch, even when I can't be there.

The weather is starting to cool down here, which is a relief. The summer was brutally hot and humid. The heat even made the air feel heavy. But it's slowly easing off, and I'm grateful. I've been flying a lot lately, and we've had several long night flights. I'm getting used to it again, though it's tiring. We have a solid group of men here now, and we're settling into a good rhythm. One of the new arrivals was over in New Guinea recently – quite experienced and sharp. He's helping bring the rest of us up to speed.

As always,
Your loving son,
Don

At Baer Field the atmosphere was different: tense, more focused, and irreversible. Don played an active role in coordinating technical inspections, drafting tactical guidelines, and mentoring young pilots and crews. He understood the weight of that responsibility. Any mistake, any overlooked detail, could have serious consequences once they crossed the ocean. His experience and calm leadership were invaluable in this final phase.

Baer Field, Fort Wayne, Ind.
16 September, 1942

Dear Folks,

I suppose you noticed I have been moved again, we moved up here last week, and are settled for a short but busy stay. Looks like my last station in this hemisphere. I haven't received your weekly letter yet, but suppose it will catch up with me from Harding Field in the next few days. Marie is getting along pretty good at home, but I wish I could get to see her and Donna for a while, but that is against orders now. We can't have any wire up here, so will have to wait until I get back again. She said she would write in a few days, and send you a picture of the baby, she took quite a bunch, but it is so hard to get Donna to pose for her picture. She is going to take one picture all the way along and will send you one every once in a while so you can keep up with your Grand-daughter's progress.

I may have told you wrong as to what my address will be when we leave here, so I will repeat it now, and you won't make any mistake: 319th Bomb Gp., 439th Bomb Sqdn., A.P.O. 3070, c/o Postmaster, New York, New York.

Capt. Donald G. Smith, A.S.N. 0-399010
319th Bomb Gp.
439th Bomb Sqdn.
A.P.O. 3070
c/o Postmaster, New York, New York.

I believe I told you A.P.O. 5070 in my other letter, and it should have been 3070.

We are keeping busy, and learning something new each day, didn't know there was so much to be learned about this new airplane. They get more complicated every day. I wonder what they are going to do with the new officers coming in to learn all this stuff at the speed they are sending them through the training schools.

It really felt nice to be back in the cool climate again, after having been down in the hot climate for a couple of months. We can sleep at night without the discomfort of sweating it up. It is cool enough here at night to use at least one blanket, and makes it hard to get up in the morning.

How is everything at home? Is the winter going to make its appearance early this year? Would like to get out to Belle once more, but we can't even get overnight off to say nothing of a long enough period of time to make that trip. I looked up Phillips the other day and decided if I ever got up that way I would buzz the Hesses on the way by. Don't suppose I will ever get up there, but never can tell.

Will close for now. Hope you get this before the week end.

As ever, your loving Son,
Don

During the evenings, when operational pressure briefly eased, Don wrote frequent letters home and to Marie. This personal correspondence reflected his deep attachment to his family and his moral motivation to fight in Europe. His letters touched on the everyday realities of military life and his worries about the future – serving as an emotional anchor in a time of increasing uncertainty.

Baer Field, Indiana
25 September, 1942

Dear Folks,

Just a quick note tonight, as we are pretty busy, and I wanted to correct the address before heading out. It should now be:

Capt. D.G. Smith
439th Bomb Sqdn., ASN O-389010
A.P.O. 3052; c/o Postmaster, New York, New York

All they changed this time was the A.P.O. number, so if you update it, your mail will reach me there. You can start sending letters to that address immediately. This morning, I mailed a package home – it's addressed to me, but Dad, feel free to open it and see how it looks. It's something I mentioned while I was home, but couldn't find until I reached this post.

I also mailed you a picture of the airplanes we're flying now. So when you hear someone talk about the B-26, you'll know what they look like. They only have one tail, unlike the B-25, which had two – that's the easiest way to tell them apart.

It's been getting colder here the past few days – a clear sign that winter's on its way. I wish we were going to be here long enough to head up to South Bend and catch a good football game, but it seems we never stay in one place long enough to do anything besides fly, eat, and sleep.

Marie said she mailed you some pictures of Donna. She's really starting to look more like the rest of the family. My favourite photo is the one where she's on her tummy, looking up at the camera. Be sure to show them to Mugs, so he'll recognise her when she comes to visit her grandparents. I bet she'd really enjoy playing with Mugs in just a few years.

Well, I must ring off for now. This will probably be your last letter from this side, as I'll soon be overseas.

As ever,
Your loving son,
Don

The period at Baer Field marked the end of Don Smith's time on American soil. Soon he and his unit would be transferred to the European Theatre of Operations, where a series of dangerous missions awaited him.

The air component, without aircraft assigned, formed the vanguard of the 319th Bomb Group. This group began its journey to England as early as 27 August 1942, departing from Harding Field in Louisiana. It consisted of flying personnel who ultimately would not ferry aircraft to Europe: pilots, copilots, navigators, bombardiers, and other specialised aviation personnel. Because no crew had an aircraft assigned at that time – the formal assignments would not follow until Baer Field at the end of September – they went ahead as a troop unit by ship to the United Kingdom, while the crews of the later flight echelon would only receive their aircraft afterwards and bring them over via the northern ferry route.

Two days later, on 29 August, the group arrived at the assembly point at Fort Dix in New Jersey. There they spent several days completing administrative processing, medical examinations, and drawing additional equipment. They then embarked on one of the largest and fastest ocean liners of its time: the *Queen Mary*, converted into a troop transport. Together with some 16,000 other American servicemen, they prepared for the crossing to Europe.

On 5 September at 1500 hours, the *Queen Mary* departed New York Harbor and slipped via the Hudson River into the Atlantic Ocean. The crossing was swift and safe but took place under the constant threat of German U-boats. The exact destination remained secret until the very end. Only on the morning of 11 September did it become clear that the ship was bound for the Firth of Clyde, a deep sea inlet on the west coast of Scotland. There, the *Queen Mary* anchored off Gourock, where disembarkation began.

After arrival, the air component was sent on to the relief airfield RAF Attlebridge in East Anglia. Shortly thereafter, on 12 September, came the transfer to RAF Station Shipdham, in Norfolk, about 30km north of Norwich. This region, with its many American air bases, played a key role in preparing Allied operations in North Africa. The arrival of the air component formed part of this strategic build-up.

In the weeks that followed, they trained intensively, orientated themselves, and above all waited for the arrival of the aircraft from America. On 7 October 1942, an important moment occurred: for the first time since their departure from Louisiana, members of the air and ground components met again on British soil. This reunion boosted morale and improved cooperation between flying and support personnel.

They could not stay long, however. On 21 October, the air component received new marching orders. Everything was packed, farewells were said to Norfolk, and by train they headed once more towards Gourock in Scotland. The next day they boarded another troopship, the *Orbita*. Where the voyage would lead was again kept strictly secret. Over the following days, a large convoy formed, consisting of dozens of ships protected by a heavy naval escort. On 26 October at 23:30, the convoy left the Firth of Clyde and set course south – towards a new and decisive theatre of war.

While the air component was already on its way to Europe in early September 1942, the ground component of the 319th Bomb Group began its own, parallel route towards the front. This group formed the indispensable backbone of the unit and consisted of technical personnel, aircraft mechanics, radio operators, drivers, administrative staff, logistics specialists, medical staff, communications experts, and kitchen personnel. Without them the aircraft could not fly, the crews could not eat, and the mission could not succeed.

On 21 September 1942, the entire ground component departed Harding Field, Louisiana, for Camp Kilmer in New Jersey – one of the largest staging areas for American troops bound for Europe. There they were equipped, medically checked, and prepared for an adventure full of uncertainties.

Two days later, on 23 September, preparations were completed and the men boarded the *Queen Mary*, the iconic troopship that had earlier carried the air component to Europe. Once again, thousands of American servicemen were aboard, each with his own story and destination. The *Queen Mary* left New York Harbor at 07.00 on 27 September.

The aircraft that would eventually be assigned to Captain Donald Smith was a Martin B-26A Marauder with serial number 41-17751, built by the experienced aircraft manufacturer Glenn L. Martin Company of Middle River, Maryland. The aircraft was part of an early production series under Army Contract W-535-AC-16137, an agreement drawn up during 1941 as part of the rapid build-up of American air power. The unit price of this advanced medium bomber was a hefty $153,154 – a considerable sum by wartime standards and a reflection of the B-26A's advanced aerodynamics, powerplant, and armament. The Marauder was known for its high landing speed, short wingspan, and cruise speed – characteristics that made the aircraft both loved and notorious among airmen.

The official receipt date by the United States Army Air Forces was 25 July 1942, which formally placed the aircraft on the Air Forces' inventory. From that moment, it began a path of technical inspections, test flights, and preparatory transfers among various fields on the American mainland. In the ensuing months, the aircraft was flown between, among others, the Glenn Martin factory, Middletown Air Depot, Harding Field (Louisiana), and ultimately Baer Field in Indiana.

At Harding Field, the aircraft underwent further tests, engine checks, radio installations, and balancing procedures. It served there as part of operational preparation and training flights but did not yet receive a definitive destination. Only on 26 September 1942, while at Baer Field was the aircraft formally assigned to the overseas ferry operation, destined for employment in Europe and North Africa. Baer Field was the central departure point for trans-Atlantic aircraft deliveries, and from there Captain Donald Smith's ferry flight via the northern route to the United Kingdom began.

To Don, this aircraft meant more than metal and engines; it was the instrument of his first contribution to the global Allied war effort. He was part of the Flight Echelon of the 319th Bomb Group, which, as part of preparations for Operation Torch, would be sent via Great Britain to North Africa.

Although Don was formally assigned to B-26 Marauder 41-17751 at the end of September 1942, the maintenance card shows that the aircraft had flown much earlier – among other dates on 7 and 9 March 1942. These early flights in March and later in 1942 were conducted by test pilots, civilian ferry crews, or instructors – not by Don Smith, who was only later linked to this aircraft in the context of Operation Torch. Besides, in March 1942 he was in full training for the Doolittle Raid.

The first test flight on 7 March 1942 took place from the Martin factory at Middle River, Maryland. As usual, this was a standard factory acceptance flight, conducted by a Glenn L. Martin Company test pilot. Later the same day, the aircraft was ferried to Atlanta by a so-called C.C.C. pilot – Contract Civilian Crew, a civilian ferry crew in the employ of Ferrying Command. Such transfer flights were often performed by commercial or temporarily seconded pilots.

The flights on 9 March 1942, during which the aircraft called at Baer Field and Westover Field, were presumably handled by Air Corps instructors, engineering pilots, or trainees within the framework of distribution and training.

Although the aircraft was officially received by the United States Army Air Forces on 25 July 1942, it was not assigned to a permanent crew in the weeks thereafter. In that transitional period, the aircraft was flown by civilian ferry crews, test pilots, or Air Forces instructors, transferring it among fields such as Middletown and Harding Field. These flights served to verify, adjust, and prepare the aircraft for its eventual overseas employment.

Both the aircraft of the flight echelon and the previously deployed personnel of the 319th Bombardment Group – who had already departed for Great Britain by ship at the end of August 1942 – were never intended to remain in England. Their ultimate destination was French North Africa, where the group would take part in Operation Torch, the first large-scale Allied amphibious landing on the African continent. England served merely as a temporary staging ground.

The group was assembled, received, and prepared in Britain for the next stage of their move south. The aircraft of the flight echelon, including Don Smith's, arrived in early October 1942 via the northern ferry route, landing at RAF bases such as RAF Attlebridge and Horsham St Faith in Norfolk. The ground and air personnel who had travelled by ship earlier were already there or were soon reunited with the arriving crews.

After a short period of regrouping, technical inspection, and additional briefings, the aircraft were to continue south from their English bases to North Africa – via Land's End, St Eval, and Gibraltar – to become operational from airfields such as Tafaroui and Maison Blanche near Algiers. The entire 319th Bomb Group was thus intended to serve as a tactical bombardment unit providing air support for the Allied forces landing in Algeria and Morocco on 8 November 1942.

In early October 1942, a total of fifty-seven B-26 Marauder aircraft and their crews assembled at Baer Field (Fort Wayne, Indiana) for the perilous transatlantic crossing to England. They formed the Flight Echelon of the 319th Bombardment Group, composed of:

- 14 aircraft from the 437th Bombardment Squadron
- 14 aircraft from the 438th Bombardment Squadron
- 15 aircraft from the 439th Bombardment Squadron
- 14 aircraft from the 440th Bombardment Squadron

The aircraft did not depart as a single formation but flew individually, as soon as each was technically ready and the weather permitted.

The Flight Echelon of the 319th Bombardment Group primarily followed the northern ferry route using aircraft from the four squadrons, with the 440th being the least represented on this path.

The northern ferry route was as follows:

Baer Field (Indiana, USA) → Presque Isle (Maine, USA) → Goose Bay (Canada) → Bluie West 1 (Greenland) → Reykjavik (Iceland) → Prestwick (Scotland)

The 310th and 319th Bombardment Groups were the first American medium bombardment units deployed to the Mediterranean Theatre during Operation Torch. The 310th flew B-25 Mitchells, while the 319th became the first unit to operate the B-26 Marauder in a combat zone.

Later, an additional fifteen aircraft made the crossing using the southern route, again representing all four squadrons, though the 440th was the most heavily represented this time.

To carry as much equipment as possible, the crew of each aircraft was reduced to four men: pilot, copilot, navigator, and radio operator. Don's aircraft was loaded to capacity with spare parts, tools, and essential gear for the unit – at the expense of defensive crew or armament. This heavy load made the aircraft sluggish and less manoeuvrable in an emergency.

Preparation for the ferry flight was chaotic and far from streamlined. Baer Field had been designated a Concentration Command – the central assembly and departure point for crews, aircraft, and supplies. On paper, it was to function as the coordination hub from which the group would begin its overseas transfer. In reality, the base was woefully unprepared for the task.

Baer Field had little to no experience of preparing an entire combat group for deployment – let alone in making B-26 Marauders ready for a transatlantic crossing. The ground personnel stationed there were accustomed to training aircraft and light planes, not to medium bombers like the B-26, which were complex, demanding, and maintenance-intensive. There was an acute shortage of spare parts, proper tools, qualified technicians, and above all – experience.

Moreover, crews and aircraft were assigned randomly on-site. Many pilots met their plane – and their new crew – for the first time only days before departure. There was scarcely any time for joint training, for standardising procedures, or for learning one another's strengths and weaknesses. Some Marauders arrived straight from the factory, having never flown a proper test flight. In some cases, crews had to install extra fuel tanks, fine-tune radio systems, and check weapon mechanisms themselves – often without any technical support.

The result was a tense departure from a base that looked more like a logistical bottleneck than a military springboard. The 319th Bomb Group would begin its mission with minimal preparation, in a new type of aircraft, over an untested ferry route. The men knew they were about to make history – but also that they would be doing so without a safety net.

The crews received detailed briefings on the planned northern route, emergency procedures over open water, icing hazards, and the use of radio direction-finding stations. Each aircraft carried extra navigation charts, a survival kit, oxygen bottles, emergency rations, and thermal clothing – for what awaited them was no ordinary training flight.

Captain Donald Smith flew from Westover Field to Presque Isle Army Air Field in Maine, near the Canadian border, on 4 October 1942. The flight of roughly 1,600km passed largely over the northeastern United States. Although relatively safe, it demanded full concentration. Crews flew either in small groups or entirely solo, depending on weather conditions and aircraft readiness. Along the way, they passed over Buffalo, Albany, and Bangor, adhering strictly to assigned air corridors to avoid conflicts with other air traffic.

Presque Isle was no ordinary stopover: it was the gateway to the Atlantic crossing. Here, each aircraft underwent one last thorough inspection. Radar and weather teams collected the latest data on conditions over Canada, Greenland, Iceland, and Scotland. Crews often had to wait days for a favourable 'weather window' before attempting the next leg. During that time, they slept in barracks, wrote letters home, repaired minor technical issues, and discussed among themselves who might be allowed to depart first.

For the men of the 439th Squadron – and especially for Don and his crew – Presque Isle marked the true beginning of the adventure and the growing realisation that this was no longer a training mission. The next time they took off, they would be heading towards Canada and then over the ocean itself. The war was calling, and the B-26s stood ready.

Once the aircraft of the 439th Bombardment Squadron were ready at Presque Isle, the crews waited for a suitable 'weather and navigation window' to begin the next leg – the crossing to Goose Bay, Labrador,

Canada. This flight, about 1,100km, was the first step into rougher, more remote territory. Pilots followed a predetermined route, using radio beacons and visual landmarks along Canada's eastern coastline. Don flew this leg on 6 October 1942, leading his crew through increasingly hostile skies.

Although relatively short, the flight crossed vast forests and sparsely inhabited areas where any engine failure or navigation error could be fatal. The Marauders therefore preferred to fly by day, in small groups or solo, depending on radio frequencies and weather conditions. Goose Bay, Labrador, Canada, was still a new military base in 1942, freshly developed as a launching point for transatlantic ferry flights. Here, aircraft were inspected, refuelled, and prepared for the most difficult stages to come: Greenland and Iceland.

For many crews of the 439th – and for Don's men in particular – Goose Bay marked the moment when the ferry mission truly became an Atlantic venture. From the moment they left Presque Isle, the flight became a battle against the elements – storms, ice, and unpredictable weather turned the northern route into a gruelling ordeal. Aircraft were frequently delayed for days in Canada and Greenland due to weather conditions.

After their stay in Goose Bay, where aircraft were refuelled and checked and crews prepared for the difficult flight over icy waters, the B-26s took off for Bluie West 1, an American air base on the west coast of Greenland near Narsarsuaq, on 8 October 1942 – including Captain Donald Smith and his crew. The distance between Goose Bay and Bluie West 1 was roughly 1,200km. The route passed over desolate and rugged terrain with minimal navigational aids. Because of unpredictable Arctic weather, crews often had to wait several days for a safe 'window' to attempt the crossing. Icing, low clouds, and strong crosswinds made this one of the most dangerous legs of the entire ferry route.

Bluie West 1 was still relatively new in 1942 but was vital to ferry operations. It served as the springboard to Iceland (Reykjavik), the next stop on the way to Britain. In Bluie West 1, crews had to tie down their B-26s at night because of wind gusts reaching 150 miles per hour. Before take-off, engines and wings had to be defrosted with ground heaters before they could even attempt to fly.

The flight was anything but comfortable. The aircraft roared and shuddered continuously, with almost no room to move and no facilities for basic needs. Anyone who needed to urinate had to rely on a simple hose or makeshift can, and otherwise had no choice but to endure it. The long hours over the grey ocean were harsh and unrelenting.

After their difficult passage to Greenland, the crews of the 439th Bombardment Squadron – among them Captain Donald Smith's crew – faced their next challenge: the crossing of the frigid waters between Bluie West 1 and Reykjavik, the capital of Iceland. This flight, about 1,300km, again took them over open ocean, in a region notorious for sudden weather changes, turbulence, and poor visibility. Captain Donald Smith flew this leg on 10 October 1942.

The B-26 Marauder was not a long-range aircraft, and although equipped with extra fuel tanks, every mile over the freezing water carried risk. Radio contact with other aircraft or ground stations was often limited, and navigation errors could prove fatal. Reykjavik Airport, built in 1940, served as a crucial stopover for American ferry flights en route to Europe. Here, the crews caught their first glimpse of the European war theatre, even if only briefly. After rest, resupply, and a final weather check, they prepared for the last leap towards the British Isles.

After the stop in Reykjavik, Iceland, the B-26 Marauder crews of the 439th Bombardment Squadron faced the final and most symbolic leg of their ferry flight: the crossing to Prestwick, Scotland – the entry point to the European continent for countless American aircraft during the war. Don's unit flew this leg on 11 October 1942, completing the perilous transatlantic crossing that had begun nearly two weeks earlier in Indiana.

In total, this transatlantic journey consisted of five to six flying stages, covering nearly 6,000km. Yet the crossing seldom went as planned. Unpredictable Arctic weather – fog, gale-force winds, snow, and ice accumulation on the wings – often delayed departures by several days. Technical issues with the still relatively new B-26 Marauder, the limited number of maintenance teams along the route, and the challenge of coordinating group flights – usually in formations of two to six aircraft – further extended the overall journey time. While the actual flying time amounted to roughly five days, a realistic schedule allowed for seven to ten. The northern ferry route demanded not only skill but also patience, endurance, and improvisation from every crew that dared to cross the Atlantic.

Ultimately, 55 of the 57 aircraft from the 319th Bomb Group reached Greenland. As the weather worsened, difficulties mounted, and several planes were forced to halt their journey – or were lost entirely. Three aircraft disappeared during their attempt to reach Iceland. Only thirty-five Marauders completed the leg to Reykjavik, and thirty-four aircraft eventually landed safely at RAF Horsham St. Faith in England. One overshot England and mistakenly landed in enemy-held territory.

Captain Donald Smith's aircraft, B-26 Marauder 41-17751, was among those that arrived safely. Prestwick Airfield, on the west coast of Scotland, was specifically equipped to handle these transatlantic delivery flights. There, the Marauders were once more inspected, crews were debriefed, and they received their first orders in Europe. From Prestwick, Scotland, Don and his crew flew onward to RAF Horsham St Faith – arriving around 13 October 1942 – where they joined the rest of the 439th Bombardment Squadron.

RAF Horsham St Faith had originally opened in 1939 as a Royal Air Force bomber station, home to aircraft such as the Blenheim and the Wellington. In 1942, the airfield was upgraded to accommodate larger, heavier bombers – including the American Martin B-26 Marauder. Its flat terrain, proximity to Norwich, and convenient transport links made it an ideal staging base for American units passing through.

For the 319th Bomb Group, RAF Horsham St Faith became a place of consolidation and preparation. The Marauders that had arrived via the northern route were regrouped for the first time since leaving the United States. Test flights were carried out, final mechanical checks completed, and formation and gunnery exercises conducted. Don participated in several of these early test flights, ensuring his crew and aircraft were ready for operations. Although their stay was brief, it marked a pivotal moment: for many, it felt like the calm before the storm.

Despite its short duration, the stay at RAF Horsham St Faith was crucial. The base represented the transition from training to combat readiness – a convergence point where men, aircraft, and orders finally aligned before the group's baptism of fire. Contrary to popular belief, the 319th Bomb Group was never stationed at RAF Shipdham. That airfield, also located in Norfolk, was occupied later in 1942 by B-24 units of the 44th Bomb Group. The 319th's B-26 Marauders were based solely at RAF Horsham St Faith and, briefly, at RAF Attlebridge. There is no evidence that any part of the group's flight echelon operated from RAF Shipdham.

The transfer of the 439th Bomb Squadron took place in several stages. Don and his crew were among the first to arrive in early October as part of the so-called Flight Echelon. Here they carried out training flights and final preparations. Around 20 October, the squadron moved officially to RAF Attlebridge, becoming fully operational there on 23 October. The B-26s were flown over the short distance between the two bases, while the remaining personnel and equipment followed in ground convoys. RAF Attlebridge had only recently been upgraded with new concrete runways, hangars, and expanded facilities suitable for medium bombers like the Marauder.

Originally built in 1941 as a grass airfield for the RAF, Attlebridge was extensively modernised in 1942 to accommodate larger aircraft and US units. Before becoming the permanent home of the 466th Bomb Group (in 1943), it was used in October–November 1942 as a temporary training and coordination site for the 319th. The facilities were still rudimentary: maintenance sheds and barracks stood beside wooden huts and tents.

The men of the 439th and 440th Squadrons were quartered in basic Nissen huts, heated by small coal stoves. The cold, damp autumn air of East Anglia made living conditions harsh, but camaraderie kept morale high. For many, it was their first real glimpse of the English countryside and climate. Meals were served in makeshift mess halls – coffee, eggs, corned beef, and baked beans were staples – and occasional contact with curious locals offered brief relief from the monotony. Sanitary facilities were primitive. Latrines and washrooms were housed in separate wooden huts without heating, offering only cold water and the most basic amenities.

On 22 October 1942, the technical and logistical detachments of the 319th left England aboard troopships bound for North Africa, as part of the massive Torch convoy. Mechanics, supply officers, drivers, armourers, and other ground personnel sailed from ports such as Liverpool, bound for the provisional airfields at Tafaroui and Maison Blanche near Algiers. Their departure marked a new phase for the pilots and aircraft that remained behind at RAF Horsham and RAF Attlebridge. After the ground personnel had departed the remaining flight crews – including Don – had to maintain their own quarters, latrines, and even their aircraft. There was no hierarchy in such chores: if you could fly, you could also sweep, haul coal, or clean latrines. It was part of the rhythm of military life – discipline and self-reliance kept the Air Force running. Life on the bases took on a new atmosphere – less structured, more uncertain. Ferry Command units of the US 8th Air Force, and occasionally RAF detachments, stepped in to provide temporary technical help. Pilots and flight engineers often performed their own maintenance: checking tyres, topping off oil, patching minor leaks. The crews knew they were on their own now, and every bolt, wire, and tank was double-checked before flight.

RAF Attlebridge had three runways arranged in a triangular pattern, typical of British airfields of the period. The main strip (02/20) was paved and long enough – about 1,800m – to handle the powerful but temperamental B-26 Marauder. The other two (07/25 and 12/30) served as secondary runways, depending on wind or maintenance needs. Not all taxiways and dispersal areas were complete; some sections were still gravel or mud. After rain, the paths between dispersal points turned to sticky sludge, and it was not uncommon for men to lose a boot in the mire while walking to their aircraft.

At the heart of the base stood the control tower, a concrete structure topped with a glass observation room. From here, air controllers oversaw the flight line, runways, and weather. The tower was equipped with radio gear, signal pistols, charts, and meteorological instruments. Pilots such as Captain Donald Smith filed their flight plans there and received take-off clearance. The tower was the nerve centre of every operational day, especially during test flights or as the ferry movement to North Africa drew near.

Each day, briefings were held in a simple hut, where crews received updates on the upcoming ferry route to North Africa, weather forecasts, air defences over the Channel, and formation procedures. The mood was tense but professional. Maintenance teams worked around the clock, checking engines, installing auxiliary fuel tanks, and calibrating radios to Allied frequencies. Captain Smith, known for his calm leadership, personally supervised the inspection of his aircraft, ensuring that every system was in perfect working order before departure.

Beyond the technical and operational aspects, there was also a focus on mental readiness. Many crews had never flown under combat conditions. Officers gave motivational talks, maps of Gibraltar and North Africa were studied, and scenarios were rehearsed: what to do in case of a ditching at sea, a loss of course, or engine trouble over water. Gradually, the group became a cohesive unit, aware that their first mission would not be a drill, but an actual leap into war.

Evenings in the mess hall offered brief respite. Dinner – often canned vegetables, meat, mashed potatoes, and plenty of coffee – was followed by small moments of recreation. The men played cards, read newspapers or letters from home, or listened to crackling BBC broadcasts on the radio. Occasionally, an old Hollywood comedy was shown in an improvised room, giving everyone a short break from tension.

Although RAF Attlebridge was only a brief stop on the way to the real front, for many it became a place of memory. Here, under the curved corrugated roof of a cold Nissen hut, Don came to understand the gravity of his mission. Here stood his Marauder on wet concrete, facing south. And here, among mud, maps, and the smell of coffee, the men of the 319th began what would be their baptism by fire – the leap towards North Africa and the beginning of their real war.

During their stay in England and in the lead-up to their crossing to North Africa, the 319th Bombardment Group (Medium) was officially assigned to the newly formed Twelfth Air Force of the US Army Air Forces. This air force, commanded by General James H. Doolittle, had been created specifically for the air campaign accompanying Operation. Within the Twelfth Air Force, the 319th fell under the XII Bomber Command, responsible for coordinating medium bomber operations. Though the group was still preparing in England and would not depart with their B-26 Marauders for Algeria until 12 November, administratively they were already part of the new command. The 319th thus became one of the first American bomber groups to be deployed in the Mediterranean Theatre of Operations, with RAF Attlebridge as its final stop on British soil.

The mood at RAF Attlebridge was tense. Don knew the gravity of the mission and amid the chaos he decided to give his aircraft a name – a wry nod to the everyday absurdities of military life: SNAFU. The term, an acronym for 'Situation Normal: All Fouled (or F***ed) Up,' was common among American troops. It perfectly described the confusion and improvisation that marked their daily operations. By naming his aircraft SNAFU, Don revealed both his dry humour and his grounded realism. The name captured the uncertainty of every mission and was a deeply personal reflection of the man who flew the aircraft. Tragically, SNAFU would never reach North Africa. The name became forever linked to Don's final flight – a name that today symbolises both the harsh reality of war and the courage of those who faced it.

The men of the 319th Bomb Group, housed in cold barracks and Nissen huts scattered across the misty fields of Norfolk, were summoned for a series of important briefings. They were told that their time in

England was coming to an end: they were to prepare for a ferry flight to RAF St Eval in Cornwall – a crucial stop on their way to North Africa. British and American forces had landed in Algeria and Morocco on 8 November, and now the B-26 Marauders of the 319th Bomb Group were to make the crossing to provide air support as part of Operation Torch. The briefings took place in a wooden hut where a large map of Western Europe hung on the wall. In groups, pilots and navigators were briefed on the planned route, weather conditions, visual landmarks, the importance of radio silence, and procedures in case of formation loss or mechanical failure. Navigating over a low cloud deck in November was risky – and everyone knew it. Meanwhile, the aircraft themselves were being meticulously prepared. Although most of the ground crews had already sailed for North Africa on 22 October, enough technicians remained at RAF Attlebridge to fuel and service the Marauders. Engines were run for hours, instruments calibrated, and ferry tanks installed. Each aircraft was effectively 'armed' for a long flight over sea and unknown terrain.

For the crews, the preparation was also personal. Don and his fellow airmen packed their few belongings, laid out their flight suits, checked their maps and coordinates, and wrote – often with stiff fingers – their final letters home. Don did so on 23 October, addressing his letter to his parents in South Dakota. In the corner of the stationery, he wrote a small number '3', his way of marking it as the third letter since his arrival in England. Soldiers numbered their letters to help families keep track of the sequence and notice if any went missing. It was a small but thoughtful gesture in a world filled with noise and distance. Among the men there was no panic, but a quiet seriousness. Some read from their Bible, others sipped lukewarm coffee in the canteen, and a few cracked dry jokes – the kind soldiers use to ease the tension.

At night, few slept well. The bunks were narrow and cold, the air heavy with the smell of oil, leather, and damp clothing. Yet it wasn't only the discomfort that kept them awake. Everyone knew that this flight was more than a transfer: it was a threshold to a new phase of the war, to another continent, with unknown dangers ahead. The Marauder was a powerful aircraft, but notoriously difficult to land – and with full ferry load, even more unpredictable in fickle English weather. Moreover, this leg of the ferry operation would be flown without radio guidance, in small groups, relying solely on experience and paper charts. Many sensed that this was no training mission.

The ferry flight on 12 November appeared a logistical transfer but was, in truth, a perilous undertaking in appalling weather. RAF St Eval, on the rugged southwestern coast of England, served as a critical staging base for transatlantic and African ferry operations. The orders were clear: take off from Norfolk, fly south across England, land at RAF St Eval, refuel, and prepare for the next stage – a long flight over the sea to Gibraltar and then onward to airfields near Oran or Algiers such as Tafaroui and Maison Blanche.

At RAF St Eval, more awaited them than fuel. Final technical checks were carried out, weather forecasts reviewed, and crews briefed with new coordinates, instructions, and waiting periods. The ferry route had to be flown in stages, in formation, and under strict coordination. Small mistakes could have catastrophic consequences. Once they left England, there would be no turning back: navigational errors, poor weather, or mechanical failure could all prove fatal.

The upcoming flight was treated with utmost seriousness. The planning was tight; letters home were written in haste; aircraft were inspected; maps studied. For Don, who had already flown over Japan during the Doolittle Raid, this did not feel like an escape from danger – it was another duty, another chapter in a war that allowed no pause. He had deliberately chosen not to remain in the US as an instructor, as some other Doolittle Raiders did. He wanted to keep flying, keep contributing, keep fighting.

Because the flight to North Africa meant a permanent transfer, the men of the 319th Bomb Group took all their personal belongings aboard their B-26s. They would soon be stationed at a new base in an unknown war zone, far from England – and anything not taken along risked being lost forever. For men like Don, this was a final chance to bring a small part of their familiar world with them to the front. In the days before departure, they packed carefully: an extra set of underwear and socks, shaving gear, soap and toothbrush, some stationery and envelopes, photographs of loved ones, perhaps a Bible or a small prayer book, and a few keepsakes. Some took diaries or books to read along the way. The more practical among them added tins of meat or chocolate, extra cigarettes, or matches, knowing that supplies in Africa could be scarce.

The luggage was stowed inside the aircraft, usually near the crew positions or within easy reach in case of emergency. The B-26 was no transport plane and offered little comfort, so bags were small, often tied with ropes or straps to the fuselage. Navigators and copilots wedged their maps, tools, and notes among their personal items. For Don it was likely no different. His gear went aboard with him, carefully chosen with the awareness that it might accompany him for months or longer.

Yet the act was more than practical – it was ritual. By taking their belongings, the men of the 319th BG gave their mission a human face. They were not anonymous figures in grey machines, but sons, brothers, and fathers who carried with them small fragments of home – a bridge between the familiar and the front. For Don, it was a symbolic gesture. On 12 November 1942, he took off from RAF Attlebridge, his aircraft loaded with fuel, navigation data, and that one small bag of memories. What it contained, we may never know. But the thought that his final journey carried a piece of home makes his story all the more personal.

After the 319th Bomb Group's departure, RAF Horsham St Faith became a permanent base for the US 8th Air Force. The 2nd Air Division stationed B-24 Liberators there, and the base grew into a key hub within the American network in England. After the war, RAF Horsham St. Faith remained in RAF use for several years. In the 1960s, the site was converted into what is now Norwich International Airport. Several original buildings survived, including the control tower, which today forms part of a small memorial site. RAF Attlebridge was eventually decommissioned.

Shortly before their scheduled departure, ten crews of the 319th Bombardment Group at RAF Attlebridge were briefed on the prevailing weather conditions. The crucial meeting took place in the early afternoon, as the men made their final preparations for the flight to RAF St Eval.

The conditions that day, around 1400 hours, were far from favourable. Reports from nearby RAF Coltishall indicated light and variable winds, thick cloud cover merging into mist, and a temperature of only 7°C. The pilots were warned about severely limited visibility and the very real danger of ice formation on wings and engines, especially during take-off and at higher altitudes.* Even the seemingly light winds could alter the course of the heavily loaded B-26 Marauders – aircraft known for their power but also their demanding and sometimes treacherous flying characteristics.

* The historical weather reports were obtained from the Met Office National Meteorological Library and Archive (UK).

The briefing emphasised the seriousness of the mission. Navigators were told to review their calculations, and pilots were urged to remain constantly alert and monitor every instrument closely. A tense silence settled over the room. No man underestimated the risks. Everyone knew that the journey to North Africa began here – but no one could be certain where it would end.

Lieutenant Thomas Griffin – like Don, a veteran of the Doolittle Raid – later described their final meeting in his memoirs:

> I had the duty – and the honour – of driving Don to his B-26 that morning in a jeep. It was only a short ride, but it felt heavy with meaning. Don sat beside me, calm, his eyes fixed on the misty horizon.
>
> 'How do you feel, Don?' I asked as we drove slowly across the rain-soaked field.
>
> He smiled faintly. 'Ready enough. It's not the first time I've taken a leap into the dark.'
>
> We both understood the reference. He was thinking of Tokyo. Of April. Of the mission we had both survived.
>
> 'But this time,' he added, 'at least we know where we're going. It's just the path that's just as treacherous.'
>
> When we reached his aircraft – a B-26 Marauder he had named SNAFU, serial number 41-17751 – Don paused for a moment. His hand rested on the nose of the plane. An ironic name, perhaps, but fitting: 'Situation Normal – All Fouled Up.'
>
> I wished him a safe flight. We shook hands. His grip was firm. His gaze steady. It was the last time I saw him.

Chapter 20

The Last Entry

The weather on their day of departure was anything but ideal, as reported by several stations across southern England. Around 1400 hours, RAF Coltishall recorded a temperature of only 7°C. Near RAF Wyton, in the region where one of the aircraft would crash, it was even colder – around 4°C.* Such conditions posed a serious hazard for the Marauders, notorious for their critical flight behaviour. During the final briefing pilots were warned about potential icing on wings and engines, and the danger of disorientation in poor visibility.

On that grey November afternoon ten B-26 Marauders began their take-off run one after another, their twin engines thundering across the wet concrete of RAF Attlebridge. The main runway from which they departed, designated 09/27, faced west-southwest and was used jointly by both the RAF and the USAAF. Most of the aircraft belonged to the 319th Bomb Group's 439th Bombardment Squadron. Because of the bad weather, the aircraft at Horsham St Faith remained grounded; their departure was postponed until conditions improved.

Soon after departure, the formation disappeared into heavy cloud. The weather deteriorated rapidly – visibility dropped to almost nothing, and the carefully planned pattern of aircraft began to break apart. Within minutes, contact between crews was lost. Navigators, confined to their small compartments, struggled to maintain their bearings using instruments and dead reckoning alone. The risk of collision – or of straying fatally from the intended route – grew by the minute.

Don's Marauder, SNAFU, serial number 41-17751, was among the first to encounter trouble. Around 1500 hours, it plunged at high speed into the fields near Abbots Ripton, close to RAF Alconbury in Cambridgeshire.

---

* The historical weather reports were obtained from the Met Office National Meteorological Library and Archive (UK).

Captain Smith's aircraft was not the only loss that tragic day. Other planes were forced to divert to improvised landing fields, and some sustained damage during emergency landings. The most disastrous events, apart from the crash of Don's plane, occurred when two aircraft lost their bearings completely and – unknowingly – crossed the English Channel into occupied France. There, they were detected by German radar stations and intercepted by Luftwaffe fighters. One aircraft was shot down near Cherbourg. Among the dead was Captain Frank Tuttle, commanding officer of the 439th Bomb Squadron. Another carried Lieutenant Colonel Alvord Rutherford, commander of the entire 319th Bomb Group.

The full extent of the disaster became clear only hours later. The 439th Bombardment Squadron lost eighteen men and five B-26 Marauders that day. Captain Donald Smith was one of the five pilots who never returned. The chaos of that day marked a tragic turning point – not only for the unit but also for the operational future of the 319th Bombardment Group in North Africa. For the families of Captain Smith and his crew, there remained only the bitter realisation that he – having already survived the Doolittle Raid – had lost his life during what was meant to be a routine transfer, far from the front, but no less deadly.

On board B-26 Marauder 41-17751 were six crew members:

- Captain Donald G. Smith, pilot
- Lieutenant William T. Isenor, co-pilot
- Lieutenant Ray W. Henslee, navigator
- Sergeant Carroll F. Salter, bombardier
- Sergeant Laverne Helpingstine, radio operator and gunner
- Sergeant Robert E. Richter, flight engineer and gunner

All six men were killed in the crash.

The remains of the crew were recovered by rescue teams from the nearby RAF Alconbury. Although precise details of the recovery operation are not known, it is likely that the bodies were first identified and prepared for transfer at that base. They were then, under the supervision of Captain Joseph B. Ramsey Jr. of the 93rd Bombardment Group, transported to the American section of Brookwood Military Cemetery, southwest of London. The transfer took place on 13 November 1942. During the war, Brookwood served as the central burial site for American servicemen who died in southern Great Britain.

The formal handling of Donald G. Smith's death continued with equal precision and detachment. On 13 November 1942, the day after the crash, an official embalmer's case report was completed. The document recorded his name, rank, service number, and unit, reducing a combat-trained pilot and Doolittle Raider to a sequence of administrative fields. The cause of death was entered without elaboration: *plane crash*. No personal history followed, no account of the flight, no acknowledgement of the life that had ended – only the clinical necessities of wartime procedure.

The report focused instead on the physical aftermath. It detailed the embalming process, the quantities of fluid administered, and the preparation of the body for burial. In the remarks section, a single sentence stood out for its stark intimacy: the casket bottom was lined with sawdust, the remains saturated with formalin, wrapped in a blanket, and covered with a sheet. It was a final act of care, carried out efficiently and without ceremony, far removed from the violence that had preceded it.

Together with the casualty message sent to Washington, the embalmer's report illustrates the final transformation of Donald G. Smith from living airman to official record. His death was processed quickly, methodically, and impersonally – yet behind these forms lay a young man of 24, a husband and father, whose life had ended abruptly on an English field. The paperwork closed the case, but it could not contain the human loss that followed.

Within forty-eight hours of the crash, the loss was reduced to lines of type and transmitted across the Atlantic. On 14 November 1942, an official US Army casualty message reached Washington, listing Captain Donald G. Smith and the five men of his crew as dead. The report was terse and clinical. It recorded traumatic shock and severe burns as the causes of death and described the event simply as an aircraft crash, administratively attributed to Alconbury. There was no mention of enemy action, no narrative of the final moments, no trace of the lives behind the names. In the language of the wartime bureaucracy, six men ceased to be individuals and became entries in a register. Yet behind that impersonal message lay the violent end of SNAFU, the destruction of an entire crew, and the irreversible moment at which Donald G. Smith's journey – from the prairies of South Dakota to the skies over England – came to an abrupt and final close.

After the war, the US government offered families the option of repatriating their loved ones' remains. The family of Captain Donald G.

Smith chose to have him reinterred in his home state of South Dakota. On 21 August, 1948, a burial service was held at Pine Slope Cemetery in Belle Fourche, Block C, Lot 14, Grave 4. There, amid the prairie landscape where he had grown up, Captain Smith found his final resting place. His grave is still maintained and visited today – by relatives, local residents, and historians who continue to honour his story.

Earlier, on 23 October 1942, Don had hand-written a letter to his parents. It would be the last thing they would ever hear from their son.

> #3
> A.P.O. 3052
> 23 October, 1942
>
> Dear Family,
>
> Just a short note in case the other letter hasn't arrived yet or has been delayed. I wanted you to know that everything is fine with your son. I haven't received any mail yet, but expect to in a few days. From Marie's letters you probably know more about how your granddaughter is growing than I do.
>
> I wish we could all be together for Thanksgiving, but I guess we'll have to wait until next year, after we've taken care of Adolf & Co.
>
> Have they started calling up married men back home yet – like Harry and Harold? I suppose I wouldn't recognise the old town now, with all the boys either in the Army or working at airplane plants on the coast.
>
> Not much more news; I'll close for now, wishing that everyone at home stays well. When you write, let me know how Mugs is doing. Let him run across the dining room floor for me again.
>
> As always, your loving son,
> Don

The notation A.P.O. 3052 on Don Smith's letter of 23 October 1942, refers to the military postal address assigned to the 319th Bombardment Group

(Medium) during its temporary stationing in England. This Army Post Office code identified the group's headquarters and was also used by its component squadrons, including Don's 439th Bomb Squadron. At that time, A.P.O. 3052 was active at two locations: RAF Horsham St Faith, where the Group Headquarters was based, and RAF Attlebridge, where the 439th and parts of the 440th Squadrons were temporarily quartered.

The use of such coded postal addresses was intended to conceal the exact whereabouts of American forces while still allowing families in the United States to send mail through the military postal system. Letters often took long and uncertain routes through field post offices, censorship checkpoints, and overseas transit depots – with frequent delays or even losses along the way.

As we noted earlier, the small number '3' in the upper-left corner of Don's letter was written by his own hand. By simply adding a number to each letter, Don gave his parents a small measure of reassurance. It helped them keep the correspondence organised, but it also silently testified that he was still writing – still safe, still thinking of them. This one, marked '#3', was his third personal letter since arriving in England. Though it was just a number, it meant much more: a sign of life, a quiet bridge of affection and hope in an uncertain world.

For his parents, that small handwritten digit was more than routine. It was comfort – proof that Don still lived in their thoughts and that he, despite the distance, had not let go of home. Each numbered envelope was, in its own way, a fragile symbol of love, continuity, and endurance amid the chaos of war.

Chapter 21

Analysis of the Crash

The Individual Deceased Personnel Files (IDPFs) for Captain Donald G. Smith and his crew, obtained from the National Archives and Records Administration (NARA) in the United States, provides the most authoritative account of the crash and its aftermath. The location of the crash is given as Abbots Ripton, a village near the perimeter of RAF Alconbury. The phrase 'near this field' is used, implying that rather than the impact being on the airfield itself, it was several hundred metres beyond it. Some reports mention a 'hill' or 'obstruction', but the surrounding terrain is largely flat. It is more plausible that the aircraft struck a gently rising slope, a railway embankment, or a line of trees that was misjudged in the near-zero visibility. However, archival inquiries reveal that train services were not disrupted at the time, effectively ruling out the theory that the aircraft hit the embankment.

Local oral tradition has long pointed to the fields around Hill View and Pleasant Hill, north of Wild Goose Leys Farm near Abbots Ripton, as the likely crash area. Despite these persistent accounts, no definitive physical evidence has yet been identified. Future research – combining detailed analysis of wartime aerial photographs, targeted soil investigation, and the careful evaluation of eyewitness testimony – may eventually succeed in pinpointing the exact location where the aircraft came down.

In support of this ongoing effort, Lord de Ramsey, whose estate encompasses much of the Abbots Ripton area, has expressed his willingness to cooperate fully with further investigation. His support ensures that any future research can be conducted with both access and respect for the land involved. Moreover, a local researcher was informed by an associate of Lord de Ramsey that the aircraft is believed to have come down near Wild Goose Leys, a statement that aligns closely with long-standing local accounts and reinforces this area as the most credible focus for continued study.

The location of the crash indicates a deviation from the intended route. Instead of being on a southwest course towards Cornwall, the crash site, just a few hundred metres from RAF Alconbury, is roughly 15.5km east of the direct line from Attlebridge to St Eval. The total distance between Attlebridge and Alconbury is about 110km.

Given the weather and the number of other aircraft forced to make emergency landings that day, it is plausible that Donald Smith was also attempting to land at RAF Alconbury. Tragically, he did not reach the runway. The crash site near Abbots Ripton, just outside the base perimeter, suggests a controlled descent in near zero visibility.

All crew members were killed instantly. The impact was catastrophic: the aircraft was completely destroyed, and several bodies were so badly burned or damaged that visual identification was extremely difficult. The wreckage was quickly removed after the crash. No photographs are known to exist, no crater is visible on subsequent wartime aerial imagery, and no detailed record has been located – neither in US National Archives (NARA) nor in UK National Archives, the RAF Air Historical Branch, or local British repositories. Only a handful of fragmentary reports briefly note what occurred.

The crash of SNAFU stands as a tragic but revealing window into the hazards of wartime aviation. It illustrates how even the most skilled and experienced crews – men like Captain Donald G. Smith, who had once flown from the deck of the USS *Hornet* towards Tokyo – could be lost when extreme weather, limited technology, and human vulnerability converged in a fatal moment of misjudgement and chance.

However, another story has persisted over the years. According to this theory, Don was not 'accidentally' heading for RAF Alconbury, but was intentionally sent there for a specific purpose. The reason: on 13 November 1942 – the day after the crash – King George VI was scheduled to visit RAF Alconbury to meet American airmen and inspect their aircraft. Some have speculated that Smith's brand-new B-26 Marauder might have been chosen to represent the type to the royal party – a public introduction of the advanced aircraft to the British monarchy.

While intriguing, this theory remains unproven. No official documents or orders have surfaced linking Smith or his aircraft to the royal visit. Nor is there evidence that the 319th Bomb Group was involved in the event. Moreover, there is no indication that Smith's plane ever reached

Alconbury's runway; it crashed nearby, possibly while attempting an approach or final course correction.

Additions and Insights

Documents from the USAAF indicate that the aircraft went down in the immediate vicinity of RAF Alconbury. Through various channels I have attempted to gain access to the archives of RAF Alconbury from that period, but so far nothing has been found concerning wartime records. Nevertheless, I remain convinced that the answer to the precise crash site may lie within those archives. Should any reader of this book succeed in obtaining access to these materials, I encourage them to investigate further. Your contribution in solving this mystery would be of great value. It is possible that the exact crash location was recorded in files of the British Home Guard or local police – sources I have not been able to consult.

An internal report dated 11 December 1942, written by Bill Monroe, the Public Relations Officer (PRO) of the 319th Bomb Group, contains a striking passage about the ill-fated departure of the ten aircraft from RAF Attlebridge. As PRO, Monroe was responsible for documenting key events within the unit, maintaining internal reports, and collecting information for publication. His notes today represent a valuable historical source.

Monroe recorded:

> The weather was bad today, so we could not take off. But the planes at Attlebridge took off despite the fog and now they're scattered all over England. At least one plane has crashed and burned. It was Captain Don Smith's. I heard his ship was flying partly on instruments and partly on sight when they hit a hill and exploded.

In official USAAF documents, the loss of Captain Donald G. Smith and his crew on 12 November 1942 is recorded as having occurred during a 'training flight in England'. This classification is striking. Don's aircraft was clearly part of the northern ferry route of the operation and was about to enter an active combat zone. Yet his fatal flight, like those of his five crewmembers, was officially logged as a 'training flight'. Was this merely an administrative convention, whereby all flights over the United Kingdom were classified as training until entering the operational area? Or was it a deliberate choice to conceal the true nature of the mission, given the strict secrecy surrounding Operation Torch?

The contrast with reports of other crews departing RAF Attlebridge that day is notable; they are listed in records as 'killed during an operational mission from England'. The discrepancy suggests that Don's case may have been intentionally categorised differently – perhaps to downplay the nature of the mission, or because the loss occurred on British soil rather than over the sea.

As discussed earlier, it can be assumed that Captain Donald Smith was attempting an emergency landing at RAF Alconbury. The presumed course of his B-26 Marauder would have followed a south-southwesterly direction, suggesting that he may have been trying to reach the airfield from the northeast.

Earlier in the war, RAF Alconbury had grass runways that could be used in several directions, the most common of which ran northeast to southwest and began just south of the village of Abbots Ripton. By November 1942, however, the station had been almost completely rebuilt to the RAF 'Class A' standard, with three concrete runways arranged in a triangular pattern: Runway 06/24 (northeast–southwest), Runway 12/30 (southeast–northwest), and Runway 18/36 (north–south). None of these new strips was perfectly aligned with Abbots Ripton, though the northeast end of Runway 06 lay closest to the village, extending towards the open farmland immediately south of it.

The available evidence suggests that the aircraft came down shortly after 3.00 pm, just south of Abbots Ripton, possibly in the area around Wild Goose Leys Farm, between Pleasant Hill and the northern perimeter of RAF Alconbury. This position lies broadly in line with the approach to Runway 06, which, as noted, may indicate that Don was attempting to reach the field from the northeast. In the dense fog of that morning, it is likely that the B-26 descended too low and struck the ground short of the airfield. The precise cause of the impact – whether due to a loss of altitude in poor visibility or a collision with an unseen obstacle – remains uncertain.

Contemporary sources refer to the farm in question as Wild Goose Leys Farm/Cottage. According to the Individual Deceased Personnel File

(IDPF) of Captain Smith, the aircraft 'crashed at Abbots Ripton'. This description can only refer to the area immediately north of RAF Alconbury, where the village bordered the airfield's perimeter. Of the three concrete runways completed by late 1942, only Runway 06/24 extended to within a short distance of Abbots Ripton; the other two strips, 12/30 and 18/36, were positioned further south and did not approach the village at all.

It therefore does seem likely that Don was attempting to reach Runway 06, the principal northeast–southwest strip of the station. At approximately 1,600m in length, this was by far the longest and strongest runway at Alconbury – designed to accommodate heavy bombers such as the B-24 Liberator. For a fully loaded B-26 Marauder on a ferry flight, carrying maximum fuel and equipment, the shorter auxiliary runways would have been insufficient for a safe landing. The wording in the IDPF thus supports this assumption.

Medical information contained in the IDPF indicates that the crew suffered traumatic shock and third-degree burns, consistent with a violent impact followed by fire or explosion. Such injuries suggest that the aircraft struck an obstruction or the ground at considerable speed, igniting its fuel load upon impact. In the dense fog of that morning the crew may have believed they were correctly aligned with the runway; it is likely that the aircraft was flying at low altitude – approximately 300 to 500ft – the crew believing they were already close to the runway. The B-26 was known as a demanding aircraft to land, requiring a high approach speed of about 145mph (230km/h). With a heavy fuel load for the ferry flight, even a small misjudgement in altitude could have catastrophic results. It is probable that the landing gear was already down and the crew were attempting a visual approach through the fog when the aircraft struck an obstacle and exploded.

The bodies were recovered by personnel from RAF Alconbury and the US Graves Registration Service. The remains were almost certainly transferred to RAF Alconbury, the nearest air base with an American presence and mortuary facilities. The first registration was carried out there by the Graves Registration Service, which prepared the bodies for transport. It was standard practice for victims of crashes in the surrounding area to be taken to Alconbury for identification and preliminary care. From this base, the caskets departed for Surrey under the escort of Captain J. H. Brown Jr. of the 93rd Bomb Group, which was stationed at RAF Alconbury at the time of the accident.

Because of the nature of the injuries, embalming was impossible; the official forms stated simply, 'Impossible due to nature of death.' An emergency procedure was therefore used: the caskets were lined with sawdust, the remains treated with formalin, and then wrapped in blankets and sheets. Because of the severe burns, fingerprints could not be taken, so identification was made through personal effects, dog tags, and official Air Corps documents. Several personal items were found in Smith's uniform, including a photograph, identification cards, and US Army Air Forces papers that confirmed his identity without doubt. The remaining personal effects were secured separately.

Among the personal effects recorded by the US Army Effects Bureau was a remarkable assortment of foreign currencies. The official inventory included French, Belgian, Luxembourg, and Italian notes, together with German Marks, Dutch Guilders, Greek Drachma, and even small amounts of Russian Rubles and Scandinavian Kronen. Such diversity was not unusual among American airmen stationed on RAF bases in Britain during the months preceding Operation Torch. At that stage, the US Army Air Forces relied heavily on RAF experience in escape and evasion procedures, and British instructors – often attached to MI9 – distributed sample currency from occupied and neutral countries for training purposes. It is likely that Don's collection originated from this cooperation or through informal exchanges with RAF officers. Whether intended for instruction, survival, or simple curiosity, the presence of these notes offers a tangible glimpse into the shared preparation and Allied partnership that shaped the early American air operations in Europe.

On 12 and 13 November, the first administrative reports were prepared. The Quartermaster Graves Registration confirmed the deaths and drafted telegrams for Headquarters SOS ETOUSA and the US War Department in Washington. The caskets were marked temporarily and made ready for transport.

Chapter 22

Burial, Reburial, and Remembrance

Two days later, on 14 November 1942 at 14:00 hours, the funeral took place at Brookwood American Military Cemetery in Surrey. The ceremony was conducted with full military honours and led by Captain J.H. Brown Jr. of the 93rd Bomb Group, which was stationed at RAF Alconbury at the time. Captain Donald G. Smith was laid to rest in Plot E, Row 6, Grave 7, beneath a simple wooden cross and between his crew members, Corporal Laverne Helpingstine (Grave 6) and Corporal Robert Richter (Grave 8). The men who had fallen together were laid to rest side by side – a quiet tribute to their shared service and sacrifice. Administrative confirmation of the burial followed in June 1943.

After the war, during the large-scale repatriation programme carried out by the American Graves Registration Service, Captain Donald G. Smith's remains were returned to the United States. He was reinterred with full military honour on 21 August 1948 at Pine Slope Cemetery in Belle Fourche, South Dakota. His grave is located in Block C, Lot 14, Grave 3. He had finally returned to his home state – to the land of his youth, surrounded by the landscape and community that had shaped his family.

Of the entire crew of B-26 Marauder 41-17751 'SNAFU' (439th Bomb Squadron, 319th Bomb Group), only two members remain buried on British soil:

- Lieutenant Ray W. Henslee – buried at the Cambridge American Cemetery, Plot F, Row 7, Grave 73.
- Staff Sergeant Carroll R. Salter – buried at the same cemetery, Plot D, Row 6, Grave 47.

What makes this case especially complex is that the facts surrounding the accident have been misreported at least five times over the years in various publications. Errors – ranging from incorrect dates and locations to mistaken crew assignments – made the investigation exceedingly difficult. Only through renewed analysis of primary sources, including the IDPFs and the records of the Graves Registration Service, could the true circumstances finally be reconstructed.

Although Staff Sergeant Carroll R. Salter and Lieutenant Ray W. Henslee are both buried at the Cambridge American Cemetery in England, their names are incorrectly listed in some French publications as having perished at Les Pieux, in the Manche department near Cherbourg, France. These French references mistakenly identify them as victims of a crash in that area, when Salter and Henslee were actually members of the crew of 'SNAFU'.

The confusion likely arose because on that same day two other aircraft of the 439th Bomb Squadron *did* crash near Les Pieux. France. Their loss was later incorrectly associated with the overall casualty list of 12 November 1942, leading to the erroneous inclusion of Salter and Henslee's names in French records.

This confusion complicated the search for the true crash site of 'SNAFU'. However, the Individual Deceased Personnel Files (IDPF) held by the US National Archives (NARA) clearly confirm that both men died in England, leaving no doubt about the actual location of the accident.

What makes this case particularly puzzling is the near-total absence of other official documentation. Neither the US National Archives (NARA) nor their British counterparts contain a complete crash file for Captain Smith and his crew. Whereas other losses of the 319th Bomb Group were carefully recorded, this incident seems to have slipped through the administrative net. As several archivists have put it: 'You've stumbled upon a mystery.' Indeed, it remains so. Only the death certificates, burial records, and local testimonies preserve the memory of what happened.

Repeated requests for Missing Air Crew Reports, RAF crash reports and other official documentation have yielded nothing. With the help of dedicated researchers across archives, forums, and social media, I eventually managed to locate a handful of original American records – enough to reconstruct the event with reasonable certainty. Still, it became clear that nearly all previous publications about this crash contained factual errors: from incorrect dates and locations to misidentified crew lists. This underlines the importance of re-examining every available source and resisting the temptation to take earlier accounts at face value.

One category of records that could not be consulted for this study are the archives of the Home Guard and local police units that operated in the area at the time. These organisations were often the first to arrive at crash sites and maintained detailed logs that might contain valuable information about the precise location and circumstances of such incidents. I contacted the Imperial War Museum at Duxford and its archival department on three occasions, seeking assistance in locating any surviving Home Guard or police reports concerning the crash near Abbots Ripton. As one of Britain's foremost institutions dedicated to the preservation of wartime heritage, the museum seemed the most logical point of contact. Regrettably, no reply was ever received. It remains entirely possible that within them lie the missing fragments that could shed new light on the fate of Captain Don Smith and his crew.

I wish to express my sincere gratitude to the many individuals, local historians, and organisations in Abbots Ripton and the wider Huntingdon area for their generosity, interest, and genuine willingness to assist in tracing the crash site of Captain Smith's aircraft. Their courtesy, enthusiasm, and sense of shared remembrance made this stage of the investigation an unexpectedly uplifting experience.

While the 93rd Bomb Group was stationed at RAF Alconbury, His Majesty King George VI paid his first visit to an Eighth Air Force base on 13 November 1942. During the visit, he was shown the B-24 *Teggie Ann*, then considered to be the 93rd's leading aircraft.

On 6 December 1942, most of the group was transferred to the Twelfth Air Force in North Africa to support the Operation Torch landings. It is possible that wartime records preserved either in the 93rd Bomb Group's archives or in RAF Alconbury's own station files may contain references to the fatal accident of Captain Donald G. Smith, whose Marauder probably crashed near the airfield just one day before the king's visit. So far, however, no such documentation has been found.

I am equally grateful to the archivists and staff members in both the United States and the United Kingdom who supported these inquiries – particularly those in regional archives across Britain, whose cooperation and diligence proved invaluable in the search to pinpoint the exact crash location. Although the investigation ultimately remained inconclusive, their professionalism and goodwill were deeply appreciated.

It is thanks to the combined efforts of all these people that the story of Captain Donald G. Smith and his crew continues to resonate – both in the landscape where their fate unfolded and in the collective memory of those who still care to remember.

Chapter 23

The Message Reaches America

On 27 November 1942, a Western Union messenger arrived at the home of Marie Crouch Smith in San Antonio, Texas. He carried a telegram from the War Department in Washington, D.C. Like so many delivered across the United States during the war, it was brief, formal, and devastating in its restraint. Its language followed a fixed formula – one designed to convey loss without detail, sympathy without explanation:

> The Secretary of War desires me to express his deep regret that your husband, Captain Donald G. Smith, has been reported killed in an airplane accident over Western Europe…

No further information was provided. There was no date, no location, no account of the circumstances. With those few lines, Marie's life was irrevocably altered.

News of Don's death soon reached his parents, Arthur and Laura Smith, in Belle Fourche, South Dakota. For the town, the war was no longer an abstract conflict reported in newspapers or heard on the radio. It had claimed one of its own. Belle Fourche felt the loss deeply. A memorial service was held shortly after the telegram arrived, attended by friends, classmates, and townspeople who had watched Don grow up. Another remembrance followed at his former school in Brookings, where teachers and students gathered to honour his life and service.

When Don's remains were returned to the United States in 1948, a final funeral service was held at Pine Slope Cemetery in Belle Fourche. He was laid to rest with full military honours, the long arc of his journey – from prairie childhood to wartime pilot – finally brought home.

His memory endured locally in other ways. The senior class of 1943 at Belle Fourche High School dedicated their *Bronc Annual*, the school's yearbook named after its Bronc mascot, to Captain Smith's memory. Decades later, the town would again publicly honour him. On 18 April 2001, Belle Fourche proclaimed an official 'Captain Donald G. Smith Day', marking the anniversary of the Doolittle Raid and reaffirming his place in the town's history.

For Laura Bolte Smith, however, remembrance did not bring understanding. In the years following the war, she began searching for answers about her son's final moments. Beyond the initial War Department telegram stating only that he had been 'killed in an airplane accident over Western Europe', the family had received nothing more.

In January 1946, Laura wrote to Colonel C. Ross Greening, one of Don's former comrades from the Doolittle Raid. She had recently received a small memorial booklet titled *In Remembrance of Donald G. Smith*, and her letter combined gratitude with unresolved grief. In it, she revealed that Arthur Smith had died just six weeks after Don, unable to endure the loss. 'There was never any greater love between father and son than between those two,' she wrote, 'and my husband wasn't able to accept Don's death.'

Laura also confessed how little she still knew. She did not know whether the crash had occurred during a training flight or in combat, whether others had died with him, or even precisely where the accident had taken place. Her words reveal that the search for clarity – the need to understand what had happened – began almost immediately, driven by a family left with unanswered questions.

Colonel Greening replied on 24 March 1947. He confirmed that Don's B-26 had crashed in England as a result of bad weather, during a period when several aircraft were lost under similar conditions in preparation for Operation Torch. He wrote that the aircraft had struck a 'hillside', a description that does not align with the largely flat farmland near Abbots Ripton, close to RAF Alconbury.

From that point onward, uncertainty became part of the story. Conflicting place names, vague descriptions, and the absence of comprehensive official records – apart from the individual IDPF file – have long obscured the circumstances of the crash. Even established military institutions and archival repositories have been unable to produce definitive documentation identifying the precise crash site or reconstructing the final moments of the flight.

The result is an uncomfortable truth. Despite years of research, comparison of sources, and reconstruction of events, the full answers sought by the family remain elusive. The loss of Captain Donald G. Smith stands not only as a personal tragedy, but also as an example of how war, in its scale and urgency, can leave even its own records incomplete.

This case remains unresolved – unfinished work, left for future researchers. Every effort has been made to uncover the facts, to reconcile documents with terrain, memory with record. Yet some questions persist, suspended between what was written down and what was lived.

Appendix

The Streeter and Gregory families belong to long-established English lineages of people who migrated to North America during the early colonial period. The Streeter name originates in southern England, and the family's presumed patriarch, Stephen Streeter, settled in Massachusetts around 1639–40. As a result, the Streeter family has been present in what would become the United States for nearly four centuries. The Gregory family, likewise of English origin – with possible Scottish branches – follows a comparable colonial trajectory. Members of the family arrived in the Virginia colony as early as about 1620, giving the Gregory name a history in America that also spans more than 400 years. Both families are thus deeply rooted in the nation's past and played roles, generation after generation, in the country's development – from early colonisation to the westward pioneer movement into the Midwest and the Great Plains during the nineteenth century.

After Donald and his sister Grace were placed in an orphanage, Don's father, Charles Levi Gregory – known as Chas – relocated, according to the 1925 South Dakota census, to Madison, South Dakota. There he worked as a hired farm labourer on a small holding. Chas remarried and had two additional children. Later records indicate that he subsequently moved to the states of Oregon and Washington. After the Second World War, he was employed by a telephone company in Oregon, reportedly associated with either his wife or his son. Chas Gregory died in Spokane, Washington, on 27 September 1967.

Donald's older sister, Dorothy Gregory, lived to the remarkable age of 103. She passed away on 6 July 2019 in Miller, South Dakota. Dorothy worked alongside her husband on their farm for many years. When they retired from farming in 1977 and moved into town, she continued working in various occupations: as a cleaner, in the catalogue stores run by her son, and later in a pizzeria. She did not retire fully until the age of 93.

George, Donald's older brother, also relocated to Oregon, where he worked as a mechanic in a garage. He died in Ferry County, Washington, on 18 July 1982.

Donald's youngest sister, Grace, died on 24 August 2009 in Springfield, Oregon. She began her career as a schoolteacher in Oneida, South Dakota, and later worked at what was then known as the Springfield Medical Building, a local medical centre in Springfield, Oregon, whose name changed in later years. She subsequently retired from a position in the finance department of the city of Eugene, Oregon.

In conversations with family members, I have been informed that Chas maintained contact with his children Dorothy and George after Grace and Donald were placed in the orphanage. Whether Grace and Donald themselves had contact with their father after leaving the orphanage – and, in Grace's case, after Donald's death – remains unclear; I have found no documentary evidence to confirm such contact. It has been stated, however, that George, Dorothy, and Grace did remain in contact with one another following the death of their brother Donald.

Arthur Smith died on 24 December 1942, just six weeks after Donald's death. There is little doubt that he died of grief following the loss of his son. Multiple sources, including written testimony, attest to this.

Laura Bolte Smith died on 3 September 1963 in Belle Fourche, South Dakota. At Pine Slope Cemetery in Belle Fourche, Arthur Smith is buried beside her. Donald rests to the right of Arthur, while Mae Jean lies to Laura's left. All four are interred in Block C, Lot 14.

Marie Crouch, Donald's widow, died on 1 May 2005 in Texas. After Donald's death, she remarried. Their daughter, Donna Marie Smith, passed away on 17 October 2001 in Batesville, Arkansas.

Grandmother Nancy Andrew died on 5 March 1940 in Kingsbury County, South Dakota. All of her children, with the exception of her daughter Eva, died after the Second World War. Clarence Streeter died on 27 April 1960 in Kingsbury County; Harry Streeter on 18 October 1948 in Lake Preston, Kingsbury County; William Streeter on 20 June 1945 in Riverside, Riverside County, California; Flora Streeter on 24 April 1952 in Lake Preston; and Jessie Streeter on 27 August 1972 in Gettysburg, Potter County, South Dakota.

Mae Streeter died on 7 March 1976 in Carthage, Miner County, South Dakota, and Hazel Streeter on 4 September 1967 in Dell Rapids,

Minnehaha County, South Dakota. Both Mae and Hazel continued teaching at the Streeter School, located on land owned by their father, Clarence Streeter – the eldest brother of Eva.

The parents of Chas Gregory were both born in the American Midwest in the years following the Civil War. His father Edward (Don's grandfather) was born on 1 February 1863 in Wisconsin and died on 23 October 1952 in San Bernardino, California, having lived through nearly a century of profound social and geographic change. His mother, Edna Murphy (Don's grandmother) was born around 1867 in Iowa and passed away before 1930 in South Dakota, where she spent a significant part of her life. Together, they represent a generation shaped by westward movement, agricultural settlement, and the gradual transformation of the United States from the post-war Midwest toward the expanding West.

In the decades following the departure of the Streeter family, the landscape in Kingsbury County changed profoundly. The land on which their homestead once stood – the Streeter homestead where Captain Donald Smith was born – lay within the natural basin of Lake Thompson, a large, shallow lake in Kingsbury County, South Dakota, formed within the region's glacial prairie landscape. The lake was named after Jacob Thompson, an early settler and landowner in the area. Like so many pioneer families, the Streeters had transformed the prairie through hard labour: breaking the sod, building their homestead, raising families, and carving out a livelihood from uncertain land. During dry periods, such as the 1930s, Lake Thompson largely dried up and its bed was used as farmland and pasture – the very conditions under which generations of farmers, including the Streeters, built their lives.

From the 1980s onward, however, water levels rose steadily and dramatically. Successive years of heavy precipitation caused the lake to expand, permanently submerging large areas of surrounding agricultural land. The location of the Streeter homestead, once the birthplace of Captain Donald Smith, disappeared beneath the water during this period. What had been the product of years of labour, perseverance, and daily routine was gradually erased by a returning natural process. Where fields were once worked and buildings stood, the lake now stretches out, managed by the state of South Dakota as a recreational area used for fishing, outdoor recreation, and wildlife management. In this way, the physical trace of the homestead where Don's life began was lost, as the landscape – indifferent yet not without meaning – returned to its original, water-defined form.

Local families also preserved older oral traditions about the lake. According to family recollections, Lake Thompson last held water as early as the mid-nineteenth century, before drying out for extended periods. Such accounts, sometimes linked to events from the early frontier era, cannot be independently verified and belong more to collective memory than to documented history. What is firmly established, however, is that the land remained under cultivation well into the twentieth century, and that the later rise of the lake's water level represented a profound loss for many families. Eyewitnesses recalled how farm buildings were dismantled or moved, while others were slowly overtaken by the water. For those who lived through it, the lasting image was one of farmland and homes – shaped by generations of work – disappearing beneath the surface of the lake.

Don's life began as a deeply personal SNAFU: a situation in which everything seemed to go wrong and chaos appeared to be the norm. His childhood was marked by loss, uncertainty, and loneliness. The early death of his mother, abandonment by his father, months spent in an orphanage, and the fragmentation of his family ensured that his formative years were defined by instability and emotional deprivation. For Don, life seemed a succession of failures, each new chapter raising more questions than answers.

Yet what once appeared irreparably broken was slowly set right. Arthur and Laura Smith became far more than foster parents; they became his refuge and his home. Through their care and affection, they provided Don with what he needed most: stability, warmth, and a place to grow. They offered not only shelter, but also the freedom to pursue his ambitions and shape his future. What began as a story of chaos evolved into one of resilience and hope.

Perhaps this is the essence of Don's life journey: the understanding that even the most confused and painful circumstances can be redeemed, and that love and care can heal even the deepest wounds. His life demonstrates that a 'SNAFU' does not signify an end, but rather the possibility of a new beginning. It is a story of falling and rising again, of being lost and then found, of a future that – against all odds – ultimately found its way into the sky.

Perhaps Don chose the name ‘SNAFU’ for his aircraft deliberately. Perhaps he saw in that name a reflection of his own life: a youth marked by chaos and loss, ultimately overcome by resilience and hope. A reminder that no matter how fierce the storm, there is always a way forward.

Afterword

by Janice Evans
Daughter of Donald G. Smith's cousin

I never had the chance to meet my cousin Donald in person. He passed away long before I was old enough to ask questions about who he truly was. But his name echoed through our family like a voice from another time – a time of war, courage, and unimaginable decisions. He was 'Don', the pilot who flew across the ocean with the Doolittle Raiders and had to survive in China. A hero, certainly – but also a brother, a son, a father, and a husband. A human being.

As I grew older, I began to understand just how extraordinary his story really was. Not only because of the mission, the risks, or the honours, but above all because of what remained untold – the letters home, the silences between the lines, the absence he carried, and the absence that remained in the family after his passing.

This book has brought him to life for me – and I hope for you as well. It shows who he was, not only as a serviceman, but as a young man with ideals, responsibilities, and love in his heart. It fills in the gaps left by old photographs in dusty boxes and gives voice to the stories that were never fully told.

I am grateful to the author for the courage and dedication to reconstruct it all. For me – and for so many others – it means that Don finally has his place in the greater story. Not as a myth, but as a man.

And perhaps that is the greatest tribute we can offer someone.

Sources

Books

Chun, Clayton and Howard Gerrard (illus.), *Doolittle Raid 1942: America's First Strike Back at Japan*, Osprey Publishing, 2006.

Edwards, Sam, *The Doolittle Raid: The Untold Story of America's First Strike Against Japan*, Dutton Caliber, 2016.

Glines, Carroll V., *The Doolittle Raid*, Ballantine Books, 1964.

Glines, Carroll V., *The Doolittle Raid: America's Daring First Strike Against Japan*, Random House Children's Books, 1988.

Glines, Carroll V., *The Doolittle Raid: The Mission That Changed the War*, Smithsonian Books, 2017.

Glines, Carroll V., *The Doolittle Tokyo Raiders*, Van Nostrand Reinhold, 1967.

Glines, Carroll V., *Doolittle's Tokyo Raiders*, Van Nostrand Reinhold, 1964.

Glines, Carroll V., *Echoes of the Doolittle Raid*, Van Nostrand Reinhold, 1991.

Glines, Carroll V., *Four Came Home: The Gripping Story of the Survivors of Jimmy Doolittle's Two Doomed Raiders*, Van Nostrand Reinhold, 1969.

Goldstein, Donald M. and Carol Aiko DeShazer Dixon, *Return of the Raider: A Doolittle Raider's Story of War & Forgiveness*, Brassey's, 2007.

Greening, Ross, *Not As Briefed: From the Doolittle Raid to a German Stalag*, Texas A&M University Press, 1994.

Groom, Winston, *The Aviators: Eddie Rickenbacker, Jimmy Doolittle, Charles Lindbergh, and the Epic Age of Flight*, National Geographic, 2013.

Higbee, Paul, *The First Strike: Doolittle Raider Don Smith*, self-published.

Hoppes, Jonna Doolittle, *Jimmy Doolittle: Daredevil Aviator and Scientist*, Smithsonian Books, 2017.

Lawson, Robert L., *Target Tokyo: The Story of the Doolittle Raid*, Random House, 1943.

Lukacs, John D., *The Tokyo Raid: The First Doolittle Attack*, Da Capo Press, 2007.

Martin, Michael, *Doolittle's Tokyo Raiders: The Legendary Attack on Japan That Changed the Course of World War II*, Zenith Press, 2016.

Nelson, Craig, *The First Heroes: The Extraordinary Story of the Doolittle Raid – America's First World War II Victory*, Viking, 2002.

Nolta, George, *The Doolittle Raiders: What Heroes Do After the War*, Stackpole Books, 2015.

O'Keefe, James W., *The Other Doolittle Raid: The Rescue Mission After the Bombing of Tokyo*, Naval Institute Press, 2007.

Oldham Centennial Committee, *Oldham: Our Heritage and History, 1887–1987*, Madison, South Dakota: Leader Printing Co., 1987.

Paradis, Michel, *Last Mission to Tokyo: The Extraordinary Story of the Doolittle Raiders and Their Final Fight for Justice*, Simon & Schuster, 2020.

Rottiers, Geert, *Brave Young Men*, a reference work self-published.2024

Rottiers, Geert, *De onmogelijke vlucht*, Het Punt, 2024

Rottiers, Geert, *The Tokyo Sixteen*, Pen and Sword Books, 2025

Scott, James M., *Target Tokyo: Jimmy Doolittle and the Raid That Avenged Pearl Harbor*, W. W. Norton & Company, 2015.

Smith, Douglas V., *The Doolittle Raid and the Battle of the Coral Sea*, McFarland, 2014.

Stillwell, Paul, *Doolittle's Tokyo Raiders: The Extraordinary Story of the First American Attack on Japan*, Naval Institute Press, 2013.

Tillman, Barrett, *Jimmy Doolittle: The Commander Behind the Legend*, Regnery History, 2017.

Tillman, Barrett, *The Doolittle Raid: A 75th Anniversary Retrospective*, Osprey Publishing, 2017.

White, Thomas R. ("Doc"), MD, *Doolittle Raid Doctor*, self-published memoir.

Wukovits, John F., *Jimmy Doolittle: American Aviator*, Da Capo Press, 2003.

Other Sources

'Brush Talks' *A Journal of China* Vol.1 No.1 winter/spring 2016 p.29.

'Halsey-Doolittle Raid April 1942', General Doolittle's Report, 9 July 1942.

In the Footsteps of My Father, Doolittle Raider David Thatcher, Winter 2015–2016 by Jeff Thatcher

Donna McElroy-Hatch, the granddaughter of Lieutenant Colonel Edgar E. McElroy of Crew 13, shared memories of how her grandfather helped rescue Major Ted Lawson and Dr Thomas White from China after Lawson had recovered enough to travel. This can be found on the website of the Children of the Doolittle Raiders. https://childrenofthedoolittleraiders.com/

With thanks to the Doolittle Raid Rescue Memorial, Quzhou, China.

Online Resources

Together We Served – https://www.togetherweserved.com/
The Doolittle Raid – https://www.doolittle-raid.net
Wikipedia, several Wikipedia pages
FamilySearch – https://www.familysearch.org/en/united-states/
Find a Grave – https://www.findagrave.com/
The Hall of Valour Project – https://valor.militarytimes.com/

Various online newspapers that feature interviews and articles about the pilots who flew in the Doolittle Raid.

Facebook page The Doolittle Raid. https://www.facebook.com/profile.php?id=100093570602530

The Doolittle Raid Rescue Memorial in Quzhou, China. https://www.facebook.com/DoolittleRaidRescueMemorial

The Children of the Doolittle Raiders: https://childrenofthedoolittleraiders.com/

The author's website www.doolittle-raid.net occasionally posts updates about the pilots.

Click on 'CREWS' and then click on the respective pilot of the crew.

The Facebook page The Doolittle Raid posts daily updates also.

Acknowledgements

My deepest gratitude goes to Janice Evans, whose exceptional generosity, kindness, and unwavering support made this book possible. Throughout the entire research process, she patiently answered countless questions, shared invaluable family information, and generously granted permission to use photographs, documents, and other important archival material relating to her great-nephew, Captain Donald G. Smith. Her enthusiasm, encouragement, and willingness to help at every stage of this project have been truly remarkable. It has been a genuine privilege to work with her, and I will always be grateful for her friendship, trust, and outstanding cooperation.

My gratitude goes to Chris Brassfield, Paul Hindle, and Paul Mansfield of the Attlebridge Heritage Centre for their generous assistance and unwavering commitment to preserving the memory of RAF Attlebridge and the men of the 466th Bomb Group. Their dedication to keeping alive the remembrance of the aircrews' sacrifices ensures that history remains vivid and is passed on to younger generations. Such individuals keep the past alive in the most meaningful way. I am also deeply grateful for the interesting and insightful tour they provided, which brought the history of Attlebridge to life.

I am deeply indebted to Brenda Thompson, genealogical researcher – without her, this book would not have been possible. She shared dozens of newspaper clippings and a wealth of information about the towns and places where Donald grew up, providing the essential foundation for much of my research.

My thanks also go to Darrell and Darren Sapp, father and son, whose insights into the Streeter School and the early history of rural education in Kingsbury County were invaluable. They generously shared their knowledge of how land was divided under the Public Land Survey System, explained the practical workings of that survey framework, and provided important local perspectives on the historical presence of Lake

Thompson and other features of the surrounding landscape. For me, this was an invaluable lesson in geography, from which I learned a great deal. My sincere thanks to you both, Darrell and Darren.

My heartfelt thanks also go to South Dakota State University (SDSU) in Brookings (formerly South Dakota State College), especially to Sophie Hogan of the University Archives, the Jackrabbits football team archives, and Marianna Pavlis of the Alumni Association, whose staff offered outstanding support and helped me uncover important details about Don's college years. Their cooperation and generosity were truly exceptional.

I would like to acknowledge Dakota State University (DSU) in Madison, South Dakota – the successor to the former Eastern State Normal School – for preserving the historical records that document teacher-training activities in the 1920s, including field visits such as those described in this narrative. Publicly available archival materials helped ensure the accuracy of this section. Thank you, Abbie Steuhm,

I owe a special debt of gratitude to Jada Udager, archivist at the Tri-State Museum in Belle Fourche, South Dakota, whose generosity and professionalism made it possible for me to access Donald Smith's original letters. These letters provided an outstanding timeline of his training and early service, and without her assistance this project could never have reached its depth or accuracy. Thank you, Jada.

Warm thanks also to Janice Evans and Denise Mack, whose kindness, encouragement, and thoughtful guidance were a constant source of motivation; to Shannon Stilwell, who kindly provided me with a cherished photograph of Marie, Don's wife; and to Jordan Larkin of the Inland Northwest Special Collections at the Spokane Public Library.

My appreciation extends as well to everyone at Pen and Sword Books, whose professionalism, enthusiasm, and trust in this project have been deeply appreciated; to my editor at Pen and Sword, Karyn, whose guidance greatly improved the final manuscript; and to the team at Casemate Publishers for bringing this book to readers across the Atlantic. My sincere thanks to colleagues at both publishers, including Martin, Amy, Heather, Matthew, and John.

I am grateful to Laurie Langland, University Archivist and Archivist for the Dakotas Conference of the United Methodist Church at Dakota Wesleyan University, and to the staff of the Children's Home Society of South Dakota for their thoughtful assistance.

My thanks also go to Megan Bridge of the Northwest Museum of Arts and Culture in Spokane, my thanks also go to Cindy Chal, Chair of the Children of the Doolittle Raiders., and to the staff of Brookwood Cemetery, NARA UK, and NARA USA for their valuable help.

I gratefully acknowledge Dan Setzer, Wing Historian of the 57th Bomb Wing Association, whose knowledge of the 319th Bomb Group borders on the unbelievable.

My thanks also go to Hailey Hanzlik, Engineering Administrative Assistant for the City of Belle Fourche, who assisted me with information regarding the location of the graves and the transfer of Don's remains from Brookwood to Belle Fourche. I am likewise grateful to the staff of Brookwood Cemetery for their clear, careful, and respectful explanations. Their guidance was offered with integrity and proved to be of great value to this research.

To my sons, Niels and Mats Rottiers, who accompanied me on our journey to England – to the places where Don's final flight began and where it tragically ended. Thank you for driving me everywhere during those days in England and for making it possible to see all the places I hoped to visit. They were immensely enjoyable and deeply interesting days. Without your help, I could never have seen what I wanted to see. That the journey ultimately became a shared father-and-sons experience was an unexpected and cherished gift.

My appreciation extends to Lord De Ramsey and the staff of his estate for their kindness and cooperation, and for granting access to the land at Abbots Ripton, where the final chapter of Don's story came to an end.

My family, friends, and all those at home continually encouraged me to complete this work. My sincere thanks to Sean Evans for his correspondence and invaluable assistance in tracing the exact crash location of Don's plane. Each of the individuals and institutions mentioned here has, in their own way, contributed to the realisation of this book – and for that, I am profoundly grateful.

Finally, I would also like to sincerely thank Suzie Harrison, who works at the Cambridge American Cemetery for the American Battle Monuments Commission (ABMC), for the brief but very dignified ceremony held in memory of the two crew members of SNAFU who rest there.

Some scenes in this book, where the historical record is silent, have been reconstructed from letters, contemporary accounts, and the author's knowledge of the period to reflect events as they most likely occurred.

Photographs and letters courtesy of Janice Evans, daughter of Ruth Streeter, Don. Smith's cousin.

Appendix I

Letters

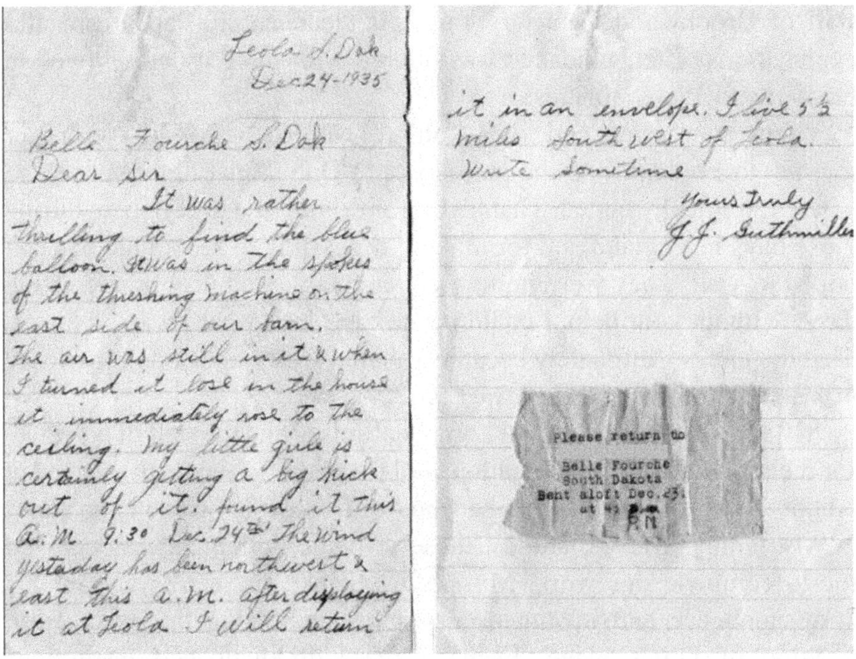

Leola S. Dak
Dec 24-1935

Belle Fourche S. Dak
Dear Sir
It was rather thrilling to find the blue balloon. It was in the spokes of the threshing machine on the east side of our barn. The air was still in it & when I turned it lose in the house it immediately rose to the ceiling. My little girl is certainly getting a big kick out of it. found it this A.M. 9:30 Dec. 24th The wind yesterday has been northwest & east this a.m. after displaying it at Leola I will return it in an envelope. I live 5½ miles South west of Leola. Write Sometime

Yours Truly
J.J. Guthmiller

Please return to
Belle Fourche
South Dakota
Sent aloft Dec.23
at 4 PM

Letter from J.J. Guthmiller of Leola, South Dakota, dated December 24, 1935, describing how he found the blue balloon released by Donald Smith in Belle Fourche during the Christmas season. Guthmiller lived about five and a half miles southwest of Leola and wrote to tell Donald of his discovery. (Private collection of Janice Evans)

Opposite: Written aboard the USS *Hornet* just days before the Doolittle Raid on 15 April 1942, this is one of the very few surviving letters from the mission. All outgoing mail was subject to strict censorship to maintain secrecy, and Don's letter was partially censored before being sent to his parents – offering a rare and human glimpse into the tense final days before the raid.

4-15-42

Dear Folks;

We have been authorized to write letters, as long as we are careful what we say, and if the censors pass it. We left in such a hurry, I didn't get a chance to write you after we were ordered away. I was lucky enough to get into San Antonio one night on the way, and while we were restricted from writing, I told Marie the next time she wrote you, she could mention I had been there. We are still on the move, so cannot give you any address where you might write me, but just as soon as possible I will write you again and give you my address.

When we left, we were supposed to be back in two months, but am afraid now it will be a little longer. I suppose Marie wrote I had received my promotion the day we left, it was dated back to February 1st, it was almost two months catching up with me. [redacted], so will have to pick it up on the return journey. Now we are [redacted] ahead of your time. This letter may be quite a while reaching the States, but it will someday make its way back to you.

I wrote Marie a note also, and just wanted to let you know everything was all right here. Having a lot of new experience to tell about when I get back, Will close for now, and until you hear from me again, don't worry about me.

Your Loving Son,
Don.

EGLIN FIELD
FLORIDA

March 18, 1942

Dear Folks;

I just rushed over from dinner, so I could find time to write you a few lines, and also so I could use the typewriter in the office, as it makes writing much easier. I received your letter last Saturday, after it had been forwarded from Columbia, and you said you didn't expect me to receive it, well I guess we were lucky, as I will be able to hear from you al least once more before we leave. Right now it looks like we will get out of here next week, as we hae everything taken care of and the planes all have been repaired. We are finishing the necessary work on the planes, along with some flying. Last week I took a trip to Houston, Texas, and I called Marie before I left, and her folks brought her over to Houston, and we were able to see her for a few minutes, we stayed over night, and flew back here the next day.

They are still shooting usewith vaccine, and by the time they finish with us, I don't expect to have any blood left, just a mixture of serum.

Well floks, I must close and run along, as the men are all getting back for work, and we are get ing reay for another mis ion, so will close for now. just wanted to let you know everything was all right, though awful busy.

As Ever, you Son,

Don

This letter was written from Eglin Field, Florida during the preparations for the Doolittle Raid on 18 March 1942. The flight to Houston was a training mission connected to the upcoming raid. Don was granted a one-day, one-night leave by the Army to meet his wife Marie in Houston, who was pregnant at the time.
This fact was exceptional, as the mission and its preparations were highly secret.

#3

A.P.O. 3052

October, 23, 1942

Dear Folks;

Another short note, just in case the other letter didn't arrive yet, or will be delayed, and I wanted you all to know everything is going well with your Son. Haven't been able to receive any mail yet, but expect to in a few days, so from Marie's letters you will know better than I how your Grand Daughter is growing.

Wish we could all be together for Thanksgiving but guess we will have to wait until next year, after we have settled everything with Adolph & Co.

Have they started calling married men from around home, like Harry & Kennedy? Suppose I wouldn't know the old town, most of the old gang in the Army, or out on the coast working in plane factories.

Not much more news, will close for now, when you write, let me know how everything is at home. Hope you all are well. Slide Mugs across the dining room floor once for me.

As ever, your loving Son.

Don.

Written from RAF Attlebridge (or possibly RAF Horsham St. Faith) on 22 October 1942, this final letter home reveals Don's longing to spend Thanksgiving with his family. He numbered it *"#3"* because it was his third letter home since arriving in England.

Appendix II

Documents

No[illegible] The data on this side *will not be* accomplis[illegible] by the Officer initiating the report in cases where the remains *are to be shipped to Brookwood American Military Cemetery for burial.* In such cases the officer, or non-commissioned officer, accompanying the body to Brookwood will sign here as custodian in transit and will deliver all 4 copies to the U.S. Officer in Charge of Burials, or to the U.S. Superintendent at Brookwood Cemetery, who will fill in this side of the form and verify same by his signature:

Joseph B Ramey Jr Capt 93 Bomb Grp APO 634
(Signature, Rank, Organization of the custodian in transit)

In all OTHER cases, in N. Ireland, England, Scotland, and Wales, the following data will be supplied and verified by the Officer initiating the report.

Burial: 1400 14 November 1942 [illegible] Military Funeral
(Time, Date, and Type Religious Service Performed)

*Cemetery in which Buried: Brookwood American Military Cemetery
(Name and Number)

Grave in which Buried: Plot No.: E Row No.: 6 Grave No.: 7

Kind of Marker: Temporary Wooden Cross

Disposition of Identification Tags: (a) Buried with the Body: None

(b) Attached to Marker: None (c) Accompanied Body to Brookwood:

Bodies Buried on Either Side:

Right: LaVerne Helpingstine, Corp., 18086337, 439 Bmb. Sq. No. 6
(Name, Serial No., Rank, Organization, and Grave No.

Left: Robert E. Richter, Corp., 37161667, 439 Bmb. Sq. No. 8
(Name, Serial No., Rank, Organization, and Grave No.)

Signature of Officer Reporting

Verified by G.R.S. Officer

*Sketch here if in isolated grave

CASKET: I.P. & C.
EMBALMING: NOT PERFORMED
NAME PLATE: INGRAHAM

PREPARE IN QUADRUPLICATE (4):
1 COPY FORCE GRS, ORIGINAL AND TWO COPIES TO CHIEF, GRS

HQ.508.—26-8-42/500m/309

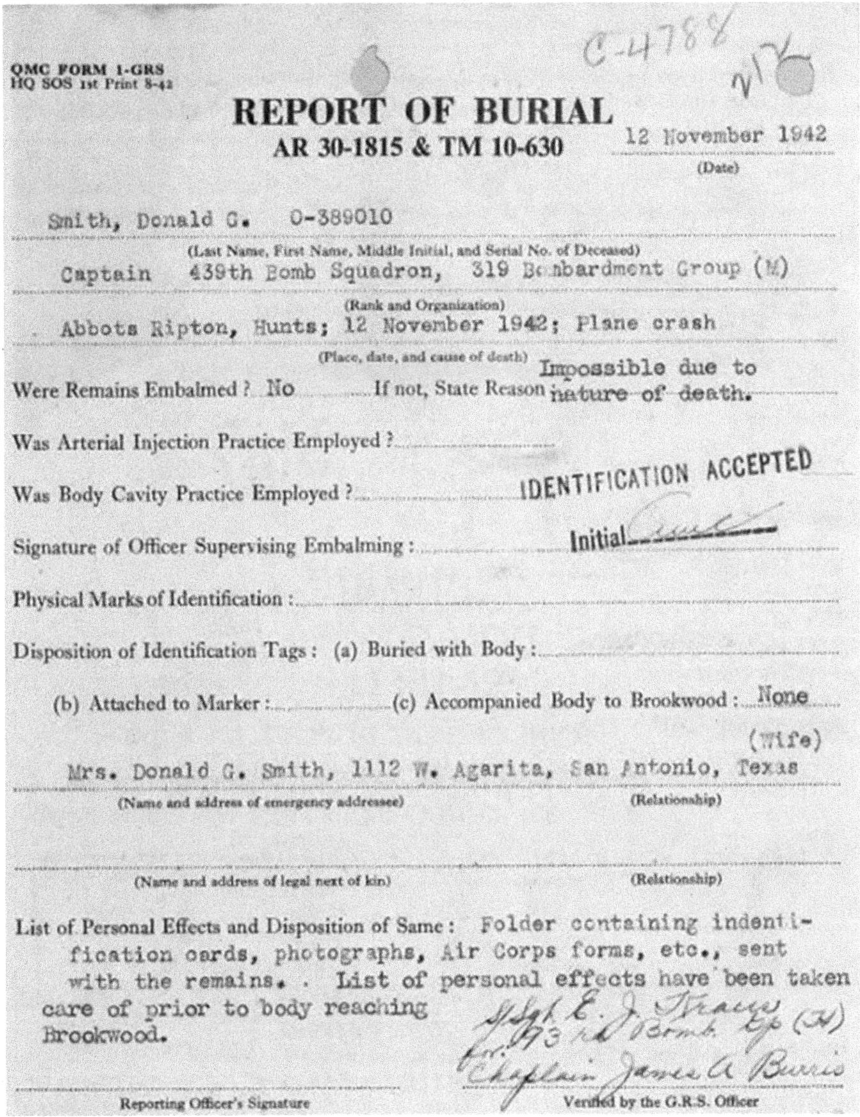

C-4788
217

QMC FORM 1-GRS
HQ SOS 1st Print 8-42

REPORT OF BURIAL
AR 30-1815 & TM 10-630

12 November 1942
(Date)

Smith, Donald G. 0-389010
(Last Name, First Name, Middle Initial, and Serial No. of Deceased)

Captain 439th Bomb Squadron, 319 Bombardment Group (M)
(Rank and Organization)

Abbots Ripton, Hunts; 12 November 1942; Plane crash
(Place, date, and cause of death)

Were Remains Embalmed? No If not, State Reason Impossible due to nature of death.

Was Arterial Injection Practice Employed?

Was Body Cavity Practice Employed? IDENTIFICATION ACCEPTED

Signature of Officer Supervising Embalming: Initial

Physical Marks of Identification:

Disposition of Identification Tags: (a) Buried with Body:

(b) Attached to Marker: (c) Accompanied Body to Brookwood: None

Mrs. Donald G. Smith, 1112 W. Agarita, San Antonio, Texas (Wife)
(Name and address of emergency addressee) (Relationship)

(Name and address of legal next of kin) (Relationship)

List of Personal Effects and Disposition of Same: Folder containing indentification cards, photographs, Air Corps forms, etc., sent with the remains. . List of personal effects have been taken care of prior to body reaching Brookwood.

S/Sgt E. J. Tracy
93rd Bomb. Gp (H)
for: Chaplain James A Burris

Reporting Officer's Signature — Verified by the G.R.S. Officer

Above and opposite: Report of Burial – Temporarily buried at Brookwood Cemetery near London, American Section. The accompanying documents also mentioned the crash location of the aircraft in England – a site that, to this day, has never been correctly identified in any publication.

Smith's personnel file remained untraceable at the US National Archives (NARA) for many years. After repeated inquiries, the author eventually obtained a copy, which revealed crucial details about the crash. Because the file had been unavailable, the exact crash location had never previously been correctly identified or published in any earlier works.

Cartoon of Lieutenant Donald G. Smith by Second World War artist Dick Kirschbaum. The drawing highlights Don's attack on Kobe, Japan, where Crew 15 flew so low during the attack on Japan that children reportedly threw stones at their aircraft. It also reflects his modesty toward the press, who he told the raid was "largely routine," and humorously notes his background as a poultry expert from Belle Fourche, South Dakota. (Private collection of Janice Evans)

Index